Gendering Spanish Democracy

The political transformation of Spain into one of the world's leading democracies is well established, yet little is known about the differences between men and women's behaviour, experience and achievements during that process. How much did the women's movement contribute to this transformation? How far have policy advocates successfully integrated gender equality into key spheres of public life? Have power relations between women and men been re-balanced? *Gendering Spanish Democracy* adopts an innovative approach, critically reviewing key institutional processes, policies and systems to reveal the way they function to promote or obstruct gender equity. Both the transition to democracy, equality law reform, and the social welfare regime are put to the test. The groundbreaking efforts of policy-makers to combat the violence, sexual harassment and low political participation that are intrinsic to women's experience are scrutinised, and the constraints on equality in the field of employment and the family critically investigated.

The authors conclude that the recent re-balancing of the gender order in Spain is unexpected and contradictory, being ultimately more effective in political rather than socio-economic arenas.

Gendering Spanish Democracy breaks new ground in applying a systematic gender perspective to the analysis of established democracies, and is the first book in English to reveal the unique features of contemporary Spain's evolving gender order.

Monica Threlfall is Senior Lecturer in Politics, Loughborough University, UK, and editor of the *International Journal of Iberian Studies*. She has edited *Consensus Politics in Spain: Insider Perspectives* and *Mapping the Women's Movement: Feminist Politics and Social Transformation in the North*. **Christine Cousins** is Principal Lecturer in Sociology at the University of Hertfordshire, UK. She is the author of *Society, Work and Welfare in Europe*, and recent journal articles on gender, employment and social policies. **Celia Valiente** is Associate Professor, Department of Political Science and Sociology, Universidad Carlos III de Madrid, Spain. She is author of numerous articles and chapters published in the US, Europe and Spain.

Routledge advances in European politics

Gendering Spanish Democracy

Monica Threlfall, Christine Cousins and Celia Valiente

Routledge
Taylor & Francis Group

LONDON AND NEW YORK

First published 2005
by Routledge
2 Park Square, Milton Park, Abingdon, Oxon OX14 4RN

Simultaneously published in the USA and Canada
by Routledge
270 Madison Ave, New York, NY 10016

Routledge is an imprint of the Taylor & Francis Group

© 2005 Monica Threlfall, Christine Cousins and Celia Valiente

Typeset in Times by Wearset Ltd, Boldon, Tyne and Wear
Printed and bound in Great Britain by MPG Books Ltd, Bodmin

British Library Cataloguing in Publication Data
A catalogue record for this book is available from the British Library

Library of Congress Cataloging in Publication Data
A catalog record for this book has been requested

ISBN 0–415–34794–7

Contents

Acknowledgements

In addition to our families and friends, we would like to thank a number of institutions and people who have contributed to making this book possible in different ways. The various archives and documentation centres of the Instituto de la Mujer, Instituto Vasco de la Mujer, Centro de Documentación de la Mujer, Institut Catalá de la Dona, Dirección de la Mujer of the Comunidad de Madrid, and of the Principado de Asturias, the Comisión de Investigación de los Malos Tratos a la Mujer, Asociación de Mujeres Juristas Themis, Centro de Ayuda a las Víctimas de Agresiones Sexuales, Mujeres Jóvenes, Centro de Investigación y Formación Feminista, Federación de Asociaciones de Mujeres Separadas, Seminario de Estudios de la Mujer of the Universidad Autónoma de Madrid, the former Ministerio de Asuntos Sociales, Centro de Investigaciones Sociológicas, Consejo Económico y Social, Fundación Mujeres, Fundación Pablo Iglesias, Fundación Dolores Ibárruri and the trade-union confederations Unión General de Trabajadores and Comisiones Obreras have all provided information and briefings at various stages of our research. So have the women's departments of the political parties Partido Socialista Obrero Español, Izquierda Unida and Partido Popular. The role of the late Fernando Claudín in providing a space for feminist debate while he was Director of the Fundación Pablo Iglesias is recognised with gratitude. Celia Valiente would like to thank colleagues at the Instituto Juan March, Universidad Autónoma de Madrid and Universidad Carlos III de Madrid for their invaluable support.

Special thanks are due to the Spanish women's movement activists who launched the whole process of women's emancipation in Spain. It is they who ultimately provided us with the material for this book. In particular, Monica Threlfall would like to thank all those who welcomed her participation in the activities of the women's movement, informed and educated her. Acknowledgements are due to, amongst others, Inés Alberdi, Jimena Alonso, Celia Amorós, Elena Arnedo, Judith Astelarra, Carlota Bustelo, Merche Comabella, Rosa Conde, Henar Corbi, Violeta Demonte, Mabi Díaz, María Angeles Durán, Concha Fagoaga, Matilde Fernández, Pilar Folguera, Mayte Gallego, Carmen García Matrán, Anabel González, Pilar

González, Patrocinio de las Heras, Alicia Herrera, Esperanza Illán, María Izquierdo, María Jesús Izquierdo, Carmen Martínez Ten, María Jesús Miranda, Kika Muñoz, Felicidad Orquín, Mari Carmen Pena, Empar Pineda, Carmen Rodríguez, Milagros Rodríguez Marín, Isabel Romero, Fini Rubio, Paloma Saavedra, Begoña San José, Marina Subirats and Francis Tarrazaga. In addition, insights and understanding were derived from illuminating discussions with, or information received from, Mariano Aguirre, Tina Alarcón, Isabel Alberdi, Cristina Alberdi, Pilar Alcobendas, Duca Aranguren, Covadonga Balbás, Delia Blanco, Susana Brunel, María Dolors Calvet, Mila Candela, Purificación Causapié, Rosa Cobo, Teresa Domingo, Pilar Escario, Giuliana di Febo, Purificación Gutiérrez, Perla Haimovich, Ana-Inés Lopez Accotto, Mary Nash, Micaela Navarro, Ludolfo Paramio, María del Carmen Pardo, Asunción Ruaño, Lola Sánchez, Geraldine Scanlon, Julia Sevilla, Constanza Tobío, Amelia Valcárcel, Elena Valenciano and Blanca Ullate.

Abbreviations

AC	*Comunidades Autónomas* (Autonomous Communities)
AEMS	*Asociación Española de Mujeres Separadas* (Spanish Association of Separated Women)
CAVAS	*Centro de Ayuda a las Víctimas de Agresiones Sexuales* (Association of Centres to Help Victims of Sexual Aggressions)
CC.OO	*Comisiones Obreras* (Workers' Commissions)
CDS	*Centro Democrático y Social* (Social and Democratic Centre Party)
CEOE	*Confederación Española de Organizaciones Empresariales* (Spanish employers' organisation)
CIS	*Centro de Investigaciones Sociológicas* (Centre for Sociological Research)
CiU	*Convergència i Unió* (Convergence and Union – Catalan nationalist party)
EE	*Euzkadiko Ezkerra* (Basque Left Party)
EU	European Union
HB	*Herri Batasuna* (Unity of the People – defunct Basque separatist party)
INP	*Instituto Nacional de Previsión* (National Insurance Institution)
IU	*Izquierda Unida* (United Left)
MDM	*Movimiento Democrático de Mujeres* (Democratic Movement of Women)
MEC	*Ministerio de Educación y Cultura* (Ministry of Education and Culture)
PCE	*Partido Comunista de España* (Communist Party)
PNV	*Partido Nacionalista Vasco* (Basque National Party)
PP	*Partido Popular* (People's Party)
PSOE	*Partido Socialista Obrero Español* (Spanish Socialist Workers' Party)
UCD	*Unión de Centro Democrático* (Union of the Democratic Centre)
UGT	*Unión General de Trabajadores* (General Workers' Union)

1 Introduction

Monica Threlfall and Christine Cousins

'Spanish machismo wilts' declared a newspaper headline when Castilla-La Mancha's autonomous regional government announced a new gender law. The vision of the flower of Hispanic manhood drooping in the arid, limitless prospect of Castile, where once roamed the chivalrous Don Quijote intent on rescuing fair maidens, surely heralds a revolution of sorts. The contents of the news item by Nash (2002) – resorting to electoral zip-lists of alternating women and men to ensure that an even balance of female and male deputies get elected to its regional parliament – is the perfect example of some of the astounding steps towards gender equity taken in recent years by Spanish individuals and institutions. Their cumulative impact means that Spain's parliament and party leaderships are now peopled by more women that in the rest of Europe excepting Scandinavia and Germany, while its law courts are increasingly presided by women judges.

How far from the singing washerwoman, hip-swinging gitana and priggish María bound for mass of earlier generations. 'Yes it is possible to change things', declared one of a group of six thousand local councillors under 30 years old on being elected (Roma 1999: 28). They are representative of a generation in which even the boys admit that girls have more of the best human qualities (Fundación Santa María 1999). Yet when it comes to filling political posts with women, enlightened male politicians decry the difficulties of finding enough willing candidates for the job, to which Angeles Ruíz-Tagle, President of the Spanish caucus of the European Women's Lobby, responds: 'They complain that we lack ambition but in fact they force us to choose between politics and the family.' When it comes to the crunch, the difficulties of combining a public with a private life are as great as ever. It is either one or the other. 'Despite all the equality laws, historically and socially the public realm is still associated with men', explains Micaela Navarro, the Socialist Party's equality spokeswoman. Margarita Uría of the Basque National Party (PNV) agrees: 'When a meeting drags on late into the evening, it's the women who seize any opportunity to phone home and you hear them chatting "Have you had your supper yet?" "Has your temperature gone down?". The men just sit there' (Ortega Dolz 2001: 11). No wonder some women choose family over career. But not many, the figures show. The queue of Spanish women seeking jobs is the longest in Europe.

Aims

At its simplest, the primary purpose of this book is to contribute to filling a void – the void of books in English about the gender dimensions in Spanish politics and society during the remarkable political, economic and social processes that took place over the last quarter of the twentieth century and into the new millennium.

At the time of writing, only one single-authored monograph on the position of women in the post-authoritarian Spanish society had appeared – *Women in Contemporary Spain* by Brooksbank Jones (1997). This explored new themes of the post-Franco period such as the extent of diversity of interests and needs among women, the new social exclusions, the tensions of balancing family and workplace, the growth of women's presence in the media, and their artistic creativity in writing and film. Our purpose is complementary, namely to address other aspects of women's experience, such as the public spheres of elective politics, public policy-making and the labour market, underpinned by analysis of underlying dynamics and structures that contribute to shaping gender relations in Spain, including women's activism, the family and the state social-security system.

Given the absence of any comprehensive study of gender in Spanish politics and society this book aims to offer English-language readers an up-to-date critical assessment of gender in the key social and political fields. In politics, it ranges from the role of women's organisations and feminist advocates in influencing political life during the last years of the dictatorship and the transition to democracy, to the progressive participation of women in Spain's new political institutions and their demands on the parties. In the world of work, it ranges from women's conquest of new positions in the labour market to the constraints of the gendered social-policy regime. And in feminist public advocacy, it discusses the articulation of new policies on harassment and domestic violence. The book ends with an acknowledgement that, while it is to some extent inevitable – given the balance of power between the sexes – that any discussion of gender will be overwhelmingly focused on women, gender relations have in fact evolved sufficiently to warrant a much deeper and nuanced examination of the role of men in household life in Spain.

The aim of 'making visible', which is also an analytical approach, was started by feminist historians in the 1970s and is still considered of vital political importance today for any attempt to challenge the masculine establishment (Enders and Radcliff 1999: 404) – in the Spanish case, the establishment of a masculine hegemonic discourse on Spanish democratisation. So the second purpose of this book is to fill the other kind of gap – the gap of recognition. The contribution of women to Spanish democratisation and social development has hardly been recognised, not to say ignored. It is no exaggeration to say that there has been a virtual void of attention in the mainstream literature to the gender implications inherent to the remarkable transformations that have taken place in Spain since the return to democracy. The literature on the political transition is abundant, yet only a handful of articles, almost exclusively written by women, have identified the presence of women and fewer still have allowed their accounts to properly integrate the gender dimension into their analysis.

The gender dimension has been overlooked both in traditional historical accounts, political-science approaches, and even by those highlighting the part played by the labour and other grass-roots social movements. Similarly, later general explanations of voting trends emerging in the new party system have paid scant attention to gendered patterns, let alone to the political preferences of different sectors of women, leaving the issues to be dealt with in books on women in politics specifically, amongst which Uriarte and Elizondo's wide-ranging edited work *Mujeres en política* stands out almost alone as a major contribution. In contrast, we highlight women's activism in two key fields: the protest and reform politics of the struggle against the Franco dictatorship and the subsequent return to democratic institutions and practices, on the one hand; and on the other, current feminist activism in party politics.

In the field of the sociology of work and welfare, the absence of work on gender has not been quite so glaring, particularly not as far as Spanish research is concerned. The explanatory paradigm in this field, comparable to the one of transition from one political regime to another, is *modernisation* and social change, where it is more difficult to ignore gender. And yet, three-volume books will include one chapter on gender issues, 800-page books will have a couple of subsections (e.g. Garde 1999: 564–567, 769–791) but at 'only' 600 pages, the whole gender question can be subsumed into a few pages on new family structures (e.g. de Miguel 1998: 442–454). Only in the more discrete area of labour market studies, where women's steady incorporation into employment is one of the key developments, does gender get the attention it deserves. Luckily therefore, the field has not suffered from a comprehensive silencing of gender questions.

Elsewhere, research coverage is not tantamount to completed stories or comprehensive explanations. For instance, it can be said that the European welfare state, and particularly that achieved by the Scandinavian countries based on the principle of social citizenship, occupied a strong position in the imaginary of citizens' collective aspirations during the consolidation of democracy. Catching up with Europe in terms of welfare services and social protection was also an aim of socialist governments in the 1980s. So the story of welfare development during this period should be formulated as one in which governments were faced with the demand to respond to new social needs and to new interest groups pressing for social-policy reforms. Yet one finds accounts of welfare-state development in the 1980s focusing only on the co-operation and conflict between a unionised workforce and its fraternal party in government (PSOE), ignoring differences in how men and women fare in the welfare state. Newly prominent social needs that disproportionately affect women (for example, the need to reconcile working and family life or rising risks of discontinuous jobs and unemployment) have not been highlighted.

Our perspective

We have called this book *Gendering Spanish Democracy*. How does one 'gender' a democracy? The verb and the participle 'gendering' have been chosen to signify the process of revealing gendered aspects of political and social phenomena, especially the aspects that might appear – to observers unaware of contemporary feminist understandings and insights – to have nothing to do with gender. Feminist research has also played on the term 'engender' (to conceive, produce or bring into existence). In her well-established text *Engendering Democracy*, Anne Philips used the metaphor to explore feminist and democratic theory and build a critique of liberal democracy. Her starting point was that feminism had major implications for the way we should think of democracy (1991: 21). Barbara Marshall in *Engendering Modernity* (1994: 2) chose it as a term that 'captures the active way in which gender is continually embedded' in the operation of social and political systems, believing that the restructuring of gender relations is a fundamental characteristic of modernity.

Chris Corrin in turn suggests that feminist perspectives consider how different ways of thinking can affect the way we see, what we 'know' and how we consider ideas about social and political change (1999: 1). After believing we could apprehend the totality of a phenomenon or system, we discover that it has a gendered dimension. There are assumptions about gender embedded in it. The same could be said for other standpoints (such as race or class) or other theoretical perspectives. Gendering is essentially a process concerned with identifying and analysing invisible or hidden sites of oppression and discrimination of women (or men, as the case may be). It is the assumptions, the 'not-knowing', that make women, the gender system and gendered phenomena invisible to the untrained eye. In this sense, gendering is a methodology, an analytical tool rather than an explanatory one, though it is informed by a conceptual lens – the lens of gender. The researcher abandons the false position of impartiality in order to ask: is there a gendered dimension to this phenomenon? Applying the lens of gender means working to make gender visible in social phenomena and political systems, and allows the researcher to ask how these differ systematically for women and men. Such research can constitute the prior stage before explanatory theory, answering the 'what' question before the 'how'. It does so by illuminating the position of women, particularly 'the processes of exclusion and inclusion of women as workers, mothers and citizens' (Siim 2000: 4). An example of this approach is the extensive work of gendering the welfare state carried out by scholars such as Jane Lewis, Iloner Ostner, Ruth Lister and Birte Siim, amongst many others.

Nonetheless, such research has concerned itself with the welfare state only, in the same way as the critiques of democracy have tended to focus on the political sphere of institutions, participation and representation. This book has a different starting point – the multi-disciplinary analysis of gender in one country. Therefore it uses the broader perspective of gendering. And while being informed by the methodology of gendering, it does not explicitly put forward a theory of 'Spanish gender' or 'women in Spain', but advocates the gendering approach because it has not been applied as a single holistic tool in the analysis of a multi-faceted polity consisting of a political system, a social system, an economic system as well as the behaviour and attitudes of collective and individual actors. We also use the term engender in its creative sense when discussing the type of new policies that have required a cultural shift in understandings of male and female interactions, such as in the workplace – the concept of 'harassment' – and in the domestic sphere – the concept of what constitutes 'violence' (a violation of women's bodily integrity and of the relationship of trust and equality between spouses and sexual partners).

Our overall goal is to move towards an identification of the Spanish gender system. The constraints on our endeavour should also be exposed. First and foremost, the lack of a well-accepted paradigm of the role and place of gender in twentieth-century democratisation, development and modernisation processes. The literature on political democratisation has tended to overlook gender as if it were a merely social phenomenon to be left to sociologists to study, and to ignore women's movements or feminist politics (Waylen 1998). The literature on modernisation and modernity might be expected to have yielded an overarching explanation, yet tends to focus on women's presence in the labour force rather too exclusively. Theorising from the discipline of women's studies has produced useful work on the sources of patriarchy, the myriad manifestations of women's oppression, the rediscovery of women's presence in history, and a lasting identification of feminist politics with the classic strategies of liberal, socialist and radical feminism. But neither academic nor third-wave feminism itself have added much by way of gendered interpretations of major social and political events and transformations in twentieth-century Europe, being engaged in more conceptual debates around difference, identity and diversity, and the body, amongst others (see Arneil 1999: Ch. 7).

Haste (2000: 22) articulates the dichotomy between modernist and post-modernist discourses of feminism in terms of the search between two different goals, 'the search for rational justice' and the 'search for authenticity'. She argues that these ostensibly polarised goals reflect the gap between 'changing key *parameters of power* within the existing system and transforming the *system*' [emphasis added]. In fact, our view is that this is a false alternative, as the former is just as likely to constitute a prelude to the latter. The two are complementary rather than dichotomous. Abstaining from working for change within the system because it does not come with a promise of deep transformations is unlikely to benefit women, neither in general nor in particular. This book is about the search conducted by feminist advocates for 'rational justice' in the Spanish political and socio-economic system, and for access to power structures in order to alter their impact, as institutional feminism has done in Spain. Yet at the same time it recognises that, crucial though they are, the rational justice of achieving certain rights and overcoming institutional discrimination is inherently limited. The search for justice is often 'insufficiently reflective about the cultural, linguistic and social processes which sustain and reproduce the taken-for-granted assumptions that underpin social institutions' (Haste 2000: 33). Rights can be eroded by lack of consensus, and discrimination return in subtle forms. Yet for reasons of space, only some reflections on such social processes can be made here, as a single book cannot hope to encompass all the diversity of feminisms and sexual politics. Our selection attempts to bring to the reader both some revisioning of past events, some insight into present policy difficulties faced by practitioners, some deconstruction of the way old and new systems work to women's advantage or otherwise, and some perspectives on the altered behaviours of key groups of women and men. Indeed, given that social and political changes occur both in stages and at a multiplicity of levels simultaneously, it is probably sterile to attempt to assign a hierarchy of importance to the different processes that can be observed. In the Conclusion we return to the question of 'transforming the system' in our assessment of the position of Spanish women today.

A few words about what has regretfully had to be left out of this book. It has not been possible to pay full attention to diversities of age, class, race and regional identity among Spanish women, though intergenerational relations are taken into account in discussions of family structures and childcare. We are aware of not engaging fully with current debates in feminist theory, in the sense of knowledge construction (Humm 2000: 60). We cannot offer an account of Spanish feminist theoretical contributions, such as they are. We are not able to include a discussion of the different strands of Spanish feminism and their respective contributions to the improvement in women's lives, reviewing the practices of independent or cultural feminism in Spain (*feminismo independiente*).

All in all, our approach is to see gender relations as a dynamic that underlies social and political processes. Unveiling it throws light on these and enables a better understanding of their complexity. This leads us to focus on women's agency, both as organised actors in nationwide political processes, and as a critical mass of individuals taking decisions and behaving in ways that constitute trends in parties, markets, households and families. In addition we look at how certain subsystems or micro-systems, such as policy-making spheres, parties or the social security system, function in ways that help or hinder the achievement of gender equity. In Part I, Gendering Democratic Spain, Chapter 2 on gendering the transition to democracy is devoted to accounts of the way women's advocates and feminists both in mass organisations and elite positions intervened forcefully in public life to advance sex equality throughout the transition period, successfully changing law and policy to the benefit of women and thereby altering our view of standard accounts of what the transition was about. Chapter 3 genders the Spanish social-policy regime, offering a critical gendered analysis of how it functions and the difficulties of delivering a more equitable deal for women engaged in earning a living, whether as homemakers or through employment. The second part 'Engendering New Policies' is devoted to policy developments, particularly to the creation of new policies on harassment (Chapter 4) and domestic violence (Chapter 5). These are examples of how feminists engendered policy-making, establishing new concepts and a new vocabulary. They faced the challenge of implementing newly designed procedures and legal precepts, and came across many unexpected obstacles that undermined their efforts. Chapter 6 discusses how feminism engendered political representation with the launch of the novel concept of gender parity in elected public posts. The third part of the book, 'Changing Gender Relations?', focuses on the extent to which individuals, both in the aggregate and acting collectively, have contributed to both altering and freezing the balance of power in gender relations in the labour market and the home. Chapter 7 analyses how women have striven for economic independence in a discriminatory labour market and Chapter 8 looks at how men's behaviour in the family has responded to the pressures for a more equal sharing of household work and care.

Our conclusions are discussed at the end of the book. The Conclusion is subtitled 'From progress to resistance?' because that reflects the dynamic tension we find between the way political and social processes in Spain have been successfully gendered and engendered on the one hand, and the way institutions, behaviours and public attitudes have also offered some resistance to change. The latter is clearest where demands to implement substantive equality are concerned. All in all, our findings are both new and surprising. The sphere that has proved most permeable to gender demands appears to be the political: institutions have undergone substantial gender equity-inspired reform, and political parties have enabled women to participate in them and to represent the public on their behalf. The labour market and the social-welfare regime have proven to contain obstacles, and display pockets of resistance, to a greater extent than was expected. Women may have changed their attitudes towards employment, and gone out to look for a job in droves, but such altered behaviour is only half the story, for in effect they found themselves joining the unemployed labour force – the largest contingent in the European Union. Lastly, the engendering of arguably the most challenging of feminist policies, on harassment and violence against women, has achieved a surprising consensus in the political and legal field, only to stumble on issues of practical implementation. More surprising still, it is the professionals of service delivery who are seen to be responsible.

We are indebted to much Spanish-language research and draw on it where appropriate throughout this book. Nonetheless, we believe that comprehensive accounts such as the one we present here are notable by their absence in Spanish as well.

References

Arneil, B. (1999) *Politics and Feminisms*, Oxford: Blackwell.

Brooksbank Jones, A. (1997) *Women in Contemporary Spain*, Manchester: Manchester University Press.

Corrin, C. (1999) *Feminist Perspectives on Politics*, London and New York: Longman.

de Miguel, J. (1998) *Estructura y cambio social en España*, Madrid: Alianza Editorial.

Enders, V.L. and Radcliff, P.B. (eds) (1999) *Constructing Spanish Womanhood: Female Identity in Modern Spain*, Albany, NY: SUNY.

Fundación Santa María (1999) *Jóvenes Españoles 1999*, cited in *España 1999*, No. 304, Madrid: Oficina de Información Diplomática, p. 12.

Garde, J.A (ed.) (1999) *Políticas sociales y Estado de bienestar en España: Informe 1999*, Madrid: Fundación Hogar del Empleado/Editorial Trotta.

Haste, H. (2000) 'Sexual metaphors and current feminisms' in A. Bull, H. Diamond and R. Marsh (eds) *Feminisms and Women's Movements in Contemporary Europe*, Basingstoke: Macmillan.

Humm, M. (2000) 'Feminisms and women's movements in the 1990s' in A. Bull, H. Diamond and R. Marsh (eds) *Feminisms and Women's Movements in Contemporary Europe*, Basingstoke and New York: Macmillan and St. Martin's Press, pp. 50–63.

Marshall, B. (1994) *Engendering Modernity*, Cambridge: Polity Press.

Nash, E. (2002) 'Spanish machismo wilts as La Mancha "guarantees" equality', *Independent*, 28 June.

Ortega Dolz, P. (2001) 'La democracia paritaria a prueba', *El País*, 28 October, p. 11.

Phillips, A. (1991) *Engendering Democracy*, Cambridge: Polity Press.

Siim, B. (2000) *Gender and Citizenship: Politics and Agency in France, Britain and Denmark*, Cambridge: Cambridge University Press.

Uriarte, E. and Elizondo, A. (eds) (1997) *Mujeres en política*, Barcelona: Editorial Ariel.

Waylen, G. (1998) 'Gender, feminism and the state' in V. Randall and G. Waylen (eds) *Gender, Politics and the State*, London: Routledge, pp. 1–17.

Part I

Gendering democratic Spain

2 Gendering the transition to democracy

Reassessing the impact of women's activism

Monica Threlfall

Introduction

One of the striking features of the way the Spanish transition to democracy has been depicted is its silence over questions involving gender, be these the activities of women's organisations, protest against the gender bias and sexism of the Francoist system, or the equality issues in constitutional, parliamentary and party politics. In all, there has been a notable absence of attention to the gender implications of the transformations that have occurred in the Spanish polity over the last two decades. Although the literature on the political transition is abundant, only a handful of articles, almost exclusively written by women, have identified the presence of

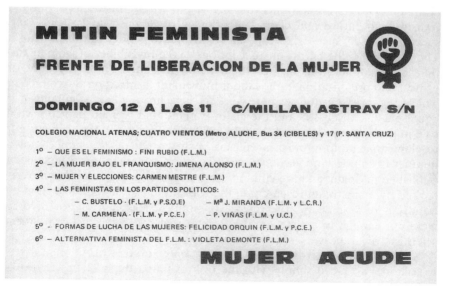

Figure 2.1 Feminist Election Rally. Leaflet distributed by the Women's Liberation Front, Madrid, 1979.

women or the influence of the women's movement. The gendered questions of the transition have been overlooked both in traditional historical accounts, in political-science approaches and even by those highlighting the part played by labour, social and urban movements. Similarly, explanations of voting trends emerging in the new party system have paid scant attention to gendered patterns of voting behaviour, or to the political preferences of different sectors of women by age, education and employment, despite their impact. Even accounts of the role of the Catholic church, where issues of divorce, birth control and abortion come up because of their salience in church–state relations (such as Brassloff 1998), avoid mentioning women and any church role in maintaining gender hierarchies.

Of course, such an absence of attention to gender in the Spanish case is not untypical of the political-science literature on democratisation in general, which has made very little mention of gender, despite evidence of the significant role women and women's movements have played in the return to democracy in some countries in Latin America (Waylen 1994: 327). In the main this oblivion reflects a fascination – both traditional and elitist – with high politics and with the leaders at its peak, where few, if any, women are to be found. Yet many of the historians and theorists of social movements who critique this way of focusing on political elites, such as Foweraker (1994), are themselves interested in grass-roots activities and labour movements featuring male protagonists, and show no interest in women's struggles either. Feminist scholarship has therefore been critical of the collective-action theorists for ignoring women's protest activities (Kaplan 1997). Even accounts that present a critique of the international transition literature and claim the primacy of Spanish civil society and social processes, such as Pérez Díaz (1993), leave gender out of the story. There appear to be hardly any exceptions to the invisibility of women and the gender dimension, one of them being Balfour's (1989) account of protest and organisation in the labour movement, centred on Barcelona, in which the presence of women workers is acknowledged, demands for equal pay are discussed and the claim is made that women played a vital role in the urban protests of the mid-1970s (Balfour 1989: 196). This is not to claim that nothing much at all has been written on the subject, for a number of sources and accounts, most often by women authors, have been published in Spain, and are cited in these pages. But they have been overlooked by mainstream research on the transition, as if a demonstration by hundreds of women for the release of political prisoners or for divorce were not enough to register on the Richter scale of historians' or political scientists' awareness.

So even at this late stage in scholarly research on the transition, one has to ask: are we faced simply with the task of filling the gaps left by traditional historians and political scientists, the tried and tested recipe called 'add-women-and-stir'? There have recently been a number of attempts at adding the missing ingredients, such as Escario *et al.*'s (1996) exploration of women's experience of the transition through a series of interviews of advocates and protagonists. There is also the remarkable collective effort of a group of current and former feminist activists to remember and to record all that was attempted and achieved, entitled *Españolas en la transición: de excluidas a protagonistas 1973–1982*, which has been an inspiration for this chapter. Using a different approach, the renowned historian of Spain, Paul Preston, has filled some gaps by turning his attention to a series of individual women both of the right and left: Mercedes Sanz-Bachiller, the head of the fascist insurgents' welfare programme during the Civil War, and the Republican socialist deputy, Margarita Nelken (2002); Pilar Primo de Rivera, eternal head of the Sección Femenina, and the Communist leader Dolores Ibárruri 'La Pasionaria' (1998). Social historians on the other hand, might try to recover overlooked aspects of ordinary women's lives and take another look at the social institutions in which they were present. But most feminist approaches today would attempt not just to 'put the women back in' to the story, but to argue that attention to gender, as opposed to female individuals, leads to an altered understanding of historical and political processes. A focus on gender both brings out the extensive connections between what has traditionally been considered 'personal' and what has passed muster as 'political', and leads inevitably to a redefinition of what constitutes 'politics'. Such a focus not only presents a more holistic and wider picture of the political process, it may also alter the picture and colour our understanding of the underlying dynamics of political change.

It is appropriate – even urgent, given the time already elapsed – for the first substantive chapter in this book to return to the activities of women's organisations in the transition to democracy in Spain, in order to reconsider their political significance. The questions this chapter seeks to explore are: how did their overall activities contribute to fortify the struggle for democracy; how far did more focused demands for gender equality alter the meaning of transition by adding a new dimension to democratic change; and how far did these subsequently lead to substantial legal and policy reforms? The chapter's wider concern, therefore, is to identify the place of a women's movement in a democratisation process. We will first address some methodological questions, and then proceed to an account of women's organisations' interactions, firstly with the politics of opposition against the Franco regime and secondly with the negotiations of the transition, constitutional settlement and democratic reforms up to 1982.

Methodological considerations

A first question is to decide on what basis to include or exclude organisations and activities in our account. Beckwith (2000: 435) has developed for international comparative purposes a definition of women's movements 'as socio-political movements that are characterized by the primacy of women's gendered experiences, women's issues, and women's leadership and decision-making' and argues that women's movements are more appropriately labelled *feminist* movements or feminist activism when they aim to transform the roles that society assigns to women and to challenge existing gendered power arrangements, and claim women's rights to autonomy and equality (following Alvarez 1990: 23 in Beckwith 2000: 437). Such a definition would, for instance, exclude the Spanish Sección Femenina because it advocated subordination to, and dependence on, men, even when some of its programmes may have brought comfort and satisfaction to not a few women (see Gallego Méndez 1983). This is because *feminist* movements, following Beckwith's overview of the research, are 'distinguished by their challenge of patriarchy [and] share a gendered power analysis of women's subordination and contest political, social, and other power arrangements of domination and subordination on the basis of gender' (2000: 437). Nonetheless, it is important to note that Kaplan (1999: 90–93) values the indirect contribution of the Sección Femenina because, even though it was a government instrument to subordinate family life to the authority of the state, it obliged women to move out of isolated domesticity into a public sphere of sorts through the obligatory Social Service (*servicio social*), and even facilitated access to political influence among women by left-wing organisations (Kaplan 1999: 101). For analogous reasons, because most definitions of feminism do not cover organised actions of women to defend *only* their class or race interests, the Spanish industrial conflicts protagonised by women workers and employees will not be covered here.

On the issue of choices regarding inclusion and exclusion, this chapter has chosen to include material on certain organisations of women as well as political mobilisations by women on the basis of the widely regarded ideas of Kaplan and Molyneux. Temma Kaplan's work on the concept of 'feminine consciousness' as a gendered form of political awareness was an invaluable contribution towards overcoming some of the difficulties in understanding this terrain. She examined how women who are identified with the role of mother or housewife can nevertheless intervene in the public life of their country, because their identity assigns them responsibilities, globally defined by Kaplan as 'to preserve life', which leads them to publicly demand the right to fulfil these responsibilities when they are threatened, which in turn can have an enormous political impact, and even revolutionary consequences. The bread riots that have broken out at different moments in history are the classic example. Secondly, there is Maxine Molyneux's well-established (1985/2001) two-level analysis of women's collective behaviour: at the level of practical gender interests when they act to defend their families, community, ethnic group or class; and at the level of 'strategic gender interests' when they act to advance their needs as a gender. Though developed in widely differing contexts, both sets of arguments are sufficiently persuasive for the chapter to have been guided towards inclusiveness in its choice of material on women's public activities, particularly since the concern of the book is with gendering a political process rather than with characterising the nature of a particular women's movement.

While previous work on women's activism in Spain (Threlfall 1985; Durán and Gallego 1986; Folguera 1988; Valiente 1995) has discussed feminism broadly within such methodological parameters, it should be stressed that this account is not mainly about the rise of feminism as such, neither its organic development nor its theoretical orientations. Its focus is, firstly, on the actions of women's groups taking place in the public domain, their mainstream political activities addressed to the authorities or the media. They should be counted as contributions to the opposition movements that eventually grew into forces capable of shaping the transition, moulding post-Francoist politics, and from 1979 onwards, taking power in a number of municipal, regional and finally national institutions. And secondly, it focuses on the linked question of the salience of gender in governmental reforms during the whole period of the transition up to 1982. It does this precisely in order to show that it is not even necessary to discuss women's activism in terms of a *hidden* presence that needs to be rescued from obscurity, nor to perceive women's activism as taking place in a private sphere, veiled from public view. It is hardly even necessary to resort to concepts of informal, ephemeral networks that come and go without being recorded and need to be recovered through oral histories (though the evidence for some of the material presented is oral), in order to gain an understanding of the role of women's activism. On the contrary, many of these events were visible, known or recorded or reported or published at the time by participants, institutions and newspapers.

Furthermore the chapter does not give much consideration to questions of size, numbers or geographical spread. Some women's organisations such as the Democratic Movement of Women (MDM) had by 1975 already held four national meetings with participants from many parts of the country, yet others clearly only ever functioned in Madrid. Precisely because so much of the familiar histories of the transition and political accounts focus exclusively on events in the capital and on peak institutions, women's activism should not be treated any differently. The materials selected are the actions directed at changing the politico-legal system in force in the last decade of dictatorship, irrespective of the size and location of the group. But it is with some regret that this account has to leave out other significant forms of women's political activism, such as prisoner support (the prisoner's wife was 'a figure present in the anti-Franco struggle from the post-war period to the seventies' (di Febo 1990: 252), and participation in labour-movement protests and strikes.

Lastly, a word on sources is required. This is not a conventional piece of historical research but the first reconstruction of the story of women's public interventions. While using a wide range of secondary and some primary sources from my personal archive, I have relied in particular on the 100-page account by Mary Salas and Merche Comabella in the collective volume *Españolas en la Transición*. This is a fascinating book because it is put together from collective memories and personal archives of former participants and protagonists, so other sources are not given, such as newspaper reports reporting the events they mention. Exact dates are often missing and it is not written in chronological order. It is nonetheless a valuable source and the integrity of the writers is not in doubt. It does raise issues about how history is made. Supposing none of the events engaged in by the feminists were reported in newspapers and no professional historian investigated them? The history of the transition would be very male-biased – and this is precisely what motivated the 32 authors of the edited volume to write the account (see Epilogue, p. 453).

The historical constraints on women's advocacy

In contrast to the trade-union movements and to socialist parties, feminist politics was hampered by several factors. Firstly, unlike other struggles, feminism lacked legitimacy as a body of thought in Spanish culture even more than it did in other European countries before the 1970s. The absolutely privileged position of the Catholic church in Spanish society and its continued influence over political life in the last century (see Brassloff 1998) enabled it to have an irresistible influence in delaying the growth of women's advocacy organisations. Catholic doctrine had created an all-pervasive, virtually monolithic image of the ideal woman, a Virgin Mary who sacrifices her son to God's will and accepts to live with the pain for ever. The effect of the use of God's authority to manipulate women's self-image and understanding of their role in life cannot be exaggerated. The need to be religious was the greatest imperative weighing on women of the nineteenth century (Scanlon 1976: 159). The counter-image belatedly offered by Spanish freethinkers in the 1930s came late and was short-lived.

Second, the position of women after the Civil War (1936–1939) became the subject of a sustained onslaught by the dictatorship, which found fascist notions of confining women to the kitchen and the care of children could be seamlessly merged with traditional Catholic beliefs (see Gallego Méndez 1983). Francoism managed to prolong for forty years a system of indoctrination into the traditional virtues of domesticated motherhood for all Spanish women through obligatory 'social service' courses run by the Feminine Section of the official Movimiento Nacional state party. The influence of such indoctrination should not be underestimated. Both Gallego (1982) and Morcillo Gómez (2000) believe National-Catholicism's impact on women derived from the way it did not deprive women of a national purpose, on the contrary, 'their agency resided, paradoxically, in their active political withdrawal' – a revealing contradiction in terms –

while 'Becoming mothers and wives constituted women's contribution to the national endeavour' (Morcillo 2000: 5). In a traditional social order, the fascists did not ignore women, but drew them in to participate in their ideal by exulting domestic drudgery and humdrum lives: young women's social service ran parallel to military service for young men as if the training were as noble for both. And the length of Franco's rule is also to be reckoned with. Printed leaflets with slogans such as 'After God, a woman must love no one better than her husband' were still being distributed by the church at least as late as 1965 (Sánchez López 1990: 102). As late as 1975 the Sección Femenina still had 349,697 women on its books as trainees (Fagoaga and Saavedra 1977: 62) and managed to avoid being abolished until May 1978 (Eiroa San Francisco 1995: 540). Feminism, labelled 'decadent, immodest and anti-Spanish', was much more virulently discredited in Spain than in other countries according to Scanlon (1990: 96). Feminist writers such as María Campo Alange (1964) and María Aurelia Capmany (1970: 29) noted that in such a context, early Spanish feminism was quite apologetic, even shamefaced (*vergonzante*), timidly suggesting changes while reassuring men they had nothing to worry about, that women would, in exchange for a few concessions, promise to remain sweet, docile and feminine.

Third, Spanish feminism, as a late developer, could not seek inspiration in its own past, looking back to an earlier stage of its history as a mass movement; nor could it rebuild itself from the broken blocks of an earlier nationwide organisation. It had no strong collective memory. It had a respectable history but a thin one with nothing as hearty as a real First Wave to flesh it out (see Scanlon 1986: 4–6, 353–354). It had in fact been nipped in the bud by fascism, as Pilar Primo de Rivera unwittingly recognised when she boasted that 'the Feminine Section was born at an opportune moment of Spanish history, precisely at the moment in which women were acquiring in Spain the momentum of growth essential to start their active insertion in society' and proceeded to undermine it systematically for decades (author's translation of Primo de Rivera 1963, quoted in Scanlon 1986: 354).

Lastly, Spanish feminism faced a further hurdle in the attitudes of the democratic and socialist opposition. Most democrats were ignorant even of liberal feminism as a political question, and throughout the 1970s the left parties remained committed to Marxist dogma about women's liberation being a deviation from the more urgent task of bringing down the dictatorship and building socialism. Isolated by their clandestine life and themselves ideologically dependent on orthodox Marxist views about the working class, the left parties learned to accept that working women in industry might be discriminated against, but viewed the rural and non-employed women as inherently lacking in political awareness, only understanding that women could be oppressed by capitalism but not by men or the power system.

Women in the political sphere

Nevertheless, Spanish feminism did have a tradition, both in thought and culture, with two important nineteenth-century figures Concepción Arenal (1820–1893) and Emilia Pardo Bazán (1851–1921) making an unusual impact through their social reforms and novels, respectively. The question of women began to be more widely debated after 1870 (Scanlon 1986; di Febo 1990) and again at the time of the First World War (González Calbet 1988: 51), with María de Maeztu (1882–1948) distinguishing herself as an educationalist. While early Spanish feminism has also been characterised as lacking in vigour (Scanlon 1986), Spanish women were nevertheless politicised by the upheavals of the 1930s and the Civil War, and thereby acquired a history of political activism. Campaigners María Lejárraga de Martínez Sierra, Margarita Nelken, Clara Campoamor and Victoria Kent distinguished themselves by advocating equality in the 1930s, using their position as women deputies in parliament between 1931 and 1936 (García Méndez 1979), though, according to one view, they were also suspicious of women's attachment to the church (Morcillo Gómez 1988: 60), believing this to make them unlikely supporters of Republican causes. Their feminism fitted into an egalitarian discourse rooted in bourgeois liberalism (Scanlon 1990). The Second Republic gave women the vote in 1931 and also took up women's issues in an enlightened manner, introducing some of Europe's earliest gender equality stipulations in the 1931 Constitution and later legal reform (see Scanlon 1986: 261–319; Morcillo Gómez 1988: 65). And, paradoxically, during the Civil War Spain had two powerful women political leaders, Dolores Ibárruri of the Communist Party of Spain (PCE) and the anarchist Federica Montseny (member of the workers' union CNT and the political organisation Iberian Federation of Anarchists (FAI)). They played a role on the national and even international stage, but also served the cause of women. Dolores Ibárruri was President of *Mujeres Antifascistas* (Anti-fascist Women, later Women against War and Fascism) that galvanised women to join the struggle. Montseny, the first woman cabinet minister in Europe, decriminalised abortion during her period as Minister for Health.[1]

After the Civil War, the closure and disbanding of all the organisations engaging women, the abolition of legal equality and the introduction into law and social practice of comprehensive and explicit discrimination under the auspices of traditionalist fascist and Catholic thinking were incalculable setbacks to further political participation, as all progress was lost (Scanlon 1990: 96). Nevertheless, the dictatorship years (1939–1977) did not represent a complete parenthesis of inactivity for political women. Individual and organised women continued to play a political role in the post-war resistance movements in a variety of ways, as di Febo (1979) Scanlon (1986) and Kaplan (1999) have amply shown.

Women's organisations in pre-transition politics

The Franco regime was profoundly uncomfortable with any form of voluntary association between Spanish citizens that was not controlled by the state party the National Movement (*Movimiento Nacional*) or the church. This means that even mundane civic activity that would be taken for granted in a democracy was banned. Even when it was decided in 1957 to allow certain associations to function, they had to apply for a permit by handing in a series of documents to the Interior Ministry's National Office of Associations (*Delegación Nacional de Asociaciones*) and could have it revoked at any time.[2] The conditions for legalisation were so stringent that most of the women's groups that subsequently came into *de facto* operation did not pass muster and could not be legalised till the late 1970s (Salas and Comabella 1999: 26) as they were deemed too political. In other words, as far as the authorities were concerned, women organising for change were just as much of a threat to them as any other type of grass-roots organisation.

Nonetheless, four solid early women's organisations passed muster and laid the foundations of the later women's movement. In 1960 the aristocratic writer María Lafitte, countess of Campo Alange, set up the first solid organisation devoted to 'the condition of womanhood', consisting of seminar groups of highly educated women, which lasted for 26 years, publishing three pioneering books in the 1960s and 1970s (Salas and Comabella 1999: 27). To maintain its hard-won legality it could not be politically active, but nevertheless caused a stir in 1970 at the first and only women's conference of the official Francoist Feminine Section when its delegate spoke out in favour of equality in education and 'classes with boys and girls' – the term 'co-education' being unmentionable (Salas and Comabella 1999: 28). Such attempts to engage with officialdom and its particular brand of liberal feminism allowed it to survive but not to flourish at the time (Brooksbank Jones 1997: 3). In the later 1970s, renamed the Seminar of Sociological Studies on Women (SESM), it participated in feminist political struggles.

The second influential group was the Spanish Association of Women Lawyers (*Asociación Española de Mujeres Juristas*) headed by María Telo. It had started public activity as early as 1969 when it organised, to considerable media attention, the first annual conference of the International Federation of Women Lawyers in Spain, in which the 'limitations on Spanish women's legal capacities' featured quite prominently, though the organisers feared the proceedings might be suspended at any moment (Ruiz 1999: 139–142). The Spanish women lawyers then succeeded in pressing their case with the Minister of Justice and to gain an audience with Franco himself on 4 March 1970. They wore full legal dress in the hope that he would take them, and their report, more seriously. He was polite but made no promises (Salas and Comabella 1999: 51). Nevertheless, the association was legalised in 1971 and successfully pressed for four women lawyers to be included in the Justice Ministry's Commission to revise the outdated Civil Code. The lawyers were influential enough for the resulting draft bill to actually propose eliminating all forms of sex discrimination – a rather remarkable achievement – but the Francoist unelected national assembly (*Las Cortes*) threw out the bill on 29 May 1974. The following year, after no less than 59 articles had been redrafted, Law 14/1975 of 2 May was passed (Franco Rubio 1982a: 419). Women ceased to be legal minors and regained some employment rights, though *patria potestad* (marital authority) remained in the husband's hands. This achievement was all the more noteworthy considering that none of the illegal opposition political parties active at this time had demanded such legal reforms or proposed amendments to any bills emanating from the undemocratic government (Salas and Comabella 1999: 64). The case illustrates the reluctance of mainstream male oppositions to work with gender issues under the dictatorship. Even the Communists, who accepted the need to gain concessions for workers by bargaining with the illegitimate state syndicate, as Comisiones Obreras did quite successfully, remained insufficiently aware of the mobilising potential of gender discrimination.

The third organisation to highlight is the AEMS (*Asociación Española de Mujeres Separadas* – Spanish Association of Separated Women) a support group that became legal in 1974 for operation throughout the whole country and was granted recognition by the Archbishopric of Madrid-Alcalá. This was crucial since the archbishoprics controlled the ecclesiastical courts that heard the petitions for legal separation, whereby in the absence of divorce, couples were able to legalise arrangements after the *de facto* breakdown of a marriage, without being allowed to remarry. When the Secretary to the Vatican administration, Monsignor Casaroli, passed through Madrid on 1 November 1973 (Brassloff 1998: 62), the still illegal AEMS managed to gain entry to the Nuncio's palace and slip him a letter denouncing the practices of the Spanish Ecclesiastical Courts, which discriminated against women even within the narrow confines of the law on legal separations (Salas and Comabella 1999: 54). Accusations included the charge that annulments could be bought and false evidence concocted (Brassloff 1998: 162, fn. 38).

The fourth legal organisation worth mentioning is APEC, devoted to the cultural advancement of women. Legalised in 1974, it allowed both men and women to be members. Its most memorable event was held shortly after, when it persuaded the North American feminist Betty Friedan to come to Madrid and present her best-selling book *The Feminine Mystique* before a multitudinous audience gathered at the prestigious Juan March Foundation. The authorities did not pluck up the energy to ban or disband it (Salas and Comabella 1999: 46) despite the size of the gathering being well beyond what they usually allowed.

Alongside such organisations, which managed to function within the confines of the system, a radically different project was taking shape. The Communist Party had been trying to launch a women's organisation (similar to its several 'mass fronts') as early as 1962, but had not been wholly successful in a difficult year, except in Barcelona where women members of the Catalan Communist Party (PSUC) launched the Democratic Assembly of Women of Sant Medir in tandem with the Workers' Commissions (Moreno 1988: 93). Three years later, various regional networks in Madrid, Zaragoza, Valencia, Basque Country, Galicia and Catalonia came together to found the most openly political women's organisation of the period: the Democratic Movement of Women (*Movimiento Democrático de Mujeres* – MDM). Its first General Assembly was held in Barcelona (Moreno 1988: 93). Combining feminist positions with the aim of mobilising women to take part in general actions against the regime,[3] it was open to all and attracted a variety of women from left-wing parties, though the core remained close to the still heavily ostracised Communist Party, which allowed the party to exercise 'ideological hegemony' over it (Abril and Miranda 1978: 220).

The MDM was to remain illegal for over a decade, most likely owing to its lingering connections with the Communist Party, but despite its lack of freedom to act in public, it managed – remarkably for 1967 – to persuade no less than 1318 or 1518 signatories (sources differ) to support its petition 'For the Rights of Spanish Women', which was addressed to the regime and sent directly to Franco's deputy vice-president (Moreno 1988: 95). It raised what was at the time a daring list of issues, demanding crèches, equal opportunities for young women to go to university, equal pay, birth control and divorce. The following year the MDM started a monthly newspaper *Women and Struggle (La Mujer y la Lucha)* which it distributed by hand in factories and markets (Salas and Comabella 1999: 30). Later 'their' was inserted before 'Struggle', a significant move towards recognising that women could fight on their own behalf.

The MDM was to maintain a regular level of activity for 12 years, and grow sufficiently strong to launch a series of initiatives that earned it media interest. Lock-ins in churches and hunger strikes by the relatives of prisoners[4] were designed to draw attention to prison conditions. There were short protests in markets, brandishing pots and pans or empty food containers painted with slogans against price rises and the lack of crèches, schools and parks. There were lightning street demonstrations demanding freedom and democracy in which women protestors cut off the traffic for a short while, sometimes wearing black veils or armbands. Some women tried to address the crowd coming out of church: after a few minutes, the speaker would quickly don a wig and disappear into the group protecting her (Salas and Comabella 1999: 31). One particularly notable event was the 300-strong women's demonstration held on 3 November 1970, which was the same day as the Workers' Commissions' day of struggle to demand amnesty for political prisoners, a day that was 'evidence of the widening solidarity of opposition forces' (Preston 1986: 27). In 1971 and 1972 the MDM campaigned on behalf of the persecuted US black activist Angela Davis, sending protest telegrams and distributing leaflets.

Due to its numerical strength and ability to draw on its own publicity resources (Pardo 1988: 134) the MDM was able to produce a mass of posters and leaflets and become influential in the growing, yet still illegal, women's movement. But its lack of legal status hampered its activities, and to remedy the constraint, it concentrated on spreading its politico-feminist message (Pardo 1988: 134) among the network of *legal* Associations of Homemakers (the word 'women' in the title had been disallowed). The Homemakers had been allowed to function as part of the government's 1970 populist drive to broaden its appeal among ordinary people (Salas and Comabella 1999: 40). The MDM's tactic was successful in that a further five new Associations were created in 1969/1970 under the 'home-making' umbrella. The initial success was quickly followed by a setback when the new feminist-infiltrated Associations attempted to influence the outcome of a government-sponsored International Congress of Women that year. Shocked by the infiltration, the government's Family Department refused to legalise further homemakers' associations for quite a time, and the conference proved to be the first and last of the Feminine Section's attempt to appear to promote women's real concerns.[5]

In 1972 the Castilian Association of Homemakers and Consumers (*Asociación Castellana de Amas de Casa y Consumidoras*) was founded by a mixed group of women including regime supporters. Some MDM women were able to gain membership with the intention of changing its orientation, which they did with the aid of its open-minded president Carmen Jiménez Sabio. From spring 1974 to mid-1975 it built up a network of 19 delegations, local branches of the Association in Madrid and surrounding towns, which it was allowed to do without seeking further government permission, having been granted the right to function in the region of Castile. The Castilian Association even obtained a permit to open premises right in the centre of Madrid (Calle Goya, 28), from which it was able to launch a plethora of semi-tolerated public activities, thereby reaching out to many more women. It had 776 women members in this period (Salas and Comabella 1999: 42). The political feminists' strategy of infiltrating an organisation devoted to housewives can be loosely compared to that deployed by genuine worker trade unionists and the Communist Party since the late 1950s, namely of infiltrating the legal official state trade union (*sindicato vertical*). It had been so effective that it had allowed a nationwide trade-union confederation to be built, the Workers' Commissions (*Comisiones Obreras*).

Legalised associations could issue statements, give interviews and edit newsletters, and the Homemakers were no exception. They were even supported by government grants from its III Development Plan budget, discussed in the Cortes in 1972 (Franco Rubio 1982b: 413). In February and October 1974 some of them wrote to the Minister of Justice and Home Affairs (*Gobernación* at the time) requesting a long list of penal reforms be enacted (Salas and Comabella 1999: 42). In October 1974, the Homemakers took the risk of publicly criticising the mayor of Madrid after he had rudely scoffed at the idea that a married woman should be allowed to work. Nonetheless, the boundaries of what one could openly demonstrate against were closely guarded and unpredictable. They would never know when the police might step in and ruin their carefully planned activities: the complete programme for a month of activities to attract and educate homemakers was banned by the Chief of Police in May 1974 (Salas and Comabella 1999: 43), and a month later in June a press conference organised to publicise their newly written manifesto on the right to equality, which called for social change, saw a government envoy arrive to announce it had been summarily suspended (Salas and Comabella 1999: 42). Members of these Associations were sometimes arrested, even though the dictatorship could not prevent them from using the opportunity to denounce such detentions to the Chief of Police and the media, and to galvanise support from other organisations, such as the church-inspired workers' clubs (HOAC), neighbourhood and parish organisations, and Colleges of liberal-minded professionals.

Having such innocuous-sounding legal organisations of rank-and-file women was useful to the wider women's movement as well as to the opposition. Kaplan underlines the paradox that they were formed as government-friendly organisations to draw women in, but as 86 per cent of Spanish women were homemakers in 1970, the Associations could not avoid including many working-class women, which proved to be the former's political undoing. As daily life was hard in the poor neighbourhoods with their lack of sewerage or rubbish collection, sometimes even of running water, their unpaved roads, minimal health, transport and telephone services, not to mention schools and recreational facilities, the task of fostering support for the regime proved fruitless. Many Associations became politically autonomous, transformed into an 'important instrument of rupture' with the regime (Kaplan 1990: 99–100).

The activity of the Amas de Casa can be related to those of the *Asociaciones de Vecinos*, the neighbourhood associations which had also been given legal status in 1964, but only flourished in the 1970s when they became a vehicle for protest (see Castells 1977). The impulse came from 'the depths of social grievances and the absence of democratic means of rectifying them' as the town councils were in the hands of appointed Falangist mayors and their cronies, often linked to real estate interests (Balfour 1989: 195). They promoted rapid urban development and neglected social infrastructures. Significantly, Balfour considers that women played a vital role in these urban protests in Barcelona (Balfour 1989: 196) because a kind of division of labour occurred, with labour agitation in the hands of men who had neither the time nor could afford the added risk of victimisation for playing a prominent role in residents' associations. This accounts for the 'prevalence of women in actions of protest' (Balfour 1989: 197).

The preceding material shows that for the pre-transition period women mobilised both as feminists and as homemakers, illustrating both *feminist* and well as *feminine* awareness. Kaplan's insights regarding the latter were inspired in part by women's role in the Barcelona upheavals and the transport boycott after the ticket price rise of 1951 (Kaplan 1982).[6] Later, as seen above, women in the 1970s organised as homemakers and planned neighbourhood demonstrations against price rises and the lack of urban amenities. They also had a history of protest and risk-taking in defence of political prisoners, particularly but by no means always, when these were close relatives, in a way that linked family survival with political engagement, as di Febo has shown (1979). However, it would be incorrect to ignore the fact that some of the activists of the Homemakers and neighbourhood organisations were either non-party feminists trying to reach out to homemakers whom they saw as oppressed, recruiting them 'to the sisterhood' as it were, or they were women clandestine members of left-wing parties such as the Communist Party and various new left groups. Indeed, the goal of the MDM (and of other party-linked women's organisations such as the ALM) was, arguably, to integrate 'feminine' with 'political' consciousness, while that of the Feminist Liberation Front (FLM) was to connect feminine with feminist awareness and feminism with the political struggle – all in the context of fighting the dictatorship and its patriarchal legacy. It would require a far more detailed study with much fresh research to unravel the complex mesh of motivations, interests and types of organisation, yet profound disatisfaction with their living conditions, whether induced by male oppression or the dictatorship's neglect, was undoubtedly the trigger and feminism provided the 'training school of political action' (Escario *et al.* 1996: 296) for a new generation of women who were to become, as the following account shows, highly influential.

The second wave

In the mid-1970s feminism re-emerged with surprising vigour, responding with alacrity to the new political opportunities opened by the slackening of political repression and the return of certain freedoms allowing feminists to work semi-clandestinely. When the Platform of Feminist Organisations wanted to publicise the common programme of its 28 organisations in February 1975, it called a secret press conference – something of a contradiction in terms – in the Madrid pub *Oliver*. The democratically inclined press played ball and gave the event the publicity the Platform wanted (Salas and Comabella 1999: 85).

At the beginning of 1975 the recently created Platform of Feminist Organisations of Madrid was able to join forces with the Homemakers'

Associations to launch an initiative that depended on their being able to deploy larger numbers of women: the boycotts of food markets. The successful market boycott of 20 February 1975 to protest against price rises was widely seconded by many women's organisations, and even though the authorities declared it a failure, the papers published just enough pictures of empty stalls and streets for readers to perceive that it had really happened. The regime's response was swift. It issued a three-month ban on any activity for all of the 28 women's organisations seconding the boycott, and also closed the offices of the University Women's Association and the Friends of Unesco Club. This sparked another reaction, this time from the President of UNESCO in Paris, who expressed concern. The boycott organisers then found it easy to gather support from a swathe of opposition and church groups to protest against the government's measures, sending thousands of signatures to the Prime Minister, the Justice and Interior Ministries, the National Movement state party, the Episcopal Conference and even to the UN (Salas and Comabella 1999: 55, 85–86). Discussing the ban in the Cortes, a procurator suggested the Homemakers' Associations were being manipulated by 'extremist clandestine groups' and should be given more support by the regime to avoid such influences (Franco Rubio 1982: 415).

On the eve of Franco's death that same year, 20 Homemakers' Associations again wrote to the Prime Minister drawing his attention to the rising cost of living, unemployment, homelessness, the deficiencies of the school system, poor conditions for women workers, and discriminatory passages in the Civil, Penal and Commercial legal Codes. This showed that, despite their title, the Homemakers Associations were able to express concerns that were acceptable to ordinary women apart from overt regime supporters. They were also clearly political in the conventional sense. Even hand-typed and stencilled leaflets distributed in working-class neighbourhoods by the local Homemakers' organisation placed the immediate cause of the protest – the rise in the official price of a loaf of bread – in the context of the repressive actions of the government, the lack of democracy, unelected councillors and discrimination against women, and called citizens of both sexes to join local organisations for freedom and democracy (de la Torre: 1975/6).

In the post-Franco continuity period from December 1975 to July 1976, various protests continued to be organised, including some by women workers of the Fiesta, Simago and Induyco plants about sex discrimination (Alvarez *et al.* 1977: 17, 21). The Associations of Homemakers were probably one of the few groups who drew specific attention to the cases of women workers who had been unjustly fired, punished or discriminated against by employers such as Danone, Simago and Rok (Salas and Comabella 1999: 43).[7] It was common for the Comisiones Obreras trade unions to call protests, but they had not fully come to understand the specific problems of women workers.

The United Nations' initiative to call 1975 International Women's Year, the first official year to draw attention to women's lot around the world, could not have come at a better time for the developing Spanish women's movement. General Franco was already a very sick man, expected to die before the year was out. It was a time of opposition resurgence and the Spanish question was once again on the international agenda, as it had been at the end of the Second World War in the 1946–1949 period when measures to bring down the Franco regime were considered. The United Nations' call provided a protective umbrella under which many liberal-minded reformist and opposition organisations were able to network more openly and make the preparations for a series of events that the regime was, by then, less likely to repress, given their UN connection.[8] 1975 became the 'key year in our recent political history' (Pérez-Serrano and Rubio 1999: 136). This view is not meant to play down the extent of clandestine work in previous years,[9] simply it was the year Spain's gender problem 'arrived' on the political scene.

Yet just as the preparations were in full swing, the government tightened security in its 27 August decree-law on the prevention of terrorism, which introduced even harsher penalties for unlawful association. New acts of armed struggle by ETA and the FRAP (Revolutionary Front for Popular Action, a non-Basque armed group) took place, suspects were seized and sent before a Council of War, and once more death penalties were passed – five of them. This led to an immediate international outcry, yet the ailing Franco refused to reprieve the five, provoking further reactions and the likelihood of new military court hearings. In this climate the feminists organising the conference to mark International Women's Year considered suspending it, but most planning meetings went ahead despite the tense situation. Even when Franco finally died on 20 November 1975, the women's groups refused to suspend the event – after all, the UN Year was running out on the calendar. Instead the conference was to be held semi-clandestinely, with the organisers keeping quiet about it being a full-blown women's liberation event, pretending instead that it was going to be nothing more than a simple, low-key response to the UN Year (Salas and Comabella 1999: 91). However, by then the women's movement was spreading and feminism was catching on. Seventy-nine legal organisations spanning seven provinces had subscribed to a collective manifesto 'For Women's Liberation: Programme of the NGOs of the Spanish State' (Salas and Comabella 1999: 87). That caused some of the political parties to sit up and show an interest in an area of legal and policy renewal over which they still had misgivings and confused ideas (Moreno 1977: 44).

The First Conference for Women's Liberation was finally held on 6–8 December 1975, only a fortnight after Franco's death, with c.500 participants from 15 local and nationwide organisations and women from about one third of Spain's 50 provinces, a notably broad spread for a non-legal event by a new type of organisation in a poor security climate. Many of the organisations had not passed the legality test owing to their ties to the illegal parties. The conference turned out to be one of the very first mass meetings to protest against the new King's excessively selective pardon for political prisoners announced only 11 days before. It drafted a telegram to the King demanding a general amnesty for political prisoners and protesting at the previous day's baton charges and arrests of demonstrators at the gates of Carabanchel men's prison, which the telegram described as a 'massacre' (Secretariado Nacional de Asociaciones de mujeres 1976: 5). It called for the abolition of the anti-terrorist decree law and, importantly, rejected any policy emanating from a non-elected government that did not guarantee democratic freedoms (Moreno 1977: 25, 148). The King was presiding over just such an unelected government and continued to do so for another year and a half until after the June 1977 elections. The tone of their protests showed that the women's movement shared many of the attitudes of the Spanish left at the time, both in their indignation that so few prisoners had been released, and in their sceptical view of Juan Carlos's intentions (see Preston 1986: 78). The conference's policy-oriented conclusions also denounced the lack of democratic rights, thereby adding its voice to the growing chorus of popular demands for change, and in a key 'political document' it expressed the participants' desire to be 'co-protagonists in the task of marshalling in democratic change' and to be part of 'the alternative being offered to the Spanish public' at the time (text of conference documents in Moreno 1977: 148, 151).

Significantly, the event ended with a communiqué expressing solidarity with all *women* prisoners held throughout the country – in fact this was one of the few times that attention was ever drawn to the existence of women *political* prisoners as well as women imprisoned for 'women's crimes'. Rarely was interest in their lot ever shown, whereas their male counterparts received publicity, expressions of support and solidarity actions, often organised by their womenfolk or women's organisations. Those convicted of women's crimes also tended to be overlooked because they were designated as common criminals, being ordinary women who had fallen foul of laws designed to ensure their continued subordination to men, by resorting to birth control, performing or receiving abortions, or using their bodies for gain or for sexual pleasure outside marriage. These were all issues that only came to be conceived as 'political' during the next decade, when their so-called offences were abolished one by one after feminist pressure.

Early post-Francoism

At Franco's death, Spanish women were still an oppressed gender. Socialised into subordination by the Feminine Section, presented with marriage and motherhood as the only socially acceptable role, forced to give up an independent income on marriage, unable to control their fertility or pregnancies, yet deprived of parental authority over their children, threatened with the charge of 'abandonment of the home' if they escaped from under the marital roof, and with imprisonment if they started a relationship with another man – in such a context, most women had in fact learnt to buckle down and resign themselves, encouraged by the weekly lecture from the pulpit and whispered advice from the confessional, in the belief that they were, after all, doing God's will and emulating the Virgin Mary whose name they all bore.[10]

For many it was a golden cage, yet a vociferous minority thought otherwise and knew that with the crumbling of the dictatorship their time had come. 1975 had served to bring the women's movement out into the open, and the year had ended in a buzz of political excitement. Not a month later in January 1976 two thousand women marched down Goya Street in Madrid demanding equality in all spheres (Alvarez *et al.* 1977: 17). Amnesty demonstrations were held: one in front of Yeserías women's prison in March was broken up by the police and another of 200–400 women in July managed to circle the prison several times and let off balloons with the word amnesty scrawled on them, intended to float over the courtyard and be seen by the inmates (Salas and Comabella 1999: 96–97). There were around 350 women in prisons at the time, and a further 400 confined to the special institutions for the 'protection of women'.

The new annual celebration of International Women's Day was launched on 8 March that year. The MDM gave a press conference on the day to present its re-drafted statutes in a successful bid for legalisation,[11] and opened public premises the following year. For the first time the many women's advocacy organisations were ready to unite into a powerful pressure group and the Secretariat of the non-governmental organisations that had organised the conference took on a new role as the co-ordinating body for the whole movement (called Platform of Madrid Women's Organisations and Groups).[12] Feminism also caught on in Catalonia where the First Catalan Women's conference held in May 1976 brought together over four thousand women representing around a hundred different groups who agreed to a united manifesto, a fact that won them the respect of the Catalan Communist Party, according to one participant (Escario *et al.* 1996: 224–225).[13]

In July 1976 the King finally announced his endorsement of a transition to democracy in a speech made while on a visit to the United States and the repressive first government of the monarchy was dismissed on his return. A new prime minister was appointed according to the procedures laid down by Franco. Adolfo Suárez soon announced his intention to find a way out of the political crisis and began contacts with the opposition in the autumn of 1976. In fact, feminists were already making an impact on the still illegal parties of the left, persuading the Communist Party (PCE) to hold its first conference on the woman question in October (Abril and Miranda 1978: 221) and the Socialist Party (PSOE) to formally commit itself to women's liberation during its 27th Party Congress in December that year. The abortion question hit the headlines on 3 October 1976 when *El País* launched its weekend colour supplement with the cover story 'To London for an abortion', reporting on the 20–30,000 women who made the journey every year to avoid the risk of a prison sentence in Spain. It was the first time that a report on this, 'the other pilgrimage' as it was ironically referred to at the time, had appeared in the press and it 'fell like a bomb'.[14] The Association of Women Lawyers organised an international conference in December 1976 on the legal situation of women in which one of its members, the radical feminist Cristina Alberdi, gave a paper defending the decriminalisation of abortion. Though she gained public recognition and later became Minister of Social Affairs in González's cabinet of 1993–1996, such daring was not to the liking of all at the time, and caused a rift in the Association (Salas and Comabella 1999: 52) as many women lawyers still feared the consequences of mentioning abortion. A month earlier, the *Plataforma* had collected signatures calling for the abolition of the law on adultery and handed them in to the Ministry of Justice on 15 November. Only a week later, on 24 November, around a thousand women, organised by the *Plataforma*, held an unauthorised march down Eloy Gonzalo Street calling for the derogation of the discriminatory Penal Code articles and for divorce. The riot police were waiting for them at Glorieta de Quevedo crossroad and charged them with batons and tear gas (Salas and Comabella 1999: 98).

On issues of law and order, the government remained erratically repressive and even legal women's organisations were sometimes banned from holding political meetings. An event entitled 'Woman and Democracy' called for November 1976 on the premises of a Catholic school was cancelled on several consecutive occasions by the civil governor of Madrid (Salas and Comabella 1999: p. 33), on orders from the Interior Minister. That month, Suárez was involved in delicate negotiations with the old guard of Francoist *procuradores* (appointed members of the 'organic', rubber-stamping legislative assembly) to secure approval for his bill to initiate a process of democratisation, which was eventually passed by them in mid-November. In order to secure the acquiescence of the National Movement, the recalcitrant right and the military to a change of system, Suárez had let it be understood that the Communist Party would not be legalised, and it is arguable that such public activity by the MDM, still considered to be under the influence of its Communist Party members, represented a threat to the government's delicate political negotiations. In fact, none of the parties of the left felt able to back Suárez's reform plan and called for abstention when it was put to a referendum on 15 December 1976. The MDM seconded the call in their appeals to women and so did the Castilian Association of Homemakers (Salas and Comabella 1999: 44). But the left lost this contest heavily, as abstention was only about 15 per cent, whereas the yes vote amounted to 78 per cent. Despite Suárez gaining legitimacy for reform, his approach to civil liberties remained repressive. In January 1977 a further demonstration by many hundreds of women in front of the Ministry of Justice on the opening day of the trial of a woman prosecuted for adultery was 'brutally repressed' with the police forcefully removing the demonstrators from the area (Salas and Comabella 1999: 97).

In early 1977, while the opposition parties argued with the government over their legalisation and the electoral law that was to open the way to the first democratic elections, new groups of women began to form. The first Conference of Working Women was organised by the MDM in February, attracting about four hundred workers from almost all branches of industry. Testimonies of the exploitative conditions under which women worked were heard publicly for the first time (Salas and Comabella 1999: 33) and gender segregation in the labour market was emphasised. Networking between women's advocates, the trade unions and the Communist Party (PCE) led to the launch of the first women's department of the Comisiones Obreras trade-union confederation. Such demands for equality at work later influenced the negotiations of the 1980 law enshrining the new Workers' Statute (*Estatuto de los Trabajadores*) in which sex equality became a formal, though not a very substantive, principle.

In the build-up to the first democratic elections of 15 June 1977, the MDM and other women's organisations such as ADM (*Asociación Democrática de la Mujer*) worked to help women to discuss the issues of the day and persuade them to vote. The Castilian Association of Homemakers opened an advice centre and distributed leaflets to women explaining how to register and how the balloting would work on the day. It was unclear how anonymity could be preserved since all the parties' ballots were laid out at the polling station and officials could see which party list voters picked up. Many women feared the officials would make a note of which ballot they chose.[15] Women's organisations recommended a vote for 'democratic' parties and for whichever best defended women's interests (Salas and Comabella 1999: 34) as a way of recommending a vote for the left parties favouring sex equality. At that stage there was no women's party, nor would the majority of the organisations, excepting the radical feminists, have recommended a vote for a gender-based party, given their links to the democratic and left parties of the day. In fact, only two committed feminists were fielded in sufficiently good positions to win Carlota Bustelo for the PSOE and María Dolores Calvet for the PCE.

The Constitutional period

Together with moderates from the old regime and reformist democrats, Adolfo Suárez put together a new party called Union of the Democratic Centre (UCD) and won the 1977 election, casting off his status as a mere appointee for the legitimacy of elected office. After the elections, the socialist-feminists developed a strategy for working inside the parties, as feminist caucuses, seeking leverage over policy-making or at least a consultative role, as well as simply hoping to persuade male and even female party colleagues of the worth of equality policy, with a view to hastening and improving any forthcoming legal reform to be debated in the new parliament. Over the years, the strategy was successfully played out in the case of the Socialist party PSOE (Threlfall 1998) and to a lesser extent in the Communist Party, which was hampered by its limited number of parliamentarians (varying from four to 23) and by its increasingly acrimonious internal factional splits. But this was not the only stance available to women's advocates. The centre-reformist UCD governments proved permeable to a small band of moderate women's policy advocates, including a handful of career civil servants. In addition, professional women such as lawyers formed feminist lobbies. Organisations practising independent feminism increased their influence on the basis of sheer numbers and the merits of their causes, though in retrospect this strategy was not as successful as it could have been compared with other countries (Valiente 1995).

Nonetheless, a range of women's policy advocates made an impact on the parliamentary politics of the transition and attempted to influence its historic constitutional settlement. Practical new services for women such as advice centres, birth-control provision and refuges against violence became some of the first social services to be set up by the early pre-autonomous governments and the first democratically elected town councils. The expanded agenda of gender issues then led to the creation of new policy-making offices in the central administration, and eventually to the creation by law of the central *Instituto de la Mujer* and its 'daughters' throughout the country.

The following account highlights the way gender questions were to be repeatedly addressed by policy-makers and the public during the key stage of political development that followed the return to democracy, reflected in a series of law reforms that altered the basis of gender relations. Even though the whole politico-legal system needed an overhaul, the notable phenomenon is the extent to which policy-makers were forced to include gender equality issues alongside their debates on the reorganisation of the state. The UCD government came under pressure from women's organisations to move well before the new Constitution was finally agreed. The Constitutional period 1977–1978 actually oversaw a rebalancing of gender relations, though this remained politically veiled rather than the subject of media headlines. Despite the silence, a full new legal deal for women emerged out of the struggle for consensus among the democratic parties.

The government came under co-ordinated pressure from groups targeting family law, who submitted unified legal-reform proposals to the government and new parliamentarians (Various Authors 1977). In December 1977 the new pressure group, the Single Mothers' Association

(Asociación de Madres Solteras), was launched. Modelled on the Separated Women's association, it campaigned for equal treatment of so-called 'illegitimate' children and gave evidence to the parliamentary Codification Commission drafting the new bill on filial matters. In addition to rights, the Single Mothers demanded practical services such as nurseries rather than charity handouts, using the slogan 'no privileges, only justice' (Salas and Comabella 1999: 72–73), with new kinds of non-judgmental services to replace the old charitable institutions such as the infamous *Patronato de Protección a la Mujer* (Foundation for the Protection of Women), whose immediate closure topped their demands. The Patronato was alleged to run its homes for single mothers like prisons guarded by nuns who made the residents feel shameful and controlled their money. They were treated like minors when in fact their inmates had not committed any crime (Various Authors 1977).

The right to use birth control was another area of legal struggle and activists brought about government reforms at an early stage of the transition. In fact, pressure for birth-control services had started well before Franco's death, as the first underground 'family planning' and sexual-health centre had been opened in 1974 by a group of volunteer doctors, nurses and psychologists, the best known being Dr Elena Arnedo, a socialist-feminist. Known only by its street location (*'Planning de Federico Rubio'*), it survived on private donations and its clients found it by word of mouth. Strangely, it was never called, visited or charged by the police. This remarkable initiative spawned similar centres in two working-class industrial suburbs of Madrid, Vallecas and Vicálvaro. Other socialist-feminists had been working on the PCE to commit itself to free access to contraception and a Communist-linked centre, the *Instituto de Medicina Social* in Madrid, had been created as a result. Later Dr Arnedo and PSOE women activists were able to persuade the party to commit itself to setting up further birth-control centres – probably a unique initiative in the history of social-democratic parties. The PSOE's first party-funded centre opened at the end of 1977 with Alfonso Guerra, Deputy First Secretary of the party, present at the launch.[16] A National Federation of Family Planning Associations followed in the same year to assist individuals and couples to maximise the number of wanted pregnancies and to further sex education (Salas and Comabella 1999: 74).

Thus, in a radical departure from traditional party practice, the Spanish left-wing parties became directly involved in the provision of contraception services because women members pressured them into it. When it came to debating the draft bill in parliament, feminist deputies spoke in favour of decriminalisation, with Carlota Bustelo eloquently defending the PSOE motion on 6 July 1978. Yet it was not agreed by consensus of the two chambers.[17] It had to be referred to the mixed Congress/Senate Committee for redrafting, and finally passed in the autumn of 1978 becoming Law 45/1978 of 7 October.

In a separate development, the UCD government was also becoming aware that it needed to be seen to address policy on women's issues. In the summer of 1977 Mabel Pérez-Serrano, the President of the Association of Separated Women, was invited to join the new Minister of Culture Pío Cabanillas in forming a government office to deal with such policies, the awkwardly named Sub-directorate for the Feminine Condition. The directorate was effective in liaising with the Ministry of Health over birth control and planned to use the Ministry of Culture's own community social centres to publicise the benefits of family planning. Curiously, the officials of the Ministry of Health under the UCD had already taken a surprisingly pragmatic, non-ideological stance on the subject, carrying out discreet fact-finding visits to the still illegal Federico Rubio centre and anticipating future training needs by organising a first Seminar on Family Planning as early as June 1977 – strictly speaking an illegal act[18] (Bannel and Pérez-Serrano 1999: 310–313). Anticipating parliamentary approval, the Sub-directorate of the Feminine Condition took pains to prepare a set of five publicity leaflets on contraception, printed half a million copies and waited for the abrogation of the relevant parts of the Penal Code. By the time they were given official permission to distribute the leaflet, it was discovered that a male under-secretary at the Ministry had taken it upon himself to have them destroyed! (Bannel and Perez-Serrano 1999: 316–317).

The new law decriminalised the sale, publicity and advertising of contraceptive methods, but penalised their being dispensed other than in accordance with the regulations. Together with Royal-Decree 2275/1978 of 1 September allowing the Ministry of Health to set up Family Orientation Services to advise on contraception, the way was open for women finally to be able to control their fertility. The new freedoms allowed the Castilian Association of Family Planning to set up its own centres. They started with the working-class district of Vallecas, where the initiative could count on the support of the 'respected progressive' community activist Father Llanos (Brassloff 1998: 64) as well as of the 'red bishop' Alberto Iniesta. Church premises were available for meetings and women were encouraged to bring along their husbands so as not to think of family planning as only women's business (Salas and Comabella 1999: 76).

Nonetheless, women's rights advocates did not hail the law as a great victory. Many thought that contraception should have been decriminalised much earlier, given the already widespread disregard for the law by the public – and even by a government department, as noted above. Little did they know that the opening of the much-heralded Family Services was to proceed at a snail's pace, and not at all in many areas, pending a fundamental health reform that the UCD never managed to design. Instead, the independent, non-profit and local-government sectors, whether responding to organised pressure or simply filling a gap in the market, stepped into the breach to provide the most-needed services.[19]

Neither could the government be trusted to propose the right kind of law reform without feminist input. An early draft of one of its bills planned to reduce the status of adultery from a crime to an offence of 'public scandal', naively not realising that this would be worse, since not only a husband but also any member of the public would have been able to denounce a suspected adulteress without serious evidence. The Democratic Association of Women quickly proposed amendments (Salas and Comabella 1999: 49), which were eventually taken on board. Another proposal of the Sub-directorate of the Feminine Condition that was criticised by feminists was the 1978 draft of a law which would oblige women to complete an obligatory period of 'Civil Service' consisting of employment training – supposedly an improvement on the recently abolished fascistic 'Social Service' training for motherhood. The Democratic Association of Women opposed this at an early stage, dubbing it a 'sophisticated new form of machismo' (ADM 1978: 27). The Sub-directorate boasted that forcing male conscientious objectors to do the civil service as well made it mixed-sex and therefore egalitarian (Subdirección de la Condición Femenina 1978). Sacramento Martí and María Salas were among those who made representations to the Sub-directorate (ADM 1978: 28) and the initiative never saw the light of day.

Despite such hiccups, several important laws regulating aspects of gender relations were passed in 1978. Law 22/1978 of 26 May abolished Articles 449 and 452 of the Penal Code, eliminating the offence of adultery for women and 'keeping a mistress' for men. Law 46/1978 of 7 October regulated the offences of sexual intercourse with a minor and abduction, making these offences against persons (not only females) and reducing the age of victimhood, which gave young boys a new level of protection and shielded children from a younger age. It is worth noting that the practice whereby legal representatives and guardians of abused minors could offer a pardon to the rapist and sexual abuser on behalf of their charges was abolished (Perez-Serrano and Rubio 1999: 140) – a chilling reminder of just how unprotected victims had been.

The Constitutional debate

In the constituent period from mid-1977 to the end of 1978, public politics was dominated by the drafting and approval of the new Constitution. Lacking an overall majority, Suárez made the wise decision to stay above the fray by delegating the drafting to a multi-party parliamentary committee in which he took no part, although his party the UCD had three out of its seven members. The unspoken goal was to search for a historic reconciliation though consensus. Many feminist groups, and virtually all the Madrid-based ones, took an active interest in the debate over the new Constitution, lobbying the President of the Cortes and their contacts among the deputies with amendments that would favour women's rights

(Federation of Feminist Organisations of the Spanish State 1978; *Movimiento Democrático de Mujeres 1978*; Various Authors 1978).

While the Constitutional Committee accommodated some of their demands, feminists were to receive only partial satisfaction in the 1978 text. Three Articles were welcomed by all as clear gains: §14 (equality), §32 (divorce), §35 (equal pay), with some including §23 (access to the media by social groups). The re-introduction of a gender non-discrimination provision in §14 was particularly welcome as it expressed a loyalty to the 1931 Constitution, and reiteration of the principle in the context of employment was also praised. But the Women's Liberation Front (FLM) and those associated with the far-left parties were gravely disappointed over two issues which were felt to be symbolic of the other parties' and the political system's untrustworthiness. Firstly, primogeniture: politicians agreed that the monarchs' son will have precedence over their daughter (§57.1) even if she the eldest, as is the case of the current Infanta, Princess Elena. Thereby a form of discrimination was permanently embedded into the political system in obvious contradiction of the same Constitution's §14. The second disappointment arose from the handling of the abortion issue, in which the left gave in and agreed to the right's form of wording ('All have the right to life ...': §15). Feminists, especially the Frente de Liberación de la Mujer, feared the courts might rule that 'all' included the foetus, thereby outlawing abortion for ever. The left's earlier draft had opened the possibility of legalising abortion by stating that 'All *persons* have the right to life' [emphasis added], which would clearly have excluded the unborn, as a baby becomes a person in law only a certain number of hours after being born.[20] The PSOE's chief Constitutional negotiator later admitted the right to abortion was bargained away in negotiations with the right (Peces-Barba 2000: 65).

In retrospect, it is all the more interesting to see how, when it came to the campaign for the Constitutional referendum of 6 December 1978, feminist groups were one of the few voices, along with Basque nationalists though for very different motives, that criticised the Constitution's failings. Feminists perceived that the broad principle of equality before the law was being violated by the text itself, not only over succession to the crown, but also in its continued protection of private and religious education. They deplored the text's overall failure to include birth control as a woman's right to control over her body, and its treatment of the right and duty to work in terms that ignored unpaid care work performed at home. They resented its apparent endorsement of a conventional family and the failure to include under its protection other forms of personal relationships, such as gay and unmarried couples and people living in communes (*sic*). They criticised the Constitution's failure to introduce divorce (§32 left it to be developed in a new law), its heterosexism (the article on marriage refers to the right of *a man and a woman* to marry) and its failure to recognise the need for co-education, which was believed at the time to be the only form of non-discriminatory education possible. The MDM criticised the document's 'silences', arguing that since the text went into so much detail on some issues, it could have spelled out other women's rights too. They did not recommend a vote either way (MDM 1978: 3). The moderately feminist Castilian Federation of Homemakers called for a yes vote and so did the far-left Union for the Liberation of Women (ULM), though for different motives, the latter arguing that if the text was not feminist enough it was because the feminist movement was still too weak and small and there were not enough male or female 'defenders' of women in parliament (ULM 1978: 5). The high-profile Women's Liberation Front (FLM) advocated abstention on the grounds that the Constitution 'would not open a door to change in our lives' (FLM 1978).

The Constitutional debate temporarily caused a rift among women's organisations. There were by then already 131 groups spread across 43 Spanish provinces, nearly the whole country (listed in González 1979: 303–310), and they were unable to unite in a single call to vote either way. Yet with hindsight one could argue that feminist expectations of the Constitution were probably too high, since no constitution has yet led to a reordering of the gender order to the extent that feminists hoped in the late 1970s. But, equally, hindsight shows that although the critical feminists were not listened to at the time, their critique has come to appear more and more reasonable over time, even prescient, as the feminists' more radical demands came back to haunt Spanish politics against all expectations. For instance, the ambiguous wording over the right to life was to lead to what was termed 'the major conflict of Spanish society' by the influential weekly *Cambio16* (No. 791, 26 January 1987, p. 12) and to a series of political rows, lawsuits and failed reforms (see Twomey 2001). The right was prompted into appealing to the Constitutional tribunal against the PSOE's already very limited 1983 abortion law, which, though passed, was never to be extended to allow social circumstances as grounds for a termination – the principle that motherhood should only take place when the mother is ready and a child is wanted was never to be enshrined in law despite later gaining social acceptance. Moreover, by the 1990s the Constitution's restriction of marriage to heterosexual couples no longer commanded consensus, and demands for single-sex unions to be recognised as equivalent to marriage increased and were accepted by several autonomy governments for administrative purposes. Lastly, the Constitution's simple reference to equality in employment was to prove wholly inadequate in facilitating access to employment for women, as the persistently higher female unemployment rates showed.

The post-Constitutional period

While the 1978 Constitution was being drafted, feminists were pushing for reform in other institutional arenas. Four women lawyers sitting on the

Justice Ministry's commission revising the Civil Code in 1978 played a role in drafting a set of bills on family law that finally reached parliament three years later. Feminists were consulted by the PSOE and PCE (and proffered their opinion even when not) commenting on every detail. María Dolores Pelayo, a Deputy for the Canary Islands, was a persistent and passionate defender of the reforms in the Cortes, introducing amendments such as on the equality of filial status of children born in and out of wedlock and those adopted (Pérez-Serrano and Rubio 1999: 144). She is credited with pushing the government and opposition sides towards consensus.

What emerged were ground-breaking laws whereby women finally achieved equality in marriage, both in the administration and ownership of acquired assets and in the exercise of parental authority (*patria potestad*) over offspring. Law 11/1981 of 12/13 May reformed the Civil Code on filiations, parental authority and marriage assets, and Law 30/1981 of 7 July eased the Code's restrictions on civil marriage, separation, annulment and divorce (Salas and Comabella 1999: 52). The existing five categories of children (legitimate, legitimated, illegitimate, natural and 'other' – *sic*) were abolished, and all received a clear right to maintenance from both parents including the non-custodial one. On coming of age, children obtained the right to change the order of their surnames to put their mother's first if they so wished (Pérez-Serrano and Rubio 1999: 144). Another long-standing demand of the feminist movement was won, namely the right of either parent to demand a paternity test to establish the legal responsibilities of a father, to be used in the all-too-frequent cases where fathers denied involvement in order to avoid child maintenance.

Divorce

In 1976 the two leaders of the Separated Women's Association (AEMS), Mabel Pérez-Serrano and Ana María Pérez del Campo, were invited to be weekly guests on what was to prove a controversial radio show discussing marriage breakdown. The public impact was so great they were threatened with violent retribution by the extremist traditionalist Catholic organisation Guerrillas of Christ the King (Salas and Comabella 1999: 57). By May 1977 the public influence of the Association had grown to the point of drawing a crowd of over two thousand people to a meeting. The ecclesiastical courts were not persuaded to reform their discriminatory practices and on 7 and 8 December 1977 an exasperated AEMS held a well-publicised sit-in of San Miguel Church demanding that cases of marital separation be moved to the civil courts. The Guerrillas of Christ the King were back, prowling around the gates in a sufficiently threatening manner for the civil governor of Madrid to send in policemen to protect the women (Salas and Comabella 1999: 59).[21] Two years later these church courts had still not been abolished. The AEMS, together with the *Movimiento Democrático de Mujeres* and the Flora Tristán Federation of Women's Associations, protested again by chaining themselves to the railings of the ecclesiastical court building, only to be arrested, confined to police cells for a period and heavily fined (Salas and Comabella 1999: 60). Pressure was kept up throughout 1980 with frequent media appearances, but divorce continued to arouse the passions of the far right and came up against the dogged reluctance of the church to give up its control over marriage.

Divorce had also been a major long-standing demand of activist women and feminists, particularly those who were already separated but had no right to remarry. More women than men request divorce in Western Europe and it was the same for Spanish legal separations at the time (Alberdi 1982: 78). From UCD to the left, several parliamentary parties had included divorce in their 1979 election manifestos. As soon as the first post-Constitutional legislature opened after the March 1979 elections, the Socialist and Communist Parties presented their bills to parliament. The AEMS and AMJ had already published their own drafts,[22] having done extensive political and legal preparatory work throughout the 1970s. They now felt considerable satisfaction at the extent to which their points had been taken into account by the Minister of Justice, the late Francisco Fernández Ordoñez (Salas and Comabella 1999: 60). The Coordinating body of Feminist Organisations of the Spanish State (*Coordinadora de organizaciones feministas del Estado español*) had their project presented to the Cortes by a male deputy and published in the official parliamentary gazette in December 1979 (Alberdi 1982: 78). The Democratic Association of Women (ADM) presented their project directly to the President of the Cortes, Antonio Hernández Gil (Salas and Comabella 1999: 49). Obviously, there was a lack of unity over preferred wordings. Bombarded with proposals, the UCD government rejected all opposition texts in October 1979 on the grounds that it would come up with its own, but then ran into internal political difficulties over the draft.

Together with education reform, the long gestation of the divorce law was accompanied by a hardening of the church's attitude towards the government. The Catholic hierarchy began to support a critical sector of UCD, hostile to Fernández Ordoñez's liberal divorce plans. It was on the verge of forming a right-wing Christian Democratic splinter group. The church dug in its heals against any form of divorce and the Opus Dei members of UCD even attempted to torpedo the bill as its made its way through the Cortes (Brassloff 1998: 105). The conservative Popular Alliance radically opposed it on the grounds that it went against the accords with the Holy See, believing that such an international treaty was of superior legal rank to a Spanish law. They were particularly incensed by the notion of divorce by mutual consent, an amendment that the bill had finally incorporated after receiving pressure from the women's organisations (Alberdi 1982: 77, fn. 13). The bill was passed on 22 June 1981 but was one of the main grievances that caused a group of UCD discontents to launch a 'Platform of Moderates' on 24 July (Preston 1986: 209–210), part of a new line-up between conservatives and right-of-centre moderates on the one hand, and liberals and the left on the other.

The far right did not accept the verdict of the parliament, and five months later on the sixth anniversary of the Caudillo's death (20 November) the Guerrillas of Christ the King struck again, attacking a large university audience engaged in a debate over divorce, throwing a Molotov cocktail into the crowd and causing burns to several participants (Salas and Comabella 1999: 61). In one sense, it is not surprising that feelings ran deep. Even sections of the public were still sceptical.[23] The indissolubility of marriage had remained unbroken both in principle and in practice throughout Spanish history with the exception of 1932–1939. So vehemently opposed to that exception had the male hierarchies of the Catholic church been that Franco had abolished divorce retrospectively in 1939, thereby creating thousands of unmarried parents and illegitimate children at a stroke (Pérez-Serrano and Rubio 1999: 158).

Equally prominent and even more controversial was the abortion question, which returned to hit the headlines almost as soon as the new Constitution was promulgated and continued to do so periodically for the next two decades. But by 1978, many women's organisations were no longer prepared to wait for the outcome of the constitutional debates and went ahead with campaigning. In June the Castilian branch of the Family Planning Association boldly asked the UCD government to decree the decriminalisation of abortion immediately in view of the growing number of women who were putting their health at risk by resorting to 'self-medication' as well as back-street practitioners. They managed to collect and publish an elite petition with over two hundred signatures of professionals and opinion-formers and though the government did not heed them, a precedent was set for the next round of protests.

The following year, under the influence of its strong feminist members' caucus, the Communist Party became the first parliamentary party to openly defend the need for an abortion law during an election campaign. They emphasised the dangers to women's health, freedom of choice and 'free and responsible motherhood' (PCE 1979). On the far left, women of the Communist Movement (MC/OIC) published their draft bill in 1979, advocating the right to abortion on demand up to 18 weeks of gestation. The March 1979 general election gave the issue more prominence than it had ever had before. Yet what most shook the government was the public's response to an attempt by magistrates to actually apply the law as it stood. Opening in Bilbao in October 1979, the trial of a group of married women of modest means, many with several children already, for involvement in abortion practices sparked off a series of protests that reflected badly on the government. In the sit-in of the Palace of Justice in Madrid hundreds of women were indiscriminately thwacked and bruised with truncheons in a municipal police charge ordered by José Barrionuevo, the PSOE local councillor responsible for security.[24] The trial dragged on for three years. Within days of opening, nearly four thousand prominent women and men[25] had incriminated themselves by declaring publicly 'I too have had an abortion' – a successful attempt to send the justice system into confusion and expose its incompetence (*Cambio16* No. 413, 4 November 1979, p. 24). The socially discriminatory effect of the law was highlighted in the ensuing furore, since anyone with a little money could get an abortion outside Spain without fear of prosecution, and only poor women were likely to face a prison sentence.

Needless to say, none of the self-incriminating *glitterati* were ever called upon to help the police with their enquiries. In all, some 25,000 signatures were collected in solidarity with the Bilbao defendants during these protests (Threlfall 1985). In March 1982, nine of the defendants were acquitted and two sentenced, and after an appeal, the latter were also acquitted in December that year (Muñoz Conde 1982). But the acquittal coincided with the sentencing of a 77-year-old male doctor for two abortions performed as far back as in 1968, unleashing more protests and a deeper legal controversy (see *El País*, 26 December 1982, pp. 11–13). By then the PSOE had been elected on a manifesto that included legalisation on certain grounds. Within a month of taking office it was prodded into making this particular gender issue the subject of one of its very first reforms, announcing partial decriminalisation as part of an urgent reform of the Penal Code (*El País*, 26 January 1983, p. 11).

Feminism in the PSOE

So far this chapter has shown the extent to which gender issues were present in transition politics in terms of feminist and women's organisations' participation in, and impact on, public life. Other arenas of political yet not-so-public life were also being influenced by the women's movement and feminist thinking, namely the political parties of the left and the trade-union confederations of Comisiones Obreras and UGT (General Union of Workers). Only glimpses of the influence on the parties have appeared in the foregoing account. These areas of the history of the period are still largely unwritten, even though many women of the Communist Party have an extensive history of effective activism. So do the women trade unionists and, to a lesser extent, the women of the far left groups, many of whom went on to have careers in the public eye.[26] A little more is known about the PSOE, and a brief summary will follow here in order to highlight the links between feminist activism of the 1970s, the policy developments that took place during the 13 years of PSOE government and the outcry against violence against women that the conservative Popular Party government faced in its second period in office (2000–2004).

During the dictatorship, the PSOE never gained the ability to influence women through mass organisations such as the Associations of Homemakers or the Democratic Movement of Women (MDM), in contrast to the PCE. It was too involved in its own reorganisation and revival after languishing under a lacklustre exiled leadership until 1974. The party's first real encounter with organised intra-party feminism can be traced to the setting up in late 1976 of a feminist group inside the party by members who wanted to raise awareness of women's rights issues. The group's sympathisers spread across various PSOE federations (the party in the regions) and their aim was to get the forthcoming 27th Party Congress of December 1976 to formally address 'the woman question'. In the event, the Catalan, Guipúzcoa and Madrid delegations to conference successfully contributed position papers on women in society (PSOE 1976), and the Conference passed a resolution resolving to fight for a slate of women's liberation demands typical of the time. It committed the PSOE to obtaining 'equal rights for women in all fields without restriction or discrimination of any kind' (PSOE undated, 1977: 8). In addition to policy commitments the feminists obtained a foothold in the party organisation with the establishment of Women and Socialism caucus (*Mujer y Socialismo*). Formally it was as a subcommittee of the Federal Executive Commission's Secretariat for Political Education, at that time headed by Luis Gómez Llorente, but he allowed it to function as an open group in which any woman could participate without prior election onto the subcommittee or any other party position, thereby skipping over internal party structures that tended to keep women at the bottom of the party hierarchy. With hindsight it was arguably the actions of women party members and their use of elective and decision-making party structures that proved effective in influencing the PSOE, reaping more gains than if they had waited for the party to simply fall under the influence of the external environment such as the 1975 Women's Year, the UN decade for Women or European second-wave feminism in general. The PSOE leadership – to a man – needed to be persuaded, and persuaded by women whom they felt were also 'one of us', loyal to the party's overall aims, in other words party members and committed socialists (Threlfall 1985, 1996, 1998).[27]

The key player in *Mujer y Socialismo*'s creation was Carlota Bustelo, a long-time member of the PSOE, active in the party during the years of clandestine work and elected to parliament in June 1977. *Mujer y Socialismo* members were feminists of varying intensity keen to develop gender policies for the party to incorporate into its overall policy and, as PSOE candidates steadily gained office from 1979 onwards, into its work in town councils and regional bodies. The strategy was based on using the opportunities for developing practical measures such as setting up family planning or advice centres for women, or drafting changes to laws and regulations. Drawn to the chance to contribute to women's advancement by virtue of their new office or their expertise as lawyers and doctors, more women from inside and outside the party 'came out' as feminists. By 1979 four Women's Advice Centres were already functioning in Andalucía under the auspices of the PSOE-led pre-autonomous government, the Junta de Andalucía (PSOE 1980–1981: 14), a pioneering move for a regional authority. The move was inspired and facilitated by the socialist-feminist member María Izquierdo (Escario *et al.* 1996: 141), for neither the Andalucían party leaders nor the government were especially sympathetic to feminism at that time, according to local feminists, but there were helpful gynaecologists willing to provide birth control (personal communications). This was by no means the only activity of the group, nor indeed of women's caucuses in the federations, but lack of space means that in the post-Constitutional stages of the transition, public actions in the cause of sex equality by any one group become far too numerous to mention.

By the time of its 29th party conference in 1981, the PSOE had adopted an extensive set of public-policy commitments towards women, advanced in general by the *Mujer y Socialismo* group of party feminists (PSOE 1981: 231–235) but fought for specifically by the feminists in the delegations sent to conference by the federations. One of the demands was to increase the profile of women's policy by creating a Women's Secretariat of the Federal Executive Commission. The leadership was reluctant, but a compromise was reached whereby the then co-ordinator of *Mujer y Socialismo*, Carmen Mestre, was included on González's slate of candidates for the Federal Executive Committee and duly elected to the portfolio named Secretary of Defence of Freedoms. Thus for the first time a declared feminist, who had been active in the independent Women's Liberation Front (FLM) just before joining the party, reached the top of the PSOE hierarchy as a result of internal feminist pressure.

Despite the appointment, the leadership was reluctant to field an extensive set of commitments to women in its 1982 election manifesto, but by then Spanish politics were moving from the transitional phase of democracy into the consolidation phase that continued in earnest with the PSOE's accession to power. Spanish democracy proved it was strong enough to withstand two changes of party in government, fulfilling Huntington's (1991) two-turnovers test. Nonetheless, just as during the transition, gender issues were to become much more salient in the 1980s and 1990s than was expected from the PSOE's low-key manifesto.

Conclusion

Let us reflect now on the process undertaken of gendering the Spanish transition to democracy. The preceding account establishes empirically the extent to which gender issues played a part in the public process. With their voices, women's organisations augmented the volume of opposition against the dictatorship and the transitional governments, thereby both swelling the mass of opposition and also extending its reach by bringing to light a form of oppression that political elites were almost wholly unaware of at the time. The struggle against women's oppression had the potential to create a new sense of identification with the democratic project in millions of people.

The activities of the women's organisations both appealed to the 'feminine consciousness' (Kaplan 1982) of many women primarily concerned with their traditional roles and also provided experiences of transformative political learning by initiating women into feminism via a commitment to the struggle for democracy, and into politics via a sense of injustice at gender discrimination. Such activities helped to politicise the female electorate in a crucial period when ordinary women, after decades of relegation to the home, approached the end of Francoism with low levels of interest in politics and a low sense of efficacy (López Pintor and Buceta 1975: 187). The numerical impact of this is hard to illustrate as much research is lacking, but it is worth mentioning that a study of gender in printed political discourse (declarations, articles, manifestos) revealed 136 discourses on women were made in the three and a half years of the 1979–1982 legislature. This proved to be higher than in the 1980s as a whole until surpassed by a marked revival in the 1993–1996 period (Gaitán and Cáceres 1995: 134).[28]

Whatever the exact contributing causes, the interesting point is that women did not become the heavily conservative voting block that had been anticipated (Cases *et al.* 1978; Threlfall 1979). Considering that the left parties had earlier disdained women as a potential source of support, it can be argued that raising the gender question at an early stage, even if at the time it made feminists appear very much in the vanguard, actually saved the left from the political trap of gender traditionalism and indifference to the rights of women that would have lost the PSOE many votes in 1982, and even more later. The feminist-organised mobilisations over the persecution of abortion practitioners and patients not only prevented a group of distressed women and men from languishing in prison for years but also undoubtedly forced a somewhat reluctant PSOE to include a pledge to decriminalise it in its manifesto – a calculated risk that in no way dented its landslide victory. Instead, sex equality became part of mainstream discourse. By the mid-1980s women as a large new political constituency had become associated with progress and modernisation.

Furthermore, the transitional political agenda was transformed, being forced to address marriage, divorce and birth control in a way that the political elites had not anticipated and sometimes struggled to avoid, in vain. It has been observed that the UCD government found little time for international or economic policy because it was too caught up in priority domestic matters. This chapter shows that domestic politics did indeed involve gendered policy developments and law reforms in no small measure, and also that feminists prevented ill-advised initiatives from coming to fruition.

Women's organisations also had a decisive influence on the achievements of the newly elected municipalities and pre-autonomous authorities by leading them to open the kind of advice and service provision centres that gave them local visibility and enhanced their legitimacy among electors and taxpayers. This was done through the parties, who were persuaded to reconsider their priorities for principled as well as pragmatic reasons.

Another kind of gender impact was the way the progressive wording of the new divorce law (lobbied for by women's organisations) had a powerful disruptive effect on the UCD and deepened internal rifts, revealing its traditional underbelly and ultimately undermining its credibility with the electorate. UCD's loss of viability in 1982 and later disappearance reconfigured the nascent four-party system into a clear-cut two-party alternation between centre-left and centre-right.

Returning to the concepts advanced in the methodological considerations for explaining women's mobilisation, this account shows how both practical and strategic gender needs fuelled women's action. Yet on balance it also suggests that strategic gender interests became prevalent, both in the claims put forward and in the solutions sought. Perhaps this was so because the account chose to privilege public manifestations and interventions in the political arena. But it is more likely that the nature of the political conjunctures examined here provided opportunities that were judged by feminist activists bent on furthering women's strategic interests to be too good to miss.

Two types of power structures to which party feminists gained access clearly stand out as key to the advancement of gender policies in the latter phases of the transition process: firstly, the institutional arenas of the national parliament, local councils and regional governments; and secondly, the internal party leadership and policy-making structures. It is important to appreciate how clearly the PSOE's developing institutional public policy on gender in the last years of the transition was a result of the impact of the organised women's group inside it, crucially backed by the presence of a wider movement as well as by influential professionals and experts. The significance of this for the future development of gender policies in the 13 years of PSOE rule should not be underestimated. In a solid social democratic party with a federal structure covering the country, organised internal debate and elective leadership processes, policy gains were solidified and built upon.

Returning to the question of why the salience of gendered questions has been overlooked in accounts of the Spanish transition, Kaplan concludes after a wide-ranging comparative review of grass-roots movements in several countries that 'because of their loose organizational forms and informal leadership styles, women's protest activities have been largely overlooked or underestimated, especially in regard to their political significance for democracy and ethical beliefs in human rights' (1997: 180).

This offers a possible explanation of why the activities of the Spanish women's organisations have been neglected in the literature on the transition. Certainly their significance for democracy was seriously undervalued, as the escalating importance attributed to civil society for post-communist democracies shows in retrospect. Yet it also leads to the question of why Kaplan believes loose organisational forms and informal leadership styles are the prevalent style of political work that women collectively engage in. The Spanish example, while not offering evidence of any tightly structured top-down women's groups, does show them successfully working within and around institutions in special periods when these were particularly malleable and involved in a process of re-legitimising themselves during the transition to democracy. Many Spanish women's organisations broke out of exclusion and marginality by working inside parties, where feminists could work informally amongst themselves as well as formally within party structures. By working in elective institutions they also worked with their rules; looseness and informality were curtailed there where groups of feminists were able to hold some institutional power and deploy resources to benefit women with specific immediate needs such as contraception and legal counsel. Nonetheless, and despite this, their achievements are little celebrated in the 'malestream' literature on the transition, a fact that can best be attributed to many authors' hazy understanding of gender.

Further questions

As to the wider, intriguing question of whether some political transitions between regimes are more prone to become permeated by gender struggles than others, further research is called for. It has been argued that the very disorderliness of politics during revolutionary upheavals does open up opportunities for women if they are organised and not frontally opposed by entrenched interests, but that such gains do not endure after the new regime has become politically consolidated (Nelson and Chowdury 1994: 16; Beckwith 2000: 450). But this was disputed early on with regard to Vietnam (Eisen 1984) and Beckwith also notes that this did not occur in Nicaragua where the Sandinista women's organisation AMNLAE co-operated with FSLN both before and after it took power (being formally the party's women's section) and gained access to political resources.

In the Spanish case, the 'disorderliness of revolution' was arguably reflected in the disorderly, multiple and conflicting demands for regime change made during the dictatorship's decline and the aftermath of Franco's death, with the initial uncertainty of a genuinely democratic outcome to the transition process. Gisela Kaplan makes the point that this was also a fight against a specific code of ethics. Spanish feminists were non-conformists and deviants in their impulse to break the prevailing gender ideals, which required a 'major conceptual revolution' (Kaplan 1992: 262–263). But the fight culminated in a profound, 'transacted' (Share 1986) break with the past, which arguably allowed feminists to build *lastingly* on the general principle of equal rights in a period when principles suddenly mattered and were fought for by key actors who wanted the most advanced democracy that could be envisaged at the time. They ended up persuaded that women's rights were part of such a project. Thus 'what was seen as a deviation from the norm is now the norm' (Kaplan 1992: 263) – a new consensus on gender equality was created.

Yet it has been argued that institutional democratisation, however principled its design, does not *necessarily* entail any democratisation of power relations in society at large, particularly not between men and women (Waylen 1994: 329). The Spanish case suggests that whether it does, or not, depends, at least in its initial stages, on an 'internal transition' within feminist advocacy groups from outsiders to insiders, from the relative powerlessness of simply making demands to the power of gaining political leverage. Thus they were able to 'reverse the cycle of women's disadvantage and powerlessness' (Coote and Pattullo 1990: 278). The Spanish case underlines the crucial importance of feminist agency and of the strategic decision to intervene in the conventional political arena. As Molyneux says of other cases, 'the process of taking women's interests out of the personal, private and non-political sphere into the public terrain of political demand-making and then of framing those demands in terms of a

Figure 2.2 Jobs – Now! International Women's Day, 8 March 1979.

redefined general interest can be an effective way of giving feminist demands a more general salience' (Molyneux 2001: 160).

The Spanish transition, as we have seen, had a rich gender dimension to it. The activities of countless feminist actors were vital in making gendered inequality visible, not to say audible; in giving gender political substance and in achieving significant concessions and reforms to lighten the weight of oppression. The rest of the book will shed light on how effective this was in the longer term by looking more closely at the specific gender policies, at the labour market, the welfare system, representative politics and the behaviour of men at home.

Law reform affecting gender relations during the transition 1977–1981*

Royal Decree-Law 23/1977 of 1 April. Abolished the National Movement and with it the Feminine Section.

Law 22/1978 of 26 May. Abolished §449 and §452 of the Penal Code, eliminating the crimes of adultery (for women) and publicly keeping a mistress (for men). Legal representatives or guardians of minors can no longer offer a pardon on behalf of their charges who have been victims of rape or sexual abuse.

Law 45/1978 of 7 October. Amended §343 and §416 of the Penal Code. Decriminalised the provision, sale, publicity or advertising of contraceptive methods, but penalised any unregulated vending.

Royal-Decree 2275/1978 of 1 September. The Ministry of Health is permitted to create Family Orientation Services which include birth control.

Law 46/1978 of 7 October. Regulates the offences of sexual intercourse with a minor, and of abduction, stipulating these to be offences against a person of either sex. Abolished references to women's virginity and decency; and reduced the age of victimhood.

Law 8/1980 of 11 March. Established the principle of equal treatment between men and women in access to employment; made any discriminatory collective-bargaining agreements, employers' decisions and individual contracts null and void.

Law 11/1981 of 13 May (*Boletín Oficial del Estado*, No. 119, 19 May 1981). Reform of the Civil Code with regard to filiations, parental authority over joint children and the 'economic regime' of marriage in which assets are to be disposed of by agreement between both spouses.

Law 30/1981 of 7 July amended the Civil Code's dispositions regarding matrimony, annulment, separation and divorce, in which both spouses have equal rights and duties.

Law of 13 July 1982 amended the Civil Code dispositions regarding nationality, so that Spanish nationality is conferred on the children of Spanish mothers and fathers equally.

continued

Constitutional provisions with a bearing on gender or sex equality*

§9.2. It befalls public authorities to promote the conditions to make real and effective the freedom and equality of the individual and of the groups s/he is part of.

§10.1 The dignity of the person, the inviolable rights inherent to it, the free development of the personality, respect for the law and the rights of others are the foundation of the political order and of social peace.

§14. Spaniards are equal before the law, and no discrimination shall prevail on account of birth, race, sex, religion, opinion or any other personal or social condition or circumstance.

*author's translation

Notes

1 The Generalitat (Catalan government) permitted abortion from 25 December 1936 and introduced an abortion service in its main hospital from March 1937. It is calculated that fewer than 1200 legal terminations of pregnancy had been performed by the end of 1938. See Nash 1983.
2 Later reaffirmed in Law 191/1964 of 24 December.
3 See MDM documents cited in Abril and Miranda 1978: 219–220.
4 For antecedents of Spanish women's activism as prisoners' wives, see di Febo (1979) and Moreno (1988: 92).
5 In 1968 it had been active in furthering law reform to allow married women to vote and stand in local elections (Brooksbank Jones 1997: 5).
6 Beall *et al.* 1989 make comparable arguments regarding women's participation in the South African struggles.
7 For a full account of the Rok conflict, see Díaz Sánchez 1999.
8 The official representation at the UN conference remained in the power of the Sección Femenina.
9 The interview techniques used in Escario *et al.* 1996 served to uncover much further evidence of early initiatives and organisation.
10 Salas (1981: 104, 113) claimed the Virgin Mary was still presented to women as an exalted model by the Catholic church, keeping them in a position of 'submission and subordination', despite theoretical equality. See also Aler Gay's (1982) pioneering deconstruction of texts, teachings and encyclicals. Virtually all Spanish women are called María, often linked to the stations of the cross (del Camino, de la Cruz), to her holy state (María Inmaculada, Concepción) or to a particular statue of the virgin (del Carmen, del Pilar), etc.
11 The MDM claimed to have 800 members in Madrid in 1976.
12 Two years later, in a significant move, it changed its name to Platform of *Feminist* Organisations of Madrid to signify a clearer identification with feminism. In 1980 both the Madrid and the Barcelona co-ordinating 'platforms' ceased to function (Kaplan, G. 1992: 26).
13 The following year the Valencian region and Basque country held their own feminist assemblies (Escario *et al.* 1996: 228).
14 The story was recounted by Aznárez in 2001.
15 The trick was to pick up several parties' ballots, take them all into the booth, tear up the unwanted ones and emerge with only the preferred party's ballot

paper, already folded, to slip into ballot box (personal observations recorded in June 1977).
16 See the personal account by Dr Elena Arnedo, one of the Federico Rubio centre's founders and promoters, in pp. 319–322 of Bannel and Pérez-Serrano 1999. The centre, an instant success, soon became self-financing and still functions today, offering a wide range of health and support services to women.
17 The UCD did not have an absolute majority in the lower house or Congress of Deputies, and was forced to govern by consensus or negotiation of pacts.
18 This probably explains why it was held far away from Madrid, in Mahon (Menorca).
19 193 independent clinics were reported by the Institute of Women to be in operation by 1984 (Threlfall 1985: 64).
20 The article was invoked by Popular Alliance in its 1983 appeal to the Constitutional Tribunal, but in fact did not prosper as the juridical grounds for outlawing abortion. The PSOE's abortion law, amended for other reasons, was passed in 1985.
21 The same who chanted 'Death to the red bishops' as Cardinal Tarancón presided over Franco's funeral and burial (Brassloff 1998: 64).
22 See Alberdi *et al.* 1977.
23 Opinion polls of the mid-1970s showed 51 per cent of women thought marriage should be indissoluble, 31 per cent said it depended and only 17 per cent said it should not, i.e. were clearly in favour of divorce (see *FOESSA 1975:* 395). But views evolved quite quickly: by 1978 only 23 per cent of women and 18 per cent of men remained opposed to dissolution, while 44 per cent of women and 54 per cent of men now favoured allowing divorce to take place (see CIS 1978).
24 This account is drawn from my first-hand observation as a participant in the sit-in. See also Escario *et al.* 1996: 334–335.
25 1300 women and 1200 men according to one count (Escario *et al.* 1996: 334).
26 Pilar Castillo, a Minister in the Popular Party governments from 1996, is but one prominent example.
27 Notwithstanding the fact that at a later stage it favoured making some high-profile appointments from outside the party, such as when Cristina Alberdi became Minister for Women.
28 Admittedly, such references may represent a small percentage compared to other issues discussed.

References

Abril, M.V. and Miranda, M.J. (1978) *La liberación posible*, Madrid: Akal.
Alberdi, C., Cerillos, A. and Abril, C. (1977) 'Líneas generales que deberían inspirar una ley divorcista' in *Ahora Divorcio*, Barcelona: Bruguera, pp. 74–81.
Alberdi, I. (1982) 'Aspectos contradictorios de la opinión de las mujeres ante el divorcio' in Various Authors, *Nuevas Perspectivas sobre la mujer*, Madrid: Universidad Autónoma de Madrid.
Aler Gay, M. (1982) 'La mujer en el discurso ideológico del catolicismo' in Seminario de Estudios de la Mujer (eds) *Nuevas perspectivas sobre la mujer*, Vol. I, Madrid: Universidad Autónoma de Madrid, pp. 232–248.
Alvarez, N., Bellido, D., Castro, M., Comabella, M., Graña, M., Pardo, R., Pérez, P. and Sáez, M. (1977) *Aportaciones a las cuestión femenina*, Madrid: Akal.
Alvarez, S. (1990) *Engendering Democracy in Brazil: Women's Movements in Transition Politics*, Princeton, NJ: Princeton University Press.

Asociación Democrática de la Mujer-ADM (1978) 'Servicio cívico temporal: una discriminación más sofisticada', Madrid: *Gaceta Feminista*, No. 2.

Asociación 'Mujeres en la transición democrática' (eds) (1999) *Españolas en la transición: de excluidas a protagonistas 1973–82*, Madrid: Editorial Biblioteca Nueva.

Asociaciones de Amas de Casa (undated, 1976/7) *Primeras Jornadas del Ama de Casa: conclusiones*, Madrid, pamphlet, 12 pp.

Aznárez, M. (2001) 'Del perejil a la píldora del día después' in *El País Especial 25 Años*, Madrid: El País, p. 156.

Balfour, S. (1989) *Dictatorship, Workers and the City: Labour in Greater Barcelona since 1939*, Oxford: Oxford University Press.

Bannel, S. and Pérez-Serrano, M. (1999) 'Mujer y Salud' in Various Authors, *Españolas en la transición: de excluidas a protagonistas 1973–1982*, Madrid: Editorial Biblioteca Nueva.

Beall, J., Hassim, S. and Todes, A. (1989) 'A bit on the side? Gender struggles in the politics of transformation in South Africa', *Feminist Review*, No. 33, Autumn.

Beckwith, K. (2000) 'Beyond compare? Women's movements in comparative perspective', *European Journal of Political Research*, 37: 431–468.

Brassloff, A. (1998) *Religion and Politics in Spain 1962–96*, Basingstoke: Macmillan.

Brooksbank Jones, A. (1997) *Women in Contemporary Spain*, Manchester: Manchester University Press.

Campo Alange, M. (M. Lafitte, condesa de) (1964) *La mujer en España: cien años de su historia*, Madrid: Ediciones Aguilar.

Capmany, M.A. (1970) *El Feminismo Ibérico*, Barcelona: Oikos-Tau Ediciones.

Cases, J.I., López Nieto, I, Ruiz de Azúa, M.A. and Vanaclocha, F. (1978) *Mujer y 15 de junio*, Madrid: Ministerio de Cultura.

Castells, M. (1977) *Ciudad, democracia y socialismo*, Madrid: Siglo XXI.

CIS (1978) Survey in *Revista Española de Investigaciones Sociológicas*, 1/78: 385–402.

Coote, A. and Patullo, P. (1990) *Power and Prejudice, Women and Politics*, London: Weidenfeld and Nicholson.

de la Torre, E. (undated, 1975/6) *Amas de casa, vecinos de Madrid, ciudadanos*, Madrid: Asociación de Amas de Hogar de La Estrella-Moratalaz, leaflet, 1 p.

de Rivera, Primo (1963) *La mujer en la nueva sociedad*, Madrid, pp. 7 and 78.

di Febo, G. (1979) *Resistencia y movimiento de mujeres en España 1936–76*, Barcelona: Icaria.

di Febo, G. (1990) 'La lucha de las mujeres de los barrios en los últimos años del franquismo' in J. Tussell, A. Alted and A. Mateos (eds) *La oposición al régimen de Franco*, Madrid: UNED.

Díaz Sánchez, P. (1999) 'Coser y luchar: las huelgas de la fábrica Rok madrileña de 1976' in A. Aguado (ed.) *Mujeres, regulación de conflictos sociales y cultura de la paz*, Valencia: Universidad de Valencia, pp. 143–155.

Durán, M.A and Gallego Méndez, M.T. (1986) 'The women's movement and the new Spanish democracy' in D. Dahleruo (ed.) *The New Women's Movement*, London: Sage, pp. 200–216.

Eiroa San Francisco, M. (1995) 'Hacia la modernización social: las mujeres en la transición' in A. Soto Carmona *et al.* (eds) *Historia de la transición y consolidación democrática en España*, Vol. II, Madrid: UNED/UAM, pp. 535–548.

Eisen, A. (1984) *Women in Revolution in Vietnam*, London: Zed Books.

Escario, P., Alberdi, I. and López-Accotto, A.I. (1996) *Lo personal es político: el movimiento feminista en la transición*, Madrid: Ministerio de Asuntos Sociales/Instituto de la Mujer.

Fagoaga, C. and Saavedra, P. (1977) *Las españolas ante las urnas*, Madrid: Pecosa Editorial.

Federación de Organizaciones Feministas del Estado Español (1978) *Los derechos de la mujer en una Constitución democrática*, Madrid: ADM, pamphlet, 7 pp.

FOESSA (1975) *Informe FOESSA 1975*, Madrid: FOESSA.

Folguera, P. (ed.) (1988) *El feminismo en España: dos siglos de historia*, Madrid: Editorial Pablo Iglesias.

Folguera, P. (1997) 'Democracy and social change' in E. Garrido, P. Folguera, M. Ortega and C. Segura (eds) *Historia de las mujeres en España*, Madrid: Editorial Síntesis, pp. 549–572.

Foweraker, J. (1994) 'Popular political organisation and democratisation: a comparison of Spain and Mexico' in I. Budge and D.M. Kay (eds) *Developing Democracy*, London: Sage.

Franco Rubio, G. (1982a) 'La contribución de la mujer española a la política' in R. Capel Martínez (ed.) *Mujer y Sociedad en España 1700–1975*, Madrid: Ministerio de Cultura, pp. 241–266.

Franco Rubio, G. (1982b) 'La contribución de la mujer española a la política contemporánea: el régimen de Franco' in R. Capel Martínez (ed.) *Mujer y Sociedad en España 1700–1975*, Madrid: Ministerio de Cultura, pp. 393–431.

Frente de Liberación de la Mujer (1978) *Porqué proponemos la abstención a las mujeres*, leaflet, 6 pp.

Gallego Méndez, M.T. (1983) *Mujer, falange y franquismo*, Madrid: Taurus.

García Méndez, E. (1979, 2nd edn) *La actuación de la mujer en las Cortes de la II República*, Madrid: Ministerio de Cultura.

Gatán, J.A. and Cáceres, M.D. (1995) 'La mujer en el discurso político', *Revista Española de Investigaciones Sociológicas*, 69/95.

González, A. (1979) *El feminismo en España, hoy*, Madrid: Zero-Zyx.

Huntington, S. (1991) *The Third Wave: Democratization in the Late Twentieth Century*, Norman, OK: University of Oklahoma Press.

Jaquette, J. (1994) [1987] *The Women's Movement in Latin America: Participation and Democracy*, Boulder, CO: Westview Press.

Kaplan, G. (1992) *Contemporary Western European Feminism*, London: Allen & Unwin.

Kaplan, T. (1971) 'Spanish anarchism and women's liberation', *Journal of Contemporary History*, 6 (2): 101–110.

Kaplan, T. (1977) 'Women and Spanish anarchism' in R. Bridenthal and C. Koonz (eds) *Becoming Visible: Women in European History*, Boston: Houghton Mifflin.

Kaplan, T. (1982) 'Female consciousness and collective action: the case of Barcelona', *Signs*, 7: 545–566.

Kaplan, T. (1990) 'Conciencia femenina y acción colectiva: el caso de Barcelona 1910–1918' in J. Amerlang and M. Nash (eds) *Historia y género: las mujeres en la Europa Moderna y Contemporánea*, Valencia: Edicions Alfons el Magnànim, pp. 267–295.

Kaplan, T. (1997) *Crazy for Democracy: Women in Grassroots Movements*, London: Routledge.

Kaplan, T. (1999) 'Luchar por la democracia: formas de organización de las mujeres entre los años cincuenta y setenta' in A. Aguado (ed.) *Mujeres, regulación de conflictos sociales y cultura de la paz*, Valencia: Universitad de Valencia, pp. 89–108.

López Pintor, R. and Buceta, R. (1975) *Los españoles de los años 70*, Madrid: Editorial Tecnos.

Molyneux, M. (1985) 'Mobilisation without emancipation? Women's interests, the state and revolution in Nicaragua', *Feminist Studies*, II: 227–254.

Molyneux, M. (2001) *Women's Movements in International Perspective*, Basingstoke: Palgrave.

Morcillo Gómez, A. (1988) 'Feminismo y lucha durante la II República y la guerra civil' in P. Folguera (ed.) *El feminismo en España: dos siglos de historia*, Madrid: Editorial Pablo Iglesias.

Morcillo Gómez, A. (2000) *True Catholic Womanhood: Gender Ideology and Franco's Spain*, DeKalb, IL: Northern Illinois University Press.

Moreno, A. (1977) *Mujeres en lucha*, Barcelona: Editorial Anagrama.

Moreno, A. (1988) 'La réplica de las mujeres al franquismo' in P. Folguera (ed.) *El feminismo en España: dos siglos de historia*, Madrid: Editorial Pablo Iglesias.

Movimiento Comunista (1979) *Proposición de Ley de defensa y protección del aborto*, Madrid: Organización de Izquierda Comunista, pamphlet, 8 pp.

Movimiento Democrático de Mujeres de Madrid (1978) *Lo que recoge y no recoge la Constitución*, Madrid: MDM, pamphlet, 8 pp.

Movimiento Democrático de Mujeres de Madrid (1979) *El programa de las mujeres*, pamphlet, Madrid: MDM, 6 pp.

Muñoz Conde, F. (1982) 'Dos sentencias para un tabú', *El País*, 26 December, p. 11.

Nash, M. (1975) *Mujeres Libres: España 1936–39*, Barcelona: Tusquets Editor.

Nash, M. (1981) *Mujer y movimiento obrero en España 1931–39*, Barcelona: Editorial Fontamara.

Nash, M. (1983) 'L'avortament legal a Catalunya', *L'Avenç*, No. 58, March, pp. 20–26.

Nelson, B. and Chowdury, N. (eds) (1994) *Women and Politics Worldwide*, New Haven and London: Yale University Press.

Pardo, R. (1988) 'El feminismo en España: breve resumen' in P. Folguera (ed.) *El feminismo en España: dos siglos de historia*, Madrid: Fundación Pablo Iglesias, pp. 133–140.

Partido Comunista de España (1979) *Porqué una ley de aborto*, Madrid: Comité Provincial de Madrid, leaflet.

Peces-Barba, G. (2000) 'The Constitutional consensus and the Basque challenge' in M. Threlfall (ed.) *Consensus Politics in Spain: Insider Perspectives*, Bristol: Intellect Books.

Pérez Díaz, V. (1993) *La primacía de la sociedad civil*, Madrid: Alianza Editorial.

Preston, P. (1986) *The Triumph of Spanish Democracy*, London: Methuen.

Preston, P. (1998) *Las tres Españas del 36*, Barcelona: Plaza y Janés, Ch. 4. 'Pilar Primo de Rivera: el fascismos y los arreglos florales', pp. 153–192; Ch. 9. 'Dolores Ibárruri: pasionaria de acero', pp. 365–416.

Preston, P. (2002) *Doves of War: Four Women of Spain*, London: HarperCollins, chapters on Mercedes Sanz-Bachiller and Margarita Nelken.

PSOE Secretaría de Política Sectorial (1980–1981, undated) *Mujer y Socialismo*, pamphlet, 15 pp.

PSOE (1981) 'Resolución 7.5 Feminismo' in *29 Congreso: Resoluciones*, Madrid: PSOE document, pp. 231–235.

Rowbotham, S. *A Century of Women*, London and New York: Viking.

Rucht, D. (2000) 'Interactions between social movements in comparative perspective' in L.A. Banaszak, K. Beckwith and D. Rucht (eds) *Women's Movements Facing the Reconfigured State*, unpublished.

Ruiz, M.R. (1999) 'La participación de las mujeres en el ámbito jurídico' in A. Aguado (ed.) *Mujeres, regulación de conflictos sociales y cultura de la paz*, Valencia: Universitad de Valencia, pp. 129–142.

Salas, M. (1981) 'El papel de la mujer en la iglesis' in M.A. Durán (ed.) *La mujer en el discurso contemporeaneo*, Madrid: Universidad Autónoma de Madrid, pp. 99–114.

Salas, M. and Comabella, M. (1999) 'Asociaciones de mujeres y movimiento feminista' in *Asociación Mujeres en la transición democrática* (eds) *Españolas en la transición: de excluidas a protagonistas 1973–1982*, Madrid: Editorial Biblioteca Nueva, pp. 25–125.

Sánchez López, R. (1990) *Mujer española, una sombra de destino en lo universal: trayectoria histórica de Sección femenina 1934–1977*, Murcia: Universidad de Murcia.

Scanlon, G. (1986) [1976] *La polémica feminista en la España contemporánea*, Madrid: Ediciones Akal.

Scanlon, G. (1990) 'El movimiento feminista en España 1900–1985: logros y dificultades' in J. Astelarra (ed.) *Participación política de las mujeres*, Madrid: CIS, pp. 83–100.

Secretariado Nacional de Asociaciones de mujeres (1976) *Primeras Jornadas Nacionales por la Liberación de la Mujer: Conclusiones*, Madrid, pamphlet, 16 pp.

Share, D. (1986) *The Making of Spanish Democracy*, New York and London: Praeger Press.

Sperling, V. (1998) 'Gender politics and the state during Russia's transition period' in V. Randall and G. Waylen (eds) *Gender, Politics and the State*, London: Routledge, pp. 143–165.

Subdirección de la Condición Femenina (1978) 'Anteproyecto de ley sobre el Servicio Cívico temporal' (extracts), *Gaceta Feminista*, No. 2, p. 29.

Tezanos, J.F., Cotarelo, R. and de Blas, A. (eds) (1989) *La transición democrática española*, Madrid: Editorial Sistema.

Threlfall, M. (1985) 'The women's movement in Spain', *New Left Review*, No. 151, June–July, pp. 45–73.

Threlfall, M. (1979) 'El socialismo y el electorado femenino', *Sistema: Revista de Ciencias Sociales*, No. 32, September, pp. 19–34.

Threlfall, M. (1998) 'State feminism or party feminism? Feminist politics and the Spanish Institute of Women', *European Journal of Women's Studies*, 5: 69–93.

Twomey, L. (2001) 'Licencia más amplia para matar: changes to Spain's abortion law and the traditionalist Catholic response' in L. Twomey (ed.) *Women in Contemporary Culture: Roles and Identities in France and Spain*, Bristol: Intellect Books, pp. 63–81.

Unión para la Liberación de la Mujer – ULM (1978) *Unión para la liberación de la mujer, ante la Constitución dice: Sí*, pamphlet, 6 pp.

Valiente, C. (1995) 'The power of persuasion: the *Instituto de la Mujer* in Spain' in

D.M. Stetson and A.G. Mazur (eds) *Comparative State Feminism*, Thousand Oaks, CA: Sage, pp. 221–226.

Various Authors (11 women's groups) (1977) *Los derechos de la mujer a la Constitución*, pamphlet, Madrid, 11 pp.

Waylen, G. (1994) 'Women and democratisation: conceptualising gender relations in transition politics', *World Politics*, 46 (April): 327–354.

Waylen, G. (1998) 'Gender, feminism and the state' in V. Randall and G. Waylen (eds) *Gender, Politics and the State*, London: Routledge, pp. 1–17.

3 The development of a gendered social policy regime

Christine Cousins

Introduction

This chapter analyses the Spanish welfare state through a gendered lens. It discusses the historical, structural and cultural factors that shaped the gendering of the social policy regime in a way that impacted profoundly on women in Spain. The chapter also contributes to our knowledge about the distinctiveness of the development of Spain's welfare state. Little has been published in the literature in English about the gendered nature of the Spanish welfare state and even the Institute of Women claimed that until the 1990s women were not considered the subject of social welfare. In fact, the extent of women's social exclusion and isolation from the rest of society was not precisely known as at that time little data was available, 'as well as this being a relatively new outlook' (Instituto de la Mujer 1992: 65).

Piecing the fragmented information together it would appear that historically and more recently women have been excluded from the social security system, unless they were able to contribute over many years to the social insurance system through their own paid employment. However, Spain has one of the lowest proportion of women in Europe who participate in paid employment, the highest levels of female unemployment in the OECD countries, high levels of women who work in irregular or temporary work and one third of the female population over the age of 16 years who claim 'homemaker' as their sole occupation. Many women, therefore, have remained outside the social security system or have only been included as dependants on their husband.

Accounts of the development of the welfare state in Spain have also been scarce in the literature in English and have been included even more rarely in comparative analyses. Spain was not included in Esping-Andersen's 1990 typology of welfare regimes, comprising the social democratic, conservative and liberal types of regimes, although in later works (1996, 1999) he argues that Spain (with other south European states) has the characteristic features of the conservative-corporatist type. Esping-Andersen's typology, however, was extended with the addition of a fourth group to include southern European countries (Spain, Portugal, Italy and

Greece) and characterised as 'Latin-Rim' or 'rudimentary' welfare states (Leibfried 1993). This, in turn, was criticised by Guillén and Matsaganis (2000) who argued that to view southern European welfare states as 'rudimentary' and 'lagging behind' north European welfare states was a misreading of their *distinctive* nature. As several other writers have demonstrated, southern European welfare states are distinctive in that they have high peaks of generosity of social protection for those in the core sectors of the labour market but huge gaps in protection for those in irregular, unstable or informal labour markets (for example, Ferrera 1996; Rhodes 1997). 'It is not that [southern European welfare states] are "behind" as a whole, but [rather] that they suffer from imbalances, giving rise to inequities and inefficiencies' (Guillén and Matsaganis 2000: 121). We return to this argument later in the chapter.

Whilst Esping-Andersen's typology of welfare regimes gave rise to a considerable literature on comparative welfare states, feminist critiques of his analysis also stimulated a substantial literature and debate on how women fare in different welfare states. Before discussing the Spanish case, it will be useful for the reader to become acquainted with the major tenets of this scholarly debate. Feminist critics focused on an important dimension of Esping-Andersen's analysis, namely the extent to which a welfare state provides 'decommodified social rights'. That is, decommodification occurs when 'a (welfare) service is rendered as a matter of right and when a person can maintain a livelihood without reliance on the market' (Esping-Andersen 1990: 22).[1] However, other writers were critical of Esping-Andersen's use of the concept of 'decommodification' which focuses mainly on the relationship between state and market. Although Esping-Andersen argues that an understanding of the welfare state must take into account how state activities are interlocked with the market's and the family's role in the provision of welfare, many writers have pointed out that he under-analyses the family's positive contribution to welfare (for example, Orloff 1993; Daly 1994). (However, see Esping-Andersen (1999) where he explicitly addresses the importance of the family). The family remains an important provider of welfare in all welfare states, even in social-democratic regimes. Therefore, the relationship between the welfare state and the family, including the unpaid domestic and caring work of women within the family, needs to be analysed in its own right.

Once gender is brought into the analysis the concept of decommodification presents difficulties. For example, not all demographic groups are equally commodified because of limited access to the labour market. Women, amongst other groups, have been historically and culturally constrained in their labour market participation and in the quality of paid employment they obtain (O'Connor 1993). Several writers have, therefore, suggested that the concept of decommodification should be supplemented or replaced with other dimensions or models (see Langan and Ostner 1991; Lewis 1992; O'Connor 1993; Orloff 1993).

Orloff (1993), for example, has argued that the decommodification concept should be supplemented with an analysis of two further dimensions of welfare states. First, welfare states differ in 'the right to be commodified', that is policies which promote women's paid employment since these enable access to individual economic independence. However, one criticism that could be made of Orloff's proposal is that a strategy of women taking on more paid work and becoming more 'like' a man also presents difficulties if it means that women retain the dual burden of paid and unpaid work. The problem with this is that whilst women do appear to be becoming more like men in entering paid work 'men seem to refuse to look more like women, in that they do not take over care work to the same extent' (Bussemaker and van Kersbergen 1994). A further problem, of course, is that many women in paid work do not earn sufficient income to provide for their own independence. The second dimension in Orloff's scheme is the extent to which welfare states enables those who do most of the domestic and caring work to form and maintain autonomous households without having to marry to gain access to a breadwinner's income or benefits.

Lewis (1992, 1993) and Langan and Ostner (1991) provide an alternative to the decommodification concept. They have shown that the strength or weakness of the male breadwinner family model and the extent to which it has been eroded in different countries can be a useful way in which to compare welfare regimes and the relation between paid and unpaid work and welfare. In the pure form of the male breadwinner model we would expect to find that 'married women are excluded from the labour market, firmly subordinated to their husbands for purposes of social security and tax and expected to care for dependants at home without public support' (Lewis 1993: 162). Lewis finds Ireland and Britain to be historically strong male breadwinner states, France exhibits a modified operation of the model and Sweden a dual breadwinner model. They recognise that the majority of families have never achieved the gendered division of labour that depended on men being able to earn a family wage. However, the strength or weakness of the male breadwinner family model can serve as an indicator of the way women have been treated in social security systems, of the level of social service provision and the nature of married women's position in the labour market.

Lewis (1992) and Langan and Ostner (1991) concentrate on women's relationship to the state as mothers or as workers, although it is possible to discern other roles. Sainsbury's work (1994), for instance, makes clear that the breadwinner model is crucial to an analysis of gender and welfare states but women's entitlements within the welfare state may be as wives, mothers, workers or as citizens. A careful analysis is therefore required to unravel the basis of the entitlements in each country. A number of dimensions of the breadwinner model are used in this chapter, for example the type of familial ideology and its influence on social policy, basis of entitlement, recipient of benefits and division of labour within the family (see Sainsbury 1994).

In addition to the insights of the above writers a further dimension to the analysis of welfare states has been suggested by Walby (1994) in relation to T.H. Marshall's concept of citizenship. Walby argues that 'Marshall's concept of citizenship opens the way to discuss the degrees of citizenship obtained by different social groups at different times' (Walby 1994: 381). While social citizenship is linked to, but different from, that of men, Walby considers that political citizenship is central to the transformation of gender relations and the shift from private to public patriarchy. As this chapter shows with respect to Spain during the period of authoritarian dictatorship, democratic civil and political rights for both men and women were absent or weak, although social rights were granted for some (mainly male) workers. The gaining of new political rights for both men and women in the transition to democracy was especially important for women in achieving civil rights, for example 'liberty of the person', family law and equal rights. This chapter supports Siaroff's (1994) claim that the late (re-)entry of women into the political process produces a distinctive welfare regime which reflects women's work-welfare experiences.

The next sections of this chapter are organised as follows. The first section aims to gender the development of welfare by considering the position of women within the Spanish welfare regime and the strong male breadwinner model of the family which underpinned social policy. Secondly, we consider the development and distinctive nature of Spain's welfare regime. Finally, some aspects of the social security system are examined and the ways in which this is gendered. The chapter does not attempt to cover in detail all areas of social policy that affect women in Spain. Such an approach is beyond the scope of a short account, even if the literature sources were available. Rather the chapter aims to examine the historical, structural and cultural factors which have shaped the way in which policy has affected women in Spain.

Women and the family during the Franco regime

De Ussel (1991) has argued that in Spain the family has never been merely a part of the daily life of its citizens. It has been granted a special eminence and has always been under the control of the Church. Whilst the Church had at times, such as during the Second Republic, lost control over many areas of social life 'it never abandoned the claim that family law fell within its orbit, either directly or via the civil power' (1991: 279). The Second Republic (1931 to 1936) had, however, brought radical changes in the legal treatment of women and the family. Church and state were separated and innovatory laws such as the regulation of abortion and divorce by consent were introduced. Women also achieved suffrage in 1931. De Ussel suggests, however, that because the legislation was in effect for such a short time its impact may have been minimal. Confirming this, Nash (1991) considers that in practice, despite important law reform, inequality still characterised the social situation of Spanish women during this short period.

After the Civil War the Church called for the abolition of divorce and the return of family law to the Church; the legislation in force before 1931 was therefore restored. Equality between legitimate and illegitimate children was removed, whilst adultery, concubines and the use of contraceptives were penalised. Religious marriage for baptised Catholics was made obligatory, the Church was given the right to adjudicate matrimonial separation and annulment, and inequality with regard to the sexes in respect of the rights outside and inside marriage was established. The state reconstituted the family and gave it a central place in the social construction of the new Spain. 'The family was the primary unit of society, a basic cell in the body politic of the state and community' (Nash 1991: 170).

Nash shows how Francoist thought generated a pronatalist ideology which viewed women as basically mothers or potential mothers. 'Female sexuality, work and education were regulated in accordance with this social function whilst motherhood was idealised and considered a duty to the fatherland' (Nash 1991: 160). The 'Perfecta Casada', the dedicated and submissive spouse and mother, was the model women. Women were 'the key to halting national degeneration through maximum development of their reproductive capacity ... Hence aspirations to work, education and self-improvement, social activity or emancipation were a threat to women's biological destiny as forgers of the nations future generations' (Nash 1991: 160, 167). Nash argues, however, that Spanish women's behaviour was little affected by this propaganda; rather the difficulties of survival in the immediate post-Civil War years appear to have led to a fall in the birth rate.[2] Only when the economic situation and living standards improved in the late 1950s and early 1960s did the birth and marriage rates begin to increase.

A strong model of the male breadwinner family existed under Franco. Unemployment benefits were payable only to the male breadwinner, and family allowances, introduced in 1938, were paid directly to the head of the family and regarded as supplementary to his income. Family bonuses were also included in his wages. These family benefits were only available to legitimate marriages and to legitimate children and were conditional on employment. Large families were allowed numerous fringe benefits and prizes were given to the largest. As in fascist Germany and Italy all these policies rewarded and compensated for paternity, at the same time reinforcing male authority within the family (Nash 1991).

A second feature of the male breadwinner model was that married women were prohibited from taking paid work following legislation of 1942. Coercive measures were introduced which obliged women to give up work on marriage. From 1938 married women had to obtain permission from their husbands to work outside the home. Several policies acted as inducements to marriage: for example *la dote* (the dowry); an economic compensation which employers gave to women when they left work to marry; nuptiality prizes given to couples; and loans granted were reduced by 25 per cent on the birth of up to four children (Nash 1991). Again these policies were similar to those introduced in Germany during the 1930s (Bock 1991).

The legal framework established by Franco with respect to marriage and the family remained unchanged until the transition to democracy and the 1978 Constitution. However, De Ussel (1991) argues that family life and sexual and social change began as early as the 1960s. Migration from the rural to urban parts of Spain, rapid industrialisation, the slow growth of women's participation in paid work and exposure to mass tourism all had their effects. Despite the illegality of contraception and the pronatalist ideology the birth rate began to fall after 1964. De Ussel (1991) notes that during the 1960s the family as an institution began to be founded on personal interaction rather than the authoritarianism of the official orthodoxy and traditional values (see also Chapter 8 of this book on men's roles). 'Political change therefore arrived (in the late 1970s) when the behaviour and attitudes of the majority of society had already transformed the Spanish family' (1991: 285). Nevertheless, despite an openness in Spanish society in the last ten years of the Franco regime, there 'were neither democratic policies nor a welfare state to provide the services women needed in order to be able to leave their homes and go out to work' (Camps 1994: 56).

The transition to democracy in the late 1970s removed most of the patriarchal laws and the legal, political, civil, personal and employment rights of women have been transformed (see Table 3.1 for the main reforms). As in other southern European countries the first set of reforms concerned the establishment of equal rights in the Constitution of 1978. The second set of major reforms, achieved under pressure from the women's movement and professional advocates, transformed the family code and family law. While family law in the past had usually generated conflict, most of the changes in the transition period were achieved with little political controversy. However, abortion has been a contentious issue and the Church has totally rejected the idea of authorising abortion at the mother's request or on social grounds (Dumon 1991), although in 1985 abortion was decriminalised in three specific areas (see Table 3.1, and also Chapters 3 and 5).

Since the transition to democracy there have been profound and rapid demographic changes, especially the fall in the fertility rate. The fertility rate has fallen from an average of 3 children per women in 1975 to 1.25 in 2003. Italy too has experienced a similar fall to 1.24 in 2003, although fertility decline had begun earlier. Decline in fertility in Spain is associated with a reduced family size, a considerable reduction in the frequency of

Table 3.1 The development of social policy for women and the family in Spain – some key dates

The Second Republic	
1931–1936	Female suffrage
	Divorce by consent
	Abortion law reform
The Franco regime	
1937	Family allowances for workers (paid to fathers)
1938	Married women had to obtain permission from their husbands to work outside the home
1938	Marriage loans (paid to male head of family)
1942	Family bonuses for workers (paid to men as a complement to salary)
1975	Abolition of permission of husband for wife to work outside the home
The transition and consolidation of democracy 1975 to the present	
1978	Equal rights of men and women written into the constitution
1978	Sale, distribution and advertisement of contraception made legal
1980	Equal pay legislation
1981	Divorce by consent
1981	Equal rights of husbands and wives
1981	Rights of children born outside and inside marriage equalised
1983	Institute of Women established
1985	Abortion-law reform[a]
1989	Parental leave introduced and maternity leave extended
1989	Tax reform – wives and husbands now taxed separately
1990	Right to family entitlement extended to families previously outside the scope of social security (including self-employed people)
1991	Family allowances means tested to those families earning under 1 million pesetas per year (approx. £5000). Level of benefits increased 12-fold.
1999	Law on parental leave

Note

a The 1985 Law permits abortion under three circumstances: when there is serious threat to the life or health of the mother; where pregnancy is the result of rape; grounds that the foetus will be born with serious handicap.

the third child, very low levels of fertility in the younger age group (20–29) and an increased delay in child-bearing (Cordon and Sgritta 2000.). In comparison with north European countries though, cohabitation rates are low, births outside marriage are low and divorce rates relatively low. Further, the proportion of lone parents and single-person households, especially among young people, is also low. For example, 1 per cent of young people below 30 live alone compared to 20 per cent in Sweden. This is related to the tendency of young people in their twenties and early thirties to live with their parents until marriage (the long family) and this pattern is also reinforced by high levels of property ownership (three-quarters own their property), the high costs of property and lack of publicly subsidised housing.

On marriage young people are likely to set up a separate residence near their parents, as intergenerational exchanges, family networks and family cohesion are highly valued (Flaquer 1999; see also Chapters 7 and 8 in this book). However, intergenerational exchanges are also necessary in the context of lack of development of welfare services. Several writers consider, however, that the 'taken for granted' nature of family life and women's traditional role within it can no longer sustain the weight placed upon it (Flaquer 1999; Cordon and Sgritta 2000; Ferrera 2000). This is in part due to the lack of public policies and support for the family (see below) and in part due to changing gender relations and women's increased participation in paid work.

For women, however, a great deal has been achieved in less than three decades. The pace of social, economic and political change has been so rapid that it is possible to distinguish a profound break in the experiences of different generations of women. Garrido (1992) speaks of the 'two biographies' of women in which the life experiences of younger and older women have progressively diverged. These experiences include increased labour-market participation, education and the decline of the birth rate.

However, one commentator has remarked 'we are aware that women have reached only legal equality and are still far away from other forms of equality . . .' (Camps 1994: 56). Two forms of discrimination are of particular importance. First, women's participation in public life, in employment, trade unions and other organisations is lower than most other European countries. The second discrimination concerns 'the double working day' – paid work and unpaid work in the home. The Institute of Women (1992), for example, found that work was still very unequally divided in the home; housewives spent over six hours a day on activities traditionally considered women's housework – cleaning, cooking, washing, shopping, sewing and childcare. Working women spent over four hours a day on such tasks and men about an hour of their time (see also Chapter 8). However, unpaid domestic work is also very unevenly distributed by social class. One survey in Barcelona found that 51 per cent of the lower-class family's needs were covered by domestic work (mainly that of women's), compared to 41 per cent of middle classes and 21 per cent of higher classes (Carrasco 1991).

The welfare regime of Spain

Giner (1985) and Sapelli (1995) have argued that the countries of southern Europe – Greece, Italy, Portugal and Spain – have, despite striking internal variations, 'an unmistakable commonality and distinctiveness within the larger framework of European society'. They find that these four countries exhibit a number of common traits with respect to their historical evolution, modes of political domination, the form and tempo of economic development and system of class relations. All four countries have experienced the imposition of a modern 'despotic regime' through authoritarian dictatorships during the twentieth century, all have made the transition to democracy (three in the 1970s) and all have had socialist governments in power for some or a large part of the post-transition period.

However, with respect to the type of welfare regime, three common features appear to stand out as most salient in their contribution to the distinctiveness of their development. These are the late timing and qualitatively different form of industrialisation and modernisation processes, the central role of the Church and the nature of the 'despotic regimes' through which all these societies have passed. It is arguably the latter, the nature of the fascist or fascistoid military dictatorships and their legacy, which has been one of the most important factors shaping the contemporary welfare regimes of southern Europe.

Esping-Andersen (1990) has argued against theories which assert democratisation or class struggle as the major determinant of social policy in capitalist societies. Rather, 'power resources' of the labour movement have had more impact on what kind of policies are developed than on whether or not social policies are developed at all. He points out that it was the conservative tradition of the ruling circles of Europe, especially the corporatist rule of the fascist dictators, but also the conservative tradition of Bismarck, which laid the historical origins of modern social policy. 'It was the conservative tradition which gave rise to the first systematic and deliberate attacks on the commodification of labour' (1990: 41). As Esping-Andersen notes in both the Catholic Church and the states of the fascist dictators, corporatism was a way of upholding 'traditional society in the unfolding capitalist economy; as a means to integrate the individual into an organic entity, protected from the individualisation and competitiveness of the market and removed from class opposition . . .' (1990: 40). Historically the welfare regimes of fascist Spain and Italy have also had much in common with that of fascist Germany. In each state public provision of welfare was initiated or extended in the absence of democracy and under authoritarian rule. Welfare rights were used as a means of social control rather than a means of extending citizenship rights or principles of equality. Social policy in these states granted social rights but these were conditional upon 'appropriate loyalty and morality of the new fascist man' (Esping-Andersen 1990: 40).

It was indeed mainly men who were perceived as citizens of these states, for these regimes 'practised a thorough-going cult of masculinity, striving to reinforce male authority in the family, to compensate male workers for paternity and to develop a new vision of paternity' (Bock and Thane 1991: 13). Family allowances (paid to men) were introduced in Germany in 1935, in Italy in 1936 and in Spain (on the nationalist side) in 1938; tax exemptions according to family size were paid to the male head of household in Italy in 1933 and Germany in 1934 and 1939; and fertility bonuses were paid to husbands in Italy in 1939 and Spain in 1943. Marriage loans were made to the male head in Germany in 1933, Italy in

1937 and Spain (on the nationalist side) in 1938 (Bock 1991; Nash 1991; Saraceno 1991).

The Catholic Church too played a central role in reinforcing the traditional role of the family and women's place within it. In Spain, the Franco regime's espousal of National Catholicism represented the exaltation and transformation into a political ideology of the Church's traditional support for natalism, familialism and female subordination (Nash 1991). As we discuss above, one of the first requests which the Church made to the new Franco regime was that family and marriage laws were returned to the control of the Church, after civilian marriage had been introduced in the Republic.

In Spain, social welfare benefits under Franco were introduced in a context in which all subordinate classes were systematically politically excluded (and selectively repressed when needed) and all independent trade unions were banned. The authoritarian rule brought political repression, a weakened sense of belonging to a political community and a restricted possibility of the development of civil society (Garcia 1993). State provision of benefits or services covered a minority of the population and, unlike north European countries, the model of a welfare state which granted social and citizenship rights to its members was not reproduced.

Franco founded a National Syndicalist state on the principles of 'unity, totality and hierarchy' (Carr and Fusi 1987: 136). Every branch of the economy was officially organised in vertical syndicates (unions), membership of which was compulsory for employers, technicians, administrative staff and workers (Carr and Fusi 1987). This was an attempt to negate class differences by bringing the two sides of industry together in a single organisation. Since few women worked during the early Franco years (for example, only 8.3 per cent of women of working age were recorded in paid employment in 1940), it was men that were so incorporated. Free trade unions were banned, as was the right to strike, but in return workers were granted job security virtually for life, and became recipients of the 'cumbersome and complex paternalism' (Carr and Fusi 1987: 138) of the social insurance system and of inadequate social services. Women were integrated into the state through the 'Sección Femenina', the female branch of the Falange state party. Obligatory period of service in the 'Sección Femenina' was established for all women, and consisted of six months of training for motherhood together with political indoctrination (Nash 1991).

Giner and Sevilla (1984) have argued, however, that Spanish Francoist corporatism was largely a sham. There were a number of fascist corporatist features, such as the vertical unions, the rubber-stamping parliament of the Cortes and the ideology that class conflict had been overcome and a harmonious pyramid of state, province, municipality and family established. However, the authors argue that it was a corporatism of exclusion, rather than inclusion, and of subordination rather than mobilisation. Spain had a weak civil society, and weakly organised interest groups. After the Civil War the groups that had supported the regime were privileged and given special protection so that status distinction and hierarchy were preserved. All other groups were made bereft of the means of organisation of their interests. 'Paradoxically, Francoist corporatism meant the "decorporatisation" of a large and subordinate part of Spanish society' (Giner and Sevilla 1984: 120).

In her study of Spanish social policy, Guillén (1992) divides the Francoist regime into two periods, 1939–1959 and 1960–1975, which also coincide with the main political and economic developments. Social policy in the first of these periods was characterised by a puny system of social insurance that offered benefits to a small proportion of the population, mainly industrial workers and their dependants. Paradoxically, some of the proposals of the Republican period were passed and hastily implemented (see Tables 3.2 and 3.3). By the 1950s the national insurance schemes co-existed with mutual aid associations, leading to duplications, difficulties of management and a squandering of resources. In the second period, reform in 1963 and 1972 (see Table 3.3) led to consolidation of the highly fragmented system, with the introduction of a system of social security related to occupational categories.

The absence of civil and political rights and therefore of working class mobilisation was perhaps the main reason for the inadequacy of publicly provided social services. Democratic expression at a local level was suppressed, local authorities were not a legitimate reflection of local interests and there was little regulation of the local economy (Garcia 1988). The suppression of class politics meant it was difficult for men to press for either a family wage or social rights. Family survival and support strategies initially compensated for weak state welfare but by the early 1970s

Table 3.2 The development of social policy in Spain 1900 to 1936: services and benefits for low-income workers covering a small proportion of the population[a]

1908	Creation of National Institute of Insurance (aimed to promote social insurance among low-income workers)
1919	Insurance of old age
1926	Insurance for maternity
1932	Insurance for labour accidents
1931–1939	Statement by the Republican constitution that it was the responsibility of the state to create a system of social insurance against illness, labour accidents, unemployment, old age, disability and maternity. However, legislation was submitted to parliament only just before the outbreak of the Civil War.

Source: Guillén 1992.

Note

a For example, only 400,000 people were covered by insurance programmes out of a population of 22 million.

Table 3.3 The development of social policy in Spain: the Franco regime 1939–1975
– some key dates in the introduction of social insurance programmes by
the state

1939–1959: Period of autarchy, international isolation and economic decline
1939   Old-age subsidy for low-income workers over 65 years or for those with
disabilities over 60 years – consolidated in 1947 as Old Age and Invalidity
Insurance Programme
1942   Health insurance for low-income workers and their dependants (coverage
30% of population in 1946 rising to 44% by 1960)

Mid-1940s
Mutual Aid Associations (providing benefits for retirement, disability, long illness,
widows and orphans and hence duplicating the insurance programmes)

1960–1974: Period of economic growth and rapid industrialisation
1961   Unemployment insurance for affiliates of retirements and illness insurance
schemes
1963   Basic Law of Social Security – a Bismarckian scheme along occupational
lines and based on contributions of the affiliates – benefits linked to
professional and occupational categories
1963   Non-contributive pensions programme for people over 70 years
1972   Reform of social security – members contributions began to be linked to
real incomes
1970   Reform of education system – mandatory and free of charge 6 to 14 years,
now 16 years

Source: Guillén 1992.

housing, education and health services were supplied mainly through the private sector (Garcia 1988, 1993). However, there were other reasons too for the inadequacy of state welfare services. First, the state's fiscal policies and, in particular, a lax tax system which led to low tax revenues, coupled with high tax evasion, not surprisingly led to low public expenditure. A second reason was the nature of the centralised, inefficient and corrupt bureaucracy which administered the limited services. The centralised administration was a source of 'clientelism' providing jobs for a large part of the 'old' middle classes. Each professional body, for example, attempted to carve out a large slice of the posts available in the state.

The reforms that accompanied the political transition to democracy in the late 1970s included the administrative reorganisation and decentralisation of the welfare system (especially to the regional level) and an increase in public sector responsibilities (see Table 3.4). However, there were a number of distinctive features of the transition period that affected the subsequent shaping of the welfare system, so that social policy developed in an incremental and piecemeal way with a high degree of continuity with the Franco regime.

First, new social actors, previously excluded from the decision-making process, were now able to participate in the debate about the future of welfare and expectations of increased public provision were high. These

Table 3.4 Political, economic and policy developments in Spain: 1975 to the present – some selected dates in the transition and consolidation of democracy

1975	Death of Franco
1976	Law of Political Reform opens the way for legislation of political parties and trade unions
1977	First democratic elections since 1936, won by centre-right UCD party
1977	Moncloa pacts – agreements on prices and incomes policies between government and political parties; trade unions; employers also agreed
1978	Constitution introduced *civil rights*, for example the right to equality, to freedom, and religious liberty; *political rights*, for example the right to freedom of expression, assembly, association, participation and strike; *socio-economic rights*, for example the right to work, to collective bargaining and to education. Socio-economic *commitments* included protection of the family, of the elderly and of health.
1978	Reorganisation of the welfare system into four independent institutes for health care, social-security benefits, social services and unemployment
1982	Socialists (PSOE) win general election and begin programme of economic rationalisation
1985	Restrictive reform on pensions
1986	Spain becomes full member of EC
1988	General strike. Pensions indexed to inflation. Expansion of unemployment protection
1989	Universalisation of health-care coverage
1991	Introduction of means-tested non-contributory benefits for pensions, invalidity benefits and family allowances
1994	Labour-market reforms, part-time work promoted
1995	Toledo Pact signed
1996	Partido Popular (PP) wins general election
1997	New social security law incorporates social pact decisions. Social Pact on labour market reforms.

new groups included the political parties, the newly legalised trade unions, the employers' associations, women's groups, health centres and advice centres. Decision making took the form of a series of 'social pacts' between these new social actors, state, political parties, business associations and trade unions, in which issues of social welfare and social security were included. However, the social pacts achieved more success in wage moderation and labour-market reform than improvements to the welfare system (Guillén 1992).

A second feature concerns the legacy of the Francoist bureaucracy. There has been as much continuity as change in the apparatus of the state (Pridham 1989). Although the political institutions changed with elections in 1977 and the Constitution of 1978, the bureaucratic inheritance from the past regime was weighty, and it remained unwieldy and inefficient. The size of the administrative apparatus was already large and this made it difficult for the democratic governments to undertake radical reform.

A third feature concerns the uncoupling of Church and political party in the 1970s (see above for the influence of the Church during the Franco regime). The Church had largely detached itself from the regime by the early 1970s, and the emergent political forces had to some extent been nurtured or assisted by the Church. No Christian Democrat party achieved widespread support during the transition. (Giner and Sevilla 1984; De Ussel 1991). The Constitution of 1978 states there will be no state religion and complete religious freedom. In practice, however, the Church has been influential in issues such as education, divorce and abortion. The fourth and probably most important feature, however, was that the transition process took place during an international economic crisis whose impact was much worse in Spain than other countries, particularly with respect to increases in unemployment and inflation. Unemployment for example increased from 4.4 per cent in 1975 to 21.7 per cent in 1985. Pressures on the transition government (UCD) to meet growing new social needs did though lead to an increase in expenditure on social protection by 50 per cent between 1975 and 1982, although it remained at a low level of 19 per cent of GDP in 1982, far lower than most European states (Mangen 1996).

When the socialist PSOE party came to power in 1982 there was a perceived need to modernise and overhaul the economy (characterised by stagnant economic growth, high inflation, high unemployment, lack of investment and a large public deficit) as well as integrate into Europe. The government faced the difficult challenge of reconciling its main aim to reduce the public sector deficit with the declared aim of achieving a European social protection system and catching up with welfare states in other European countries. Nevertheless, welfare services and coverage were expanded, especially in the areas of health and education. The health-care system was gradually universalised, its management decentralised to the autonomous communities and an increased share financed out of taxation. By the 1990s only those in the highest income bracket remained out of public coverage. Reform of public education has also resulted in universal provision for children between 3 and 16, with a large increase in university provision. Social services for the elderly, young people and children were also expanded, so that the whole population became entitled to such services (not just beneficiaries of social security as before), although income thresholds were set. However, levels of provision are low in comparative terms, as they increased from an extremely low level (Guillén and Matsaganis 2000). For example, only 3 per cent of people over 65 benefit from home-help services compared with almost 30 per cent in Scandinavian countries (ibid.). As we discuss later and in Chapter 7, the underdevelopment of social services is related to traditional forms of welfare being provided by the family which is essential for filling welfare protection gaps.

Income maintenance schemes and job creation, however, fared less well under the socialists. In 1984, with unemployment at 21 per cent, unemployment-benefit coverage was only 26 per cent of the unemployed (Mangen 1996). The 1982 election manifesto commitment to create 800,000 new jobs in four years was abandoned and labour-market reform in 1984 led to the introduction of more flexible working contracts and a rapid rise in temporary fixed-term contracts (see Chapter 7). A restrictive pension reform in 1985 reduced the replacement rate by increasing the contributory years and extending the qualifying period.

These policies increasingly alienated the trade unions and especially the UGT, which had close historical and associational ties with the PSOE party. A general strike in 1988 was concerned with the lack of unemployment cover, the level of pensions and youth employment plans. There was to be no resumption of social pacts between the unions, employers and government for almost a decade. Following the strike and in a period of economic growth the government indexed pensions to inflation and promised to raise them further until the average contributory pension equalled the minimum wage (Guillén and Matsaganis 2000). As discussed later, non-contributory benefits and pensions were introduced in 1991. The coverage of unemployment benefits was also expanded reaching 82 per cent by 1992 (see also the discussion below). As a consequence of these reforms, as well as the persistence of high levels of unemployment, social protection expenditure rose by 40 per cent between 1982 and 1993 to reach 24 per cent of GDP compared with an EU average of 28.8 per cent (Eurostat 2002).

In 1993 the PSOE formed a minority government, but efforts to meet the Maastricht convergence criteria for the single currency, unsuccessful attempts to revive the social pacts and the seemingly entrenched high levels of unemployment made budgetary restraint the prime policy concern (Mangen 1996), although unemployment fell from 1994 onwards. As discussed in the last section of this chapter, welfare reforms were therefore frequently restrictive. Since 1993 social protection expenditure as a proportion of GDP has fallen and by 1999 had reached the same level as 1990 at 20 per cent compared to an average of 27.6 per cent in the EU (apart from Finland this was the largest decline of the EU states) (Eurostat 2002). In part this decline in expenditure was due to the falling need to pay unemployment benefits (as unemployment fell) and an increase in GPD (as the economy grew), thereby making social expenditure a smaller proportion of GDP. In addition, there were restrictions on public expenditure to meet the convergence criteria for the single currency.

In 1996 the PSOE party was defeated in the election and the PP formed a new minority government, supported by regional nationalist parties such as the CIU of Catalonia. There was a change of discourse in that there was a new stress on achieving social protection reform only through economic growth and an emphasis on individual responsibility and more resort to non-governmental provision, voluntary associations and the family (Guillén and Matsaganis 2000). However, according to these authors retrenchment of social welfare and extensive privatisation programmes have so far not occurred, demonstrating the effectiveness of the opposition (parties and trade unions) in denouncing moves for welfare state cuts and the perceived electoral unpopularity of such measures.

A dominant aim of the PP government was to ensure that Spain met the convergence criteria with respect to inflation, public deficit, exchange rates and interest rates to join the single currency in 1999, a goal also shared, notably, by the trade unions. Commentators have referred to a change of strategy of the trade union leaders in the 1990s, in the context of their low membership base in declining industries, the high proportion of temporary contracts (depriving them of members), the recession of the early 1990s and their commitment to meet EMU conditions (Rhodes 2000; Royo 2002). Guillén and Matsaganis (2000) also point to a fear on the part of the unions that the PP government might act unilaterally on social reforms. Union leaders were therefore willing to engage in national social bargaining with employers and the government. Several important social pacts were signed. The first in 1995 was the Toledo Pact which led to further cuts of the replacement value of pensions and increases in the number of contributory years. This Pact was concerned with the structural problems of the Spanish social security system (given the aging of the population and falling working population) and the reforms required to guarantee its future viability. Although hailed as innovatory, as discussed below, the Pact does have significant gender implications as it strengthens existing gender inequalities. A second pact was on labour-market reform in 1997, which included a reduction in redundancy and dismissal compensations in return for the promotion of more permanent employments contracts (see Chapter 7 for an assessment).[3]

Some writers have viewed the expansion of the welfare state in Spain as 'uneven, interrupted and incomplete' (Rhodes 1997: 10), constricted by the economic crisis of the 1970s and early 1980s, by the adoption of conservative policies in the 1980s and interrupted by the recession in the early 1990s as well as retrenchment of public expenditure to comply with EMU criteria. Other writers, however, consider that there has been a 'Europeanisation' of the Spanish welfare system and social policy agenda and a pattern of welfare convergence with other European member states (Mangen 1996; Guillén and Matsaganis 2000; Moreno 2000). In particular, there has been a universalisation of entitlements to education, health and pensions. Nevertheless, there is still a marked dual system of social protection, which, as discussed in the next section, reinforces unequal and stratified forms of social protection between men and women.

Mechanisms of social exclusion

In the 1990s there was a shift from the 'Bismarckian model' of entitlement to benefits conditional on contributions made through employment to publicly funded social assistance benefits. That is, on the one hand, there is access to benefits through the social security, which requires previous contributions through an employment record, and, on the other hand, a social assistance system that is means-tested and targets those groups who do not fulfil the employment conditions required by the contributory system. For Ferrera (1996) it is the polarised character of social protection in Spain (and other southern European states) which marks one of the distinctive features of the welfare state and the most significant departure from a Bismarckian or conservative-corporatist welfare system. As discussed below, for those who occupy the core sectors of the labour market there is generous social protection, but for others in weak labour-market positions there are only meagre benefits. Spain provides no national minimum income.

In contrast to other west European countries, the insurance and assistance principles in Spain are not separated for unemployment benefits. That is, only those unemployed people who are eligible to receive unemployment benefits can receive additional benefits under the assistance principle. Thus unemployed people without previous work experience are not entitled to unemployment compensation. The two groups that are most likely not to receive unemployment benefits are women and young people.

However, the growth of temporary fixed-term employment from the 1980s (discussed in Chapter 7) had a perverse effect in that it led to an increase in unemployment coverage in the 1990s. As turnover rates have increased so has the number of people who have gained work experience and are therefore entitled to unemployment benefits. This meant an increase in the public budget deficit. The response of the government in 1992 was to increase the minimum period of contributions from 6 months to 12 months and reduce the level of benefit. The result has been a reduction in the proportion of the unemployed receiving unemployment benefit from 82 per cent in 1992 to just over half in 1999 (EIRO Oct. 1999).

The mechanism of social exclusion did not only apply to unemployment benefits, but had, until 1991, also applied to pensions, with the result that a feminisation of poverty, especially among elderly women, was found to exist. Since the quality of the pension is related to the previous length of insured employment and level of income, there were many groups of people who were excluded from a pension or who received a low level of pension which was insufficient for their needs. Three million pensioners (38 per cent of pensioners) received an income below the minimum wage in 1997 (EIRO Oct. 1999).[4] Although there has been a convergence between pension benefits and the minimum wage (which is set at a low level and has been falling relative to average wages in the 1990s), the pensions levels for widows is particularly low. The Institute of Women (1994) noted that the low level of widows' pensions is a major source of poverty for this group.

The Toledo Pact signed in 1995 (mentioned above) further tightens the links between labour-market participation and pension rights, as pensions are now dependent on longer contribution years (15 instead of eight years) and it is still based on the two forms of social security, the contributory form financed by the contributions of employers and employees and the non-contributory form financed by the state through taxation. Since women are more likely to be intermittently employed and have higher levels of unemployment and temporary contracts they are less likely to have access to a generous pension based on a life-long working pattern.

Poverty research shows that the following characteristics are associated with high levels of relative poverty – old age and a high proportion of women living alone or living in rural areas or small towns (Laparra and Aguilar 1997). In particular, households headed by women have much higher risks of poverty, especially severe poverty, and such households have been increasing since the 1980s by reason of increased separation and divorce (Carrasco *et al.* 1997).[5] The most socially excluded, however, tend to be those young adults who receive only a meagre income and no stability or social protection from their jobs. Laparra and Aguilar (1997) argue that the extension of means-tested benefits (discussed below) has failed to fully reach the most excluded mainly because they are conceived as means-tested extensions of contributory programmes.

With respect to the family, despite its importance, and despite the general commitment of the authorities to insure the social, economic and legal protection of the family written into the 1978 constitution, state financial protection of family has been almost entirely lacking. Before 1991 family allowances were the least generous in Europe – a monthly allowance of 375 pesetas for the mother (about £1.88 then) and 250 pesetas (about £1.25) for each child under 18 years, a figure that had been frozen since 1971. Since 1990 family allowances have been paid to the lowest income groups, and although the value of child benefits has increased, it still remains one of the lowest level of family benefits as a proportion of GDP in Europe (only Greece is lower). In 2000, child benefit was 24 euros per month (about £15) for each child for those in receipt of an income less than 7703 euros per year (about (£4850) (MISSOC 2001) – the meagre size of the benefits speak for themselves.

Since 1991 reforms have sought to remove some of the glaring inequalities which have affected the new poor, elderly women and families with children. In addition to the contributory system, there is now a means-tested system of non-contributory benefits for health care, pensions and invalidity benefits.[6] The number of beneficiaries of means-tested benefits increased ten-fold from 1982 to 1992 so that by 1992 more than 12 per cent of the Spanish population were recipients (Laparra and Aguilar 1997).

However Lappara and Aguilar find that these benefits barely constitute a system since they are not well integrated, overlap and suffer from an incoherence of design.

The increase in means-tested benefits has had the effect, as has been observed elsewhere, of decommodifying women who were previously excluded, but decommodifying them in different ways to men who can obtain insurance, rights-based benefits. In Spain, on average, two-thirds of insurance benefit recipients are men and almost 50 per cent of social-assistance recipients are women (Blanchard *et al.* 1995). With respect to pensions, 76 per cent of non-contributory pensions are received by women whilst men receive two-thirds of contributory pensions. Levels of assistance benefits are considerably lower and more residual than insurance benefits[7] (see also Carrasco *et al.* 1997).

Since 1989, in the context of lack of universal provision, a solidaristic conception of exclusion has entered policy debate and practice through the introduction of minimum-income schemes by the autonomous communities (see Laparra and Aguilar 1997). This is similar to the *Revenue Minimum d'Insertion* in France, but administered on a regional basis, as central government has consistently opposed the introduction of a minimum-income scheme on a national basis, partly because devolution arrangements supports such a division of powers and duties. Average benefits are low, about half of the poverty line, with large regional differences. Single mothers, although as yet a small proportion of households at approximately 10 per cent, receive no social-security benefits on a national basis but constitute between 35 and 45 per cent of those on these social-assistance programmes (Carrasco *et al.* 1997).

Conclusion

This chapter has argued that one of the distinctive features of the development of the welfare regime in Spain is the legacy of the authoritarian dictatorship of the Franco era and the way in which this affected the citizenship rights of men and women and their timing. Under Franco, social citizenship rights were 'used as a trade-off mechanism for gaining political legitimacy' (Guillén 1992: 122). The strong breadwinner model ensured that men were the recipients of social security and family benefits and that the basis of entitlement was as a worker and as head of household. Women were treated primarily as wives or mothers and married women were strongly discouraged from taking paid employment. The absence of welfare services also made it difficult for women to leave the home in order to take paid work.

However, as this chapter has demonstrated, in the past two decades there has been a catching-up process with other European welfare states, a universalisation of health care and education, and an increase in social expenditure relative to the European average. Nevertheless, the persistence and strengthening of the dual system of social protection has significant gender implications. Since half the female adult population is inactive many will be dependent on male wages or male social security benefits. For those in the labour market, high unemployment rates for some, and the large increase in the number of people now on temporary fixed-term contracts, has decreased opportunities for stable and secure employment on which the social security system has been based. Over half of women who do participate in the labour market do not have access to stable or secure incomes by reason of unemployment or temporary contracts, and if informal work is included this proportion would be even higher. The assessment of the Spanish welfare state discussed earlier in this chapter, namely that it does not 'lag behind' Europe as a whole, but rather suffers from inequities and inefficiencies, would appear to be correct. However, this assessment needs to be qualified by stating that there are pronounced gender inequities in the Spanish social security system.

In comparison with north European welfare states, the late timing of the (re)gaining of citizenship rights is perhaps one of the most distinctive features of the Spanish welfare regime. In particular, the late (re-)entry of women into the political process has meant that civil rights had first to be established and social rights, especially those concerning women's economic independence (for example, policies to reconcile paid work and family) and the ability to form autonomous households (for example, individual social security rights), are still under-developed and therefore the system remains structurally biased against women.

Notes

1 By this Esping-Andersen meant that, following Marx, when individuals offer their work on the job market, they are in effect selling their labour power as if it were a commodity that is bought and sold on a market. Welfare rights, on the other hand, provide benefits that support individuals and their families when they are unable to sell their labour, for example in the event of accidents at work, illness, old age or unemployment.

2 The birth rate declined from 3.22 in 1935 to 2.46 in 1950 in Spain and in Catalonia from 1.91 to 1.72 in the same period (Nash 1991: 164). A high number of women remained single; in 1950 45 per cent of women between the ages of 21 to 40 years were single (Garrido 1992).

3 In 2002, however, negotiations between the government and social partners on reform to unemployment benefit appeared to have broken down, and the PP government has declared unilaterally new active labour-market measures which make unemployment benefit conditional on an obligation to actively seek employment. Opposition to these measures, which are interpreted as harsh, led to a general strike in June 2002.

4 Even though there has been a recent agreement to raise pensions above the inflation rate for those who fall below the minimum wage, EIRO Oct. 1999 reports that 830,000 people will still receive monthly pensions between 40,000 and 42,000 pesetas (about £145–£153), 52,000 people will receive pensions of

between 52,000 and 62,000 (about £189–£225) and 350,000 will earn a pension of 70,000 pesetas (£255), the level of the minimum wage.

5 Carrasco *et al.* 1997 report that the proportion of households headed by women in a situation of severe poverty increased from 16 per cent to 25 per cent between 1981 and 1991.

6 Before 1991 social assistance benefits existed, but at a very low level of protection (one fifth of the minimum wage) and as a safety-net mechanism for those who were without family members to meet their need. Recipients were mainly elderly women.

7 For example, non-contributory pensions represented 54 per cent of the minimum wage in 1995 whilst the average contributory pension was just above the minimum wage (Carrasco *et al.* 1997). The unemployment insurance benefit requires a minimum contribution of 12 months and total duration of the benefit increases with contribution record. There is a minimum of 75 per cent of the minimum income increasing to 220 per cent with two or more children. The first six months pays a replacement income rate of 70 per cent and the rest of the period is 60 per cent. The unemployment assistance level is means tested and paid at 75 per cent of the minimum wage per household (see also Carrasco *et al.* 1997).

References

Blanchard, O. *et al.* (1995) *Spanish Unemployment: Is there a Solution?* London: Centre for Economic Policy Research, London School of Economics.

Bock, G. (1991) 'Antinatalism, maternity and paternity in national socialist racism' in G. Bock and P. Thane (eds) *Maternity and Gender Policies: Women and the Rise of the European Welfare States 1880s–1950s*, London: Routledge.

Bock, G. and Thane, P. (eds) (1991) 'Editors' introduction' in *Maternity and Gender Policies: Women and the Rise of the European Welfare States 1880s–1950s*, London: Routledge.

Bussemaker, J. and van Kersbergen, K. (1994) 'Gender and welfare states: some theoretical reflections' in D. Sainsbury (ed.) *Gendering Welfare States*, London: Sage.

Camps, V. (1994) 'The changing role of women in Spanish society', *RSA Journal*, August/September, CXLII (5452), London.

Carr, R. and Fusi, J.P. (1987) Spain: *Dictatorship to Democracy*, 2nd edition, London: Allen and Unwin.

Carrasco, C. (1991) *El Trabajo Domestico y La Reproducion Social*, Madrid: Instituto de la Mujer, Ministerio de Asuntos Sociales.

Carrasco, C., Alabart, A., Mayordomo, M. and Montagut, T. (1997) *Mujeres, Trabajos y Políticas Sociales: Una Aproximación al Caso Español*, Madrid: Ministerio de Trabajo y Asuntos Sociales, Instituto de la Mujer, No. 51.

Cordon, J.A.F. and Sgritta, G.B. (2000) 'The southern countries of the European Union: a paradox?', paper presented to the seminar Low Fertility, Families and Public Policies, organised by the European Observatory on Family Matters in Seville, September.

Daly, M. (1994) 'Comparing welfare states: towards a gender friendly approach' in D. Sainsbury (ed.) *Gendering Welfare States*, London: Sage.

De Ussel, J.I. (1991) 'Family ideology and political transition in Spain', *International Journal of Law and the Family*, 5: 277–295.

Dumon, W. (1991) *Families and Policies: Evolutions and Trends in 1989/90*, European Observatory on Family Policy, Commission of the European Community, Luxembourg.

EIRO (Oct. 1999) 'Spain: Agreement on pensions, disagreement on unemployment': http://www.eiro.eurofound.ie/1999/10/Features/ES9910158F.html.

Esping-Andersen, G. (1990) *The Three Worlds of Welfare Capitalism*, Cambridge: Polity Press.

Esping-Andersen, G. (ed.) (1996) *Welfare States in Transition: National Adaptations in Global Economies*, London: Sage.

Esping-Andersen, G. (1999) *Social Foundations of Post-industrial Economies*, Oxford: Oxford University Press.

Eurostat (2002) 'Social protection in Europe, statistics in focus, population and social conditions', Luxembourg: Office for Official Publications of the European Communities.

Ferrera, M. (1996) 'The "Southern Model" of Welfare in Social Europe', *Journal of European Social Policy*, 6 (1): 17–37.

Ferrera, M. (2000) 'Reconstructing the welfare state in southern Europe' in S. Kuhnle (ed.) *Survival of the European Welfare State*, London: Routledge.

Flaquer, L. (1999) 'Changes in Spanish families and the implications for employment', ESRC Seminar Series Parenting, Motherhood and Paid Work: Rationalities and Ambivalences, University of Bradford. Dept of Applied Social Sciences: http://www.staff.brad.ac.uk/aKundu/webwork/UoBparenting/flaquer.htm.

Garcia, S. (1988) 'Collective consumption and urban protest in Barcelona during the Franco era', *Critique of Anthropology*, 10 (2 and 3): 197–211.

Garcia, S. (1993) 'Local economic policies and social citizenship in Spanish cities', *Antipode*, 25 (3): 191–205.

Garrido, J.G. (1992) *Las Dos Biografías de la Mujer en España, Instituto de la Mujer*, 33, Madrid: Ministerio de Asuntos Sociales.

Giner, S. (1985) 'Political economy, legitimation and the state in Southern Europe' in R. Hudson and J. Lewis (eds) *Uneven Development in Southern Europe: Studies of Accumulation, Class Migration and the State*, London: Methuen.

Giner, S. and Sevilla, E. (1984) 'From corporatism to corporatism: the political transition in Spain' in A. Williams (ed.) *Southern Europe Transformed*, London: Harper and Row.

Guillén, A.M. (1992) 'Social policy in Spain: from dictatorship to democracy (1939–1982)' in Z. Ferge and J.E. Kolberg (eds) *Social Policy in a Changing Europe*, Frankfurt: European Centre for Social Welfare Policy and Research Campus Verlag.

Guillén, A.M. and Matsaganis, M. (2000) 'Testing the "social dumping" hypothesis in southern Europe: welfare policies in Greece and Spain during the last 20 years', *Journal of European Social Policy*, 10 (2): 120–145.

Instituto de la Mujer (1992) *Women in Figures 1992*, Madrid: Ministerio de Asuntos Sociales.

Instituto de la Mujer (1994) *Spanish Women on the Threshold of the Twenty-first Century: Report Submitted to the Fourth World Conference on Women Beijing 1995*, Madrid: Ministerio de Asuntos Sociales.

Langan, M. and Ostner, I. (1991) 'Gender and welfare: towards a comparative framework' in G. Room (ed.) *Towards a European Welfare State?*, Bristol: SAUS/SPA.

Laparra, M. and Aguilar, M. (1997) 'Social exclusion and minimum income programmes in Spain' in M. Rhodes (ed.) *Southern European Welfare States: Between Crisis and Reform*, London: Frank Cass.

Leibfried, S. (1993) 'Towards a European welfare state' in C. Jones (ed.) *New Perspectives on the Welfare State in Europe*, London: Routledge.

Lewis, J. (1992) 'Gender and the development of welfare regimes', *Journal of European Social Policy*, 2 (3): 159–173.

Lewis, J. (1993) 'Introduction' in J. Lewis (ed.) *Women and Social Policies in Europe*, Aldershot: Edward Elgar.

MISSOC (2001) 'Social Protection in the EU Member States and the European Economic Area: Situation on January 2001', DG for Employment and Social Affairs, Luxembourg: Office for Official Publications of the European Communities.

Moreno, L. (2000) 'The Spanish development of southern European Welfare' in S. Kuhnle (ed.) *Survival of the European Welfare State*, London: Routledge.

Mangen, S. (1996) 'The Europeanization of Spanish social policy', *Social Policy and Administration*, 30 (4): 305–323.

Nash, M. (1991) 'Pronatalism and motherhood in Franco's Spain' in G. Bock and P. Thane (eds) *Maternity and Gender Policies: Women and the Rise of the European Welfare States 1880s–1950s*, London: Routledge.

O'Connor, J.S. (1993) 'Gender, class and citizenship in the comparative analysis of welfare state regimes: theoretical and methodological issues', *British Journal of Sociology*, 44 (3): 501–518.

Orloff, A.S. (1993) 'Gender and the social rights of citizenship: the comparative analysis of gender relations and welfare states', *American Sociological Review*, 58 (June): 303–328.

Pridham, G. (1989) 'Southern European socialists and the state: consolidation of party rule or consolidation of democracy?' in T. Gallagher and A.M. Williams (eds) *Southern European Socialism*, Manchester: Manchester University Press.

Rhodes, M. (1997) 'Southern European welfare states: identity, problems and prospects for reform' in M. Rhodes (ed.) *Southern European Welfare States: Between Crisis and Reform*, London: Frank Cass.

Rhodes, M. (2000) 'The political economy of social pacts, competitive corporatism and European welfare reform' in P. Pierson (ed.) *The New Politics of the Welfare State*, Oxford: Oxford University Press.

Royo, S. (2002) 'A new century of corporatism? Corporatism in Spain and Portugal', *West European Politics*, 25 (3): 77–104.

Sainsbury, D. (1994) 'Women's and men's social rights; gendering dimensions of welfare states' in D. Sainsbury (ed.) *Gendering Welfare States*, London: Sage.

Sapelli, G. (1995) *Southern Europe Since 1945: Tradition and Modernity in Portugal, Spain, Italy, Greece and Turkey*, London: Longman.

Saraceno, C. (1991) 'Redefining maternity and paternity; gender, pronatalism and social policies in fascist Italy' in G. Bock and P. Thane (eds) *Maternity and Gender Policies: Women and the Rise of the European Welfare States 1880s–1950s*, London: Routledge.

Siaroff, A. (1994) 'Work, welfare and gender equality: a new typology' in D. Sainsbury (ed.) *Gendering Welfare States*, London: Sage.

Walby, S. (1994) 'Is citizenship gendered?', *Sociology*, 28 (2): 379–395.

Part II

Engendering new policies

4 Regulating sexual harassment at work

Celia Valiente

Introduction

The contention that societies are structured according to a gender system – even if it not an explicit or highly visible one – has become firmly established in feminist thought and scholarly research in a number of disciplines. The methodological approach that we are using of gendering political and social systems of a specific polity is a tool for revealing its underlying gender system. Yet if this endeavour is not to paint a picture of the system as a static structure, it needs also to factor in the new policies advocated by feminist activists and equality advocates in pursuance of remedies to the inequity and powerlessness experienced by women. This perspective will highlight the dynamic aspects of the system, how it evolves and mutates. One of the key new policies engendered by the women's movement is the creation of work environments free from such traditional forms of male–female interaction as: one-sided flirtation, requests for sexual favours, sexual stereotyping, denigration and victimisation of female colleagues.

In Spain, the concept of harassment in the workplace became established in the 1980s after its adoption by the main national gender equality institution (the Women's Institute) and the women's departments of the main trade unions. These policy actors acknowledged that unwanted sexual behaviour in the workplace occurs and is a grave problem for women. Sexual harassment invades a person's fundamental right to be treated with respect and to bodily integrity. It can cause severe stress and impact negatively on a person's job performance or become a barrier to career advancement. It constitutes a form of discrimination whose extension and seriousness justified state intervention in the field.

This chapter analyses the policy process that led to the explicit prohibition of sexual harassment perpetrated by employers in the labour law (in 1989) and the Penal Code (in 1995), and of unwanted sexual moves perpetrated by co-workers in the Penal Code (in 1999). It is argued that the main problem in this policy area is the lack of implementation of public policy. This chapter examines the elaboration of sexual harassment regulation through distinctive policy stages: problem definition and agenda setting; policy formulation; and policy implementation.[1]

Problem definition and agenda setting

In order for a public policy to become established, it is necessary for policy-makers and those in authority to be able to conceptualise a situation as a 'problem' requiring governmental intervention (Dery 1984). Conceptualisation is the prerequisite for the initial stage of policy-making, called problem definition, to get off the ground. It is particularly important in the case of sexual harassment, since the behaviour encompassed within this term had never been conceived of and therefore was not perceived as a serious issue needing action by any authorities even though it always existed (Stockdale 1991: 53). It should come as no surprise, therefore, that no specific vocabulary for sexual harassment in the workplace was available in Spain, and no legal definition had been formulated up to 1989. Problem naming makes fighting unwanted sexual advances easier, when a 'name' exists it can be defined in law, and appropriate punishment designated.

It is worth remembering that the legal system in Spain is a codified system. In common-law systems (for instance, those of the United Kingdom and the United States) judges build case law, and the importance is placed on precedent (previous cases and their outcome). In contrast, in code law systems, judges are supposed to apply the principles contained in the code and laws to each particular case. The source of law is therefore not the precedent but what is written in the codes and other pieces of legislation. This is why it was so important in Spain to reform labour laws and the Penal Code to include a clause banning sexual harassment.

The task of defining sexual harassment as a problem which deserved state attention and solutions was undertaken from the mid-1980s mainly by feminists of the Institute of Women and within the main trade unions, the *Unión General de Trabajadores* (UGT) and the *Comisiones Obreras* (CC.OO). Inspired by international examples, sexual harassment activists promoted research both about the extent of unwanted sexual advances in Spain and about the difficulties of prosecuting the perpetrators.

One of the first initiatives was taken by the Madrid section of the women's department of the UGT when it commissioned a study about sexual harassment in the city of Madrid (Calle *et al.* 1988). This study was based on interviews with a sample of air hostesses, female administrative assistants and female workers in the hotel and catering industry and in chemical and metal factories. The study showed that the overwhelming majority of the interviewees declared they had suffered 'slight' sexual harassment in the three months preceding the interviews. This occurred when another employee, a male, behaved towards a female worker as follows: whistling at her 'in a provocative manner', initiating unwanted sexual comments, topics of conversation, or dirty jokes in her presence; and/or directly making flirtatious comments to her during work time. Half of those interviewed declared that they had received unwanted sexual glances, expressions or gestures. One out of four respondents reported receiving undesired phone calls or letters of a sexual content, or unwanted propositions to go out for dinner, to have a drink, or to join in parties 'with erotic intentions'. Also one out of four interviewed reported being intentionally pinched, touched, or cornered without her consent. Finally, 4 per cent affirmed that they had 'been pressurised by a man in the workplace to maintain intimate contacts'. The study also showed that the most frequent reactions by victims were firstly to put up resistance against the harasser, and secondly to ignore the unwanted sexual advances in the hope that the perpetrator would stop (Calle *et al.* 1988: 57–58, 127). The findings of this and other studies showed that sexual harassment was widespread in Spain, a phenomenon already observed in studies of other countries (Stockdale 1991: 54; Carter 1992: 433; Fitzgerald 1993: 1071; Husbands 1993: 112).

The Institute of Women also commissioned a study (INNER 1987) based on open-ended interviews with a sample of female workers in private firms in Madrid, Barcelona, Seville and Valencia, in hotels and catering, banking and insurance, textile and clothing industries, commerce, factories and offices. It showed that few victims denounced their harasser. When victims rejected the harasser's advances, they were often victimised by being passed over for promotion, regularly reprimanded for insignificant mistakes, or assigned the most unpleasant jobs (INNER 1987: 36–37). By the second half of the 1980s, most feminist trade unionists and policy officials agreed on two points: that sexual harassment was as widespread in Spain as elsewhere; and that no adequate mechanisms in the law or within companies existed for preventing or prosecuting unwanted sexual advances whether reported or not. But both were divided over a crucial issue: the exact definition of sexual harassment.

Advocates of adopting a sexual-harassment policy agreed that the word meant unwanted sexual advances, but diverged over which specific acts constituted harassment. A minority of feminist officials and trade unionists argued that a comprehensive range of behaviour had to be included in any official definition, including lascivious glances and verbal and physical advances, and that actions had to be punished according to the gravity of the case. This broad definition was thought to be the prevalent definition in the United States. But the majority of Spanish sexual-harassment activists believed that such a broad definition exaggerated the issue and reflected what they called 'Anglo-Saxon puritanism', deemed to be alien to Mediterranean culture. Interestingly, the same objections to so-called 'Anglo-Saxon puritanism' were raised in the debates over sexual-harassment policies in other countries such as France (Mazur 1993, 1996; Smith 1996). In Spain, the so-called 'southern European culture' was portrayed in a very positive light, as a liberating culture in which people could express their sexuality – an important dimension of the self – unhindered. In Spanish culture, it was thought people frequently told jokes, touched each other and tolerated consensual sexual relations at work as well as public displays of sexual behaviour, such as openly courting, kissing and hugging in the street (to the alleged amazement of foreigners). In such a culture, it was claimed that it would be especially hard to assess whether people were behaving naturally within the bounds of their culture or harassing. In contrast, the Anglo-Saxon culture was described in negative terms, as one in which people feel forced to behave prudishly due to social control, feelings of guilt or sinfulness, or simply to the inability to enjoy life and the pleasures of sex. As a result, most Spanish advocates of a sexual-harassment policy preferred a narrower definition which excluded acts considered 'less serious' or not serious at all, for instance flirtatious glances or light innuendos. These were thought to be an inevitable component of Latin idiosyncrasy.

Feminists in the Institute and the trade unions agreed that sexual blackmail by superiors had to be punished, because they were taking advantage of their higher job status within organisations and companies to extract sexual favours from female subordinates. Nevertheless, agreement broke down as soon as the harassment perpetrated by colleagues was discussed, and the possibility of unwanted sexual advances by subordinates towards their employers was hardly debated. For the majority of feminist policy-makers, harassment by co-workers was radically different from that perpetrated by superiors because it was believed that only superiors could seriously endanger subordinates' careers within the company or in the labour market in general. This led to the consideration that women could put a stop to unwanted advances from male colleagues, as they knew that both types of harassment were offences in the United States and other countries, but again most of them argued that such a solution was an overreaction and alien to Mediterranean cultures. Consequently, the majority of Spanish advocates of sexual-harassment policy demanded punishment only for harassers who were superiors.

Most of the sexual-harassment activists interviewed for this chapter affirmed that sexual harassment is about power, not about sex. Some even argued that sexual harassment has nothing to do with sex and only with power, replicating the French discourses of the feminist movement about the issue (Bacchi 1999: 188). Therefore, these sexual-harassment activists identified a situation of harassment only when unwanted sexual moves happen in a clear context of unequal power relations (for instance, that of a male boss and a female subordinate). Only in that case did they call for state policy.

In order to understand the way in which the majority of activists were mobilised in this policy area, it is important to remember that the right-wing authoritarian regime which governed Spain from the mid-1930s until

1975 actively repressed citizens' sexualities (especially female citizens' sexualities). The last thing that sexual-harassment activists wanted was for the regulation of unwanted sexual behaviour at work to be associated with the repressive Catholic authoritarianism of the former regime. In order to be clearly distinguishable from past repression, any harassment law, they insisted, had to avoid being perceived as a state intrusion into the sexual privacy of citizens, and be seen instead as state protection against the abuse of unequal power relations, unrelated to sex. In contrast, a minority of Spanish feminists argued that all unwanted sexual advances (regardless of the position of the perpetrator) were discriminatory against women. For the mere fact of being women, women were seen in the workplace and everywhere else by perpetrators as sexual objects to be used without having to ask for consent. All unwanted sexual advances had therefore to be termed 'harassment' and to be penalised, although differently according to the gravity of the offence.

Policy formulation

Step 1: law 3/1989 of 3 March

The dilemmas and disagreements on the exact definition of sexual harassment were rather swiftly overcome without additional theoretical thinking when a 'policy window'[2] suddenly opened. The socialist government was preparing a bill which contained the following gender equality reforms: an extension of paid maternity leave, the possibility that fathers took the last weeks of this paid leave and the extension of unpaid parental leave. Feminist advocates and trade unionists decided to take advantage of this governmental move to reform legislation in order to enhance the position of women and placed pressure on the government to include the regulation of sexual harassment in this legislative reform. Their demands did not contain any aspect which could have meant a significant extra cost for employers, such as the obligation of establishing internal mechanisms in their businesses to combat sexual harassment. Probably for this reason, the demands were included in the governmental agenda unopposed.

The first skirmish in the battle against harassment was law 3/1989 of 3 March. When the bill was discussed in parliament, the main party in opposition, the conservative party *Partido Popular (PP)*, opposed any state action in this area of feminist policy.[3] The conservative deputy (member of the lower house of Parliament) Celia Villalobos argued that any measures against sexual harassment had to be negotiated between employers and trade unions in collective bargaining. She also defended the view that public policy would be useless, because sexual harassment would only decline when sexist attitudes disappeared in Spanish society and not when a bill is passed in Parliament. Her colleague, the conservative deputy Juan Carlos Aparicio Pérez, affirmed that women were already protected against unwanted sexual advances by general legislation, and that no specific regulation was required.

Advocates of sexual-harassment reform, for instance the socialist deputy Francisco Arnau Navarro, emphasised the 'educational value' of the bill, because it would send society a clear message that sexual blackmail in the workplace would no longer be tolerated. In the context of the strong social and political support for integrating Spain into the group of economically developed and politically democratic countries, sexual-harassment advocates convincingly argued that policy on sexual harassment was necessary because the matter was already regulated in the countries Spain was seeking to emulate. In fact, this argument was disingenuous, since the first legal definition of sexual harassment was developed in Spain in 1989 – in other words earlier than in other western countries. For it was not until 1992 that the Swedish government reformed the equal opportunity act to include a clause on unwanted sexual behaviour in the workplace (Elman 1996: 111). It was also in 1992 that a clause on sexual harassment was included in the Penal Code in France, and when the Parliament approved a Bill regulating sexual harassment in the workplace (Mazur 1993: 11). Nevertheless, Spanish advocates argued that Spain was lagging behind other countries in this matter, and it occurred to nobody that the opposite could be true.[4]

While the bill was being discussed in the Spanish senate, the media amply covered a debate arising from the so-called 'miniskirt ruling' given by the Lérida provincial court. An employer was fined 40,000 pesetas (approximately £150), because he proposed to a 16-year-old female employee that she should have sexual relations with him in return for extending her fixed-term contract, while putting his hands on her breast and buttocks. According to the magistrate who made the ruling, the employer had committed an offence of 'non-violent indecent assault'. Nevertheless, he also remarked in his ruling that the employee 'had provoked her employer with her specific clothing [a mini-skirt], perhaps innocently, and that he could not control himself in her presence' (*El País* 19 February 1989: 27). In a subsequent statement to the radio, the magistrate declared that the employer could not have resisted the 'provocation' because the episode 'happened in summer' and the defendant 'had perhaps eaten too much'. The employee had (*sic*) provoked 'a biological or psychological' reaction in her employer because 'it all depended on the mini-skirt. It was a matter of centimeters, and of course if the mini-skirt measured very few centimeters and was economical with the fabric, it was more provocative than another piece of clothing using more fabric' (*El País* 22 February 1989: 26). The issue of the exact size of the mini-skirt gave the media a field day and provided harassment activists further proof of how difficult it was to punish unwanted sexual advances in Spain at a time when there was still no specific regulation of the matter.

Because the party in government (the PSOE), which had presented the bill, had an absolute majority in parliament, it was approved and became law 1989 of 3 March. It contains the first specific legal definition of sexual harassment and also led to the amendment of the workers' statute, whose article 4.2.e now states 'in their jobs, workers have the right to respect for their intimacy and dignity, which includes the protection against verbal or physical attacks of a sexual nature'.[5] In Spanish law, employers' acts against the intimacy and dignity of workers are considered a very grave infringement of labour relations, and are penalised with a fine of 500,000 to 15,000,000 pesetas (approximately £1800 to £55,000).

Step 2: the 1995 Penal Code

The second legislative opportunity for feminist-policy advocates came with the reform of Penal Code. In 1994 the socialist government presented the draft of a new Penal Code to Parliament[6] as the existing one was no more than the 1848 code with substantial amendments, but they made no references to sexual harassment. Advocates of sexual-harassment reform, mainly from the trade union the CC.OO and from the United Left (IU), the second main opposition force, seized the moment to organise a campaign. In particular, pressure fell on the IU deputy who was most active in the preparatory stages of the Penal Code, Diego López Garrido, to present an amendment to the Bill to include an article prohibiting sexual harassment in the workplace.

As a result the IU tabled amendment Number 766 which prohibits sexual harassment perpetrated by any person (not only by superiors) in the workplace. The drafting accepted the amendment after modifying it in two senses, firstly so that it only referred to unwanted sexual behaviour perpetrated by superiors (not by co-workers or inferiors), and secondly they extended the prohibition to any other place where people can take advantage of a situation of superiority to obtain sexual favours, according to López Garrido.[7] Diego López Garrido defended the approval of the modified amendment in Parliament in a session in which no one raised any objections to this opportunity to include the prohibition of sexual harassment in the new Penal Code. Organic law 10/1995 of 23 November was passed with votes from all parties except the conservative PP party, who abstained for reasons which were unrelated to the sexual-harassment amendment.[8] The final wording of article 184, translated, reads as follows:

> sexual harassment occurs when a person demands favours of a sexual nature for his/her benefit or for the benefit of someone else, taking advantage of a situation of superiority of professional, educational or similar nature; and announcing to the other person explicitly or tacitly that his/her expectations in his/her professional, educational, or similar situation may be harmed if the favour is not done.

Such sexual harassment is punishable with 12–24 weekends in prison or with a fine ranging from 36,000 to 18,000,000 pesetas (that is, anything between £130 and £65,500).

In sum, by the time the socialist party lost power in spring 1996, sexual harassment in the workplace perpetrated by superiors was well established as a serious offence. In the next section we will show that this initial consensus between right and left was maintained during the PP government, not so much because of a deep commitment by conservatives to the concept or the law but simply because PP policies stayed within the bounds of law reform without ever straying into the realism of practical implementation.

Step 3: the 1999 reform of the Penal Code

Despite this the conservative government did include in its third Equality Plan the commitment to reform the law to explicitly prohibit indirect sexual harassment perpetrated by *co-workers*, as opposed to superiors (Instituto de la Mujer 1997: 78).[9] Already in 1997, the Institute for Women (nominated by the conservative party) was preparing a bill on sexual harassment in the workplace, which would define unwanted sexual moves by co-workers as sexual harassment. Many studies document that unwanted sexual advances perpetrated by colleagues are an important proportion of episodes of sexual harassment in Spain (Estudios de Mercado EMER 1994: 18; Barreto 1999: 69; Torns *et al.* 1999: 68). This bill reflected the change of position on the matter of certain people from the conservative party who were active in the policy area of gender equality, accepted and even promoted a broad state regulation on sexual harassment.

Such a change of views was probably due to international influences. Some conservative policy-makers had become increasingly aware that in other European Union member states sexual harassment perpetrated by co-workers was already explicitly unlawful, and that some conservative politicians in other countries supported this type of legal reform. It is important to note that since the early and mid-1990s gender equality has increasingly become an area of electoral competition. If in the 1980s the conservative party paid little attention to the issue of inequalities between women and men, in the 1990s the conservative party was trying to convince the electorate that it could elaborate gender equality policy as the socialist party had done, or even better. This new political choice of the conservative party was reflected in a convergence of its discourses to the discourses elaborated by the socialist party in some policy areas, for instance regarding women's waged employment (Ruiz 1999), and in actual policy-making once in office, for example with respect to sexual harassment.

The influence of the European Union and other international organisations also made some feminist trade-union leaders more favourable to the regulation of sexual harassment perpetrated by co-workers. Feminist trade unionists attended international meetings where sexual harassment (including harassment among co-workers) was amply discussed, such as when the European Commission consulted social partners on the proposal of a directive on the matter. Feminist leaders from the main trade unions pressurised the Institute of Women to legislate against sexual harassment produced by co-workers. In general, feminist trade unionists wanted that the labour law and not so much the penal law regulated unwanted sexual behaviour in the workplace. Feminist trade unionists also demanded a precise definition of sexual harassment. Feminist trade unionists included these demands about sexual harassment (among other places) in a proposal to the government and employers to sign a pact on equal opportunities for women and men (CC.OO and UGT 1997) and in the comments to the Employment Action Plan for Year 2000. The influence by feminist trade unionists on the agenda of the Institute of Women and by extension the conservative government on sexual harassment has to be understood in the context of the frequent contacts between the conservative government and social partners and the signature of several social pacts on labour matters (see Chapter 6).

The conservative government was preparing a reform of Title VIII of the Penal Code, which deals with offences against sexual freedom. At that moment, the Institute of Women proposed to reform the regulation of sexual harassment in the Penal Code, expanding the definition of the matter to include unwanted sexual moves perpetrated by co-workers and increasing the punishments of perpetrators when victims were particularly vulnerable.

Part of the legal profession opposed the government bill. For instance, in 1997, the General Council of the Judiciary, which is in charge of the regulation of the judicial system, objected that the governmental proposal to explicitly prohibit sexual harassment was legally indeterminate, vague and purely subjective (*El País* 17 September 1997: 30). The Group for the Study of Policy on Crime, which is formed by around one hundred specialists on penal law (mainly magistrates and full professors), contested the aforementioned governmental proposal. According to this group of experts, the proposed extension of the definition of sexual harassment went too far, since it included some behaviours that could not be punished by penal law, such as vulgar flirtatious comments (*El País* 11 November 1997: 28).

The governmental proposal to reform the article of the Penal Code regarding sexual harassment was hardly debated in Parliament, since it was included in a broad reform of the Penal Code on sexual violence which raised much more controversy. Very little was said by parliamentarians about unwanted sexual advances in the workplace. The socialist member of the lower house of Parliament Carmen del Campo Casasús declared that the governmental bill defining and prohibiting sexual harassment perpetrated by co-workers was 'totally incorrect', because unwanted sexual advances produced by co-workers could be prosecuted with other articles of the Penal Code, such as Article 620 on threats, coercion, slander or humiliation. It was then unnecessary to define an autonomous crime of co-workers' harassment.[10] Socialist Senator Juan Iglesias Marcelo stated that unwanted sexual behaviour advanced by co-workers should not be punished. These unwanted sexual moves were not a real threat for victims, since perpetrators and victims were at the same professional level. According to this senator, there is a serious danger for victims only when perpetrators are superiors.[11] Conservative senator María Rosa Vindel López defended the governmental proposal and reminded other senators that the prohibition of sexual harassment by colleagues was a demand advanced by some feminist groups.[12]

The efforts of the Institute of Women in favour of the extension of the regulation of sexual harassment bore fruit. Organic Act 11/1999 of 30 April reformed the 1995 Penal Code. Unwanted sexual harassment perpetrated by co-workers and subordinates was explicitly prohibited by article 184 of the aforementioned code. This type of harassment happens when, in a context of a professional or educational relationship, someone 'demands favours a of sexual nature for his/her benefit or for the benefit of someone else; this produces an objective and gravely intimidating, hostile or humiliating situation for the victim'. This indirect harassment caused by a hostile environment is punished with prison of six to 12 weekends, or with a fine of 18,000 to 9,000,000 pesetas (approximately £65 to £33,000). Punishments for sexual harassment were increased when 'the victim is especially vulnerable because of his/her age, illness, or any other circumstance'.[13]

In brief, contrary to expectations, the conservative government not only did not abolish the measures on sexual harassment undertaken by the previous socialist party but actually extended their scope. The PP-appointed heads of the Institute for Women successfully achieved acceptance of new reforms that went further than those of the previous socialist government.

Having reviewed the policy definition and formulation and analysed the policies elaborated by socialist and conservative governments on harassment, we now turn to the study of the implementation phase of these policies.

Policy implementation

After more than a decade of policy activity in the area of sexual harassment, it is already clear that the main problem regarding the official treatment of unwanted sexual moves in the workplace is the lack of implementation of the measures approved by policy-makers. As shown next, it is not known if sexual harassment is more or less prevalent now than in the past, when the matter was not regulated by legislation. The number of legal complaints is now extremely low. Nowadays, the political and social actors who consider that unwanted sexual moves in the workplace are a serious problem are the same as in the 1980s: the women's departments of trade unions and the Institute for Women. Other political and social actors (such as employers and mainstream trade unionists) are indifferent to sexual-harassment policy. The exception to this rule is the conservative party. In the 1980s, the conservative party was against state regulation of sexual harassment, but since the late 1990s some sectors of it (and the Institute for Women appointed by the Conservative government) have maintained the opposite position.

An efficient sexual-harassment policy would make episodes of this type happen less frequently than in the previous situation, when the regulation did not exist. Unfortunately, it is not possible to know whether the incidence of sexual harassment in Spain is higher or lower before and after the legal regulation of the matter. To my knowledge, no monographic study on the incidence of unwanted sexual moves in the workplace based on a representative sample at the national level is available to the general public. Nevertheless, some studies show that unwanted sexual advances in the workplace are far from uncommon. For example, in 1994, the Centre for Sociological Research (CIS) included a question on sexual harassment in a survey on family life administered to a representative sample of the Spanish adult population (CIS 1994). The question was: 'At times in the workplace, people receive unwanted sexual insinuations or propositions from co-workers or superiors. Sometimes these approximations imply physical contact, but other times these imply only sexual conversations. Has something similar even happened to you?' The answer to this question, disaggregated by sex, is presented in Table 4.1.

According to the answers to the CIS questionnaire, the majority of women (75 per cent) and men (86 per cent) say that they have never suffered sexual harassment and only 9 per cent of women and 7 per cent of men declare that they have, but the difference between women and men is very small. These figures contain two surprising answers. Firstly, that the gender gap is greater on the negative answer than on the positive:

Table 4.1 Prevalence of sexual harassment in the workplace: total, women and men, Spain, September 1994

	Total (%)	Men (%)	Women (%)
Yes	8	7	9
No	75	86	65
I have never worked	16	6	25
I do not answer	1	1	1

Source: Centro de Investigaciones Sociológicas, Study 2, 133, September 1994, question 19.

14 per cent of men do not feel able to say that they have not experienced harassment, but when it comes to the positive answer the second surprise is that the gender gap is very low. These results contrast with the findings of research done in other countries, where higher proportions of working women state that they have been victims of unwanted sexual moves in the workplace (Timmerman and Bajema 1999: 420, 425).

One cannot conclude anything definitive about the prevalence of sexual harassment in Spain from the answers to the CIS question. There are at least two reasons that make us suspect that the CIS survey seriously underestimates the aforementioned prevalence. Firstly, the question about sexual harassment was included in a questionnaire on family life. It is a topic that in principle has nothing to do with unwanted sexual moves in the workplace. Therefore, perhaps the interviewees did not have enough time to think about his/her work experiences and remember episodes of sexual harassment. Secondly, international studies show that the proportion of people who report to have suffered sexual harassment is higher in countries where the knowledge about sexual harassment is widespread and there is public discussion on the topic; and victims often resort to the legal system to find redress. These circumstances do not characterise Spain (see below).

Partial studies have documented a higher incidence of sexual harassment in Spain than the CIS study. According to a 1994 study in the region of Valencia based on a survey of a representative sample of female employees and self-employed, 12 per cent of them had suffered 'very serious' sexual harassment. It was defined as deliberate and unwanted physical contact, or as sexual blackmail (propositions of sexual relations under the explicit or implicit threat that a negative answer would have detrimental employment consequences for the woman). Twenty per cent of the women interviewed had suffered 'serious' sexual harassment (propositions of sexual relations). Forty-one per cent of the interviewed had suffered sexual harassment 'of moderate seriousness' (to devour somebody with one's eyes, flirtatious comments of strong sexual content and comments about sexual activities with an inappropriate tone. Fifty-eight per cent of the interviewed had endured sexual harassment of 'low seriousness' (lascivious glances, and physical contact such as giving pats on the back or grabbing the arm). Finally, 75 per cent of the interviewed had suffered sexual harassment of 'very low seriousness' (flirtatious comments, and dirty jokes) (Estudios de Mercado EMER 1994: 8–9, 12, 24–25).

To summarise, up till now it is not possible to know whether sexual harassment happened more or less frequently before and after the 1989, 1995 and 1999 legal regulation. In order to assess the implementation of the policy on sexual harassment, we have to look at other issues, such as the extent to which victims use the law to which we now turn.

An effective sexual-harassment policy establishes legal mechanisms that are often used to punish perpetrators and to provide victims with compensation. This is preferable to situations in which, for whatever reason, victims do not rely on the law to seek redress. Primary and secondary sources and the interviews conducted for this chapter reveal that the number of legal complaints has been extremely low (Escudero 1993: 468; Estudios de Mercado EMER 1994: 20; UGT-Departamento de la Mujer 1994: 11; Pérez 1995: 55; *El País* 13 May 1997: Sunday 2). According to the most recent data available, the number of complaints between January and March 2000 was 86 (Instituto de la Mujer 2000, data for the whole of Spain except the Basque country, Gerona and Lérida).

The low number of complaints merits attention, since it contradicts empirical evidence about the higher proportion of people who declare in opinion polls that they will file a complaint if sexually harassed. In December 1995 and January 1996, the government's Centre for Sociological Research (CIS) ran a survey on violent crime. The Spanish adult population was asked (after other questions), 'If in your workplace at a given moment you suffered any sort of sexual harassment from your boss, would you file a complaint to the police?' Two-thirds of Spanish adult women and almost half of men declared that they would file a complaint if they were sexually harassed in their workplace by a boss. One woman out of ten and more than one man out of six stated that they would not file a complaint but would speak with the harasser. Slightly less than one woman out of eight and a quarter of men would not file a complaint but instead would try to solve the problem by themselves (CIS 1995–1996 – see Table 4.2).

One caveat is necessary at this point. The question about sexual harassment was asked after many other questions about other serious crimes, such as robbery, rape or sexual assaults. The list of questions about other crimes that preceded the question on sexual harassment probably made many interviewed prone to see sexual harassment and the other crimes connected in some ways. This perceived connection may induce some of the interviewed to declare that they should file a complaint regarding sexual harassment, as they would act similarly if they were the victims of

Table 4.2 'If in your workplace at a given moment you suffered any sort of sexual harassment from your boss, would you file a complaint to the police?', Spain, December 1995–January 1996

	Total (%)	Men (%)	Women (%)
Yes	57	46	68
No, but I would speak with him/her	13	15	10
No, I would try to solve the problem myself	19	26	13
I do not know	9	10	8
I do not answer	2	3	1

Source: Centro de Investigaciones Sociológicas, Study 2, 200, December 1995–January 1996, question 28.

the other crimes. Perhaps, if the question on sexual harassment were not preceded by questions on other crimes, a significant number of Spaniards would not link them together, and would be less inclined to say that they would file a complaint if sexually harassed.

The people interviewed for this research gave me one reason that explains why many women do not file a complaint. Many victims do not conceptualise unwanted sexual advances as attacks against their intimacy or their sexual freedom nor as episodes of gender discrimination. Rather, these victims consider such sexual harassing behaviours as 'facts of life', which are certainly unpleasant but to a certain extent inevitable. The weak consciousness about sexual harassment in the Spanish population has been documented by scholarly research (Torns *et al.* 1999: 59, 73; Pernas *et al.* 2000).

It has been suggested that the greater assertiveness among Spanish women in the last few years has empowered them to stop unwanted sexual advances from their employers, colleagues and subordinates, without the need to resort to legal action. Given the experiences of women in other countries, this seems unrealistic for the majority of the victims, but perhaps not for a minority of them. In the aforementioned 1994 study on the prevalence of sexual harassment in the region of Valencia, a quarter of the women interviewed who had been harassed affirmed that they did not file a complaint because they had solved themselves the problem (Estudios de Mercado EMER 1994: 20).

The apparent characteristics of Spanish legal culture may also discourage victims of any offence (including sexual harassment) to go to court to seek redress. Surveys suggest that, generally speaking, Spanish citizens are favourable to negotiation and compromise, and opposed to litigation. Many Spaniards believe that it is better to reach a bad compromise between two contending parts than a good result after litigation. The majority of the population has never had any contact with the legal system, and believe that the courts function badly, and that in criminal trials judges proceed with partiality (Toharia 1994).

It is important to note that the general situation of the labour market has never encouraged Spanish women to actively fight against unwanted sexual behaviours in the workplace. From 1982 (when the socialist party reached power) up till now, the unemployment rate has always been above 15 per cent.[14] When jobs are so scarce, many people try to keep the job they have (even if they have to endure sexual harassment), knowing that they may not find any other.

Perhaps the most plausible explanation as to why women have not filed more complaints is the uncertainty and risks of legal action. If a woman is being sexually harassed in her workplace, she may not want to publicise it, nor may she want to prolong the period before she finds a solution. What she often wants is the perpetrator to stop harassing her and a rapid and discreet solution to the problem (Lousada 1998: 95; Martín and Martín

1999: 234–236, 242). Thus, the most discreet and effective means to stop harassment is through measures at the firm or organisational level. This would entail the establishment of internal mechanisms, such as mediators or procedures for investigation and punishment, to solve this type of conflict. The most important factors for reducing the number and gravity of cases of sexual harassment are preventive measures and guidelines within the organisation (Sánchez and Larrauri 1999: 12, 25). However, the 1989, 1995 and 1999 sexual-harassment reforms did not offer strong incentives or imperatives for firms to develop these types of internal mechanisms.

Sexual-harassment legislation may also be considered effective if it promotes the mobilisation of more social and official efforts and resources for the battle against unwanted sexual advances. With regard to sexual-harassment activists, femocrats of the Institute of Women and feminists within trade unions (and to a lesser extent within some political parties) have been the main actors involved in this policy area before and after the elaboration of the 1989, 1995 and 1999 reforms. No other social or political actor (for instance, employers, mainstream trade unionists, or state units other than the Institute of Women) have been very active in the fight against unwanted sexual moves.[15]

As for employers, their position towards sexual harassment and its regulation is a combination of ignorance and indifference. The majority of Spanish employers are of the belief that sexual harassment does not take place in their companies. Most employers also consider that it is a minor problem that does not require any investment or effort on their part. Similarly, employers' organisations have not included the fight against sexual harassment among their priorities.[16]

Like the majority of employers, the majority of trade-union delegates behaved up till now as if sexual harassment was not a problem in the companies and sectors where they represent workers. Accordingly, most collective agreements do not contain any reference to sexual harassment (Del Rey 1997: 141; De la Fuente 1998a, 1998b: 216–218; Sánchez and Larrauri 1999: 10).

Lastly, the approval of the 1989, 1995 and 1999 reforms did not lead to the mobilisation of more resources and efforts against sexual harassment within the state. Up till now, the public service has not been an outstanding actor in this battle. For instance, in 1992 only four ministries (Industry and Energy, Economy, Social Affairs, and Agriculture, Fishing and Food) made a reference to the matter in their collective agreements (*El País* 12 March 1992: 24).[17]

Two main outcomes of the regulation of sexual harassment can be identified. First of all, public awareness of the existence of unwanted sexual behaviour at work is now slightly higher than before the official treatment of the matter. There is some evidence to support this point. For instance, some newspapers publish reports on the topic now but did not do it 15 years earlier (Torns *et al.* 1999: 60).[18] Reports and debates about sexual harassment have appeared in most mass media. Of course, not all this media attention has been produced only by sexual-harassment reforms or by court decisions, but also by special events such as the trials of Clarence Thomas (who faced charges of sexual harassment made by his former employee Anita Hill in 1992, before his nomination as a US Supreme Court Magistrate), or the publication in 1994 of the Spanish translation of Michael Crichton's best-seller *Disclosure*, and the première of the film based on this book. Secondly, although the level of litigation is extremely low, litigation indeed takes place and some harassers have been punished.

Advocates of sexual-harassment policy have been explicitly asked in the interviews for this chapter if the two outcomes of the reforms (the slight increase in public awareness and the few court rulings) are so modest that they lead us to conclude that the official treatment of sexual harassment has been useless. Sexual-harassment activists have also been asked what would happen (if anything) if the prohibition of sexual harassment were suppressed in the labour law and the Penal Code.

All activists consider that the reforms are a significant policy, because these (hopefully) are (or might be) a first step in the fight against unwanted sexual behaviours in the workplace. It was very important that the laws were passed, since the official debate about the extension and gravity of sexual harassment is now closed. The inclusion of sexual harassment in the Penal Code was particularly important in this regard, because the Penal Code defines the most reprehensible behaviours in a modern society (such as killing, raping or stealing, and since 1995 also sexually harassing) and assigns them punishments. The battle about the recognition of the problem of unwanted sexual behaviour was fought and won. By approving the 1989, 1995 and 1999 reforms, law-makers publicly stated that activists were right while arguing that sexual harassment substantially contributed to women's inferior status in labour. Law-makers indicated that detractors of sexual-harassment regulation clearly underestimated the prevalence and seriousness of the phenomenon. This was a political victory for activists. Law, which is a privileged discourse (Outshoorn 1996: 6), contains now some statements of the feminist discourse. Therefore, if the 1989, 1995 and 1999 reforms were now abolished, activists would have to do what they have done since the mid-1980s: pressurise policy-makers to elaborate a sexual-harassment bill.

Conclusion

This chapter has described the policy area on sexual harassment in Spain since the 1980s. Sexual blackmail by superiors in the workplace was explicitly prohibited in the labour law in 1989 and in the 1995 Penal Code under socialist governments. Unwanted sexual moves perpetrated by co-workers were prohibited in a 1999 reform of the Penal Code undertaken by the conservative government. The legal prohibition of sexual harassment made by the socialist and conservative governments is an important gender equality policy. Policy-makers have sent society a clear message that unwanted sexual behaviour in the workplace is a reprehensible behaviour to be punished under the Spanish law. Now, the public awareness of the existence of unwanted sexual behaviour at work is slightly higher than a decade or two decades earlier.

Nevertheless, the Spanish regulation on sexual harassment has a relevant limitation, since very few victims have relied on the law to find redress. In the future, it will not be necessary to elaborate further legal reforms, although policy-makers would probably be tempted to follow this line of action in order to gain electoral support. It will be more advisable to provide support for victims and to devise mechanisms in the firms to help victims to find redress and to deter potential perpetrators. Then, unions and employers' organisations (and to a lesser extent political officials) should be the main actors in this policy area in the following years.

Notes

1 The research for this chapter has mainly consisted of analysis of secondary literature, legislation, parliamentary debates, press clippings, published and unpublished documents of political parties, trade unions, employers' organisations, the European Union and the Institute of Women, and 18 in-depth personal interviews with officials from: the Institute of Women; women's departments within trade unions; employers' organisations; policy-makers; leaders of the feminist movement; a magistrate of the Supreme Court; and legal experts specialising in cases of sex discrimination in the workplace. This chapter draws on Valiente (1998).

2 According to John Kingdom (1984: 173–174), a 'policy window is an opportunity for advocates of proposals to push their pet solutions, or to push attention to their special problems . . . these policy windows . . . present themselves and stay open for only short periods'.

3 The parliamentarian discussion of the bill can be consulted in: *Diario de Sesiones del Congreso de los Diputados, Comisión de Política Social y de Empleo*, III legislatura 16 November 1988: 12795–12817; and *Diario de Sesiones del Senado*, III legislatura 22 February 1989: 5101–5107.

4 A legal definition of sexual harassment was elaborated in other countries before Spain. For instance, sexual harassment was defined as a type of sex discrimination prohibited under Title VII (about labour discrimination) of the US Civil Rights Act in 1980 (Stetson 1991: 223–224).

5 Art. 63 of the Civil Service Act of 7 February 1964 was similarly modified.

6 The parliamentary works of the new Penal Code can be consulted in Delgado-Iribarren (1996).

7 As the work of these drafting committees is neither public nor published, reconstruction of the negotiations was done on the basis of the author's interview with Diego López Garrido (Madrid, 15 November 1996).

8 An organic law (*Ley Orgánica*) regulates, among other matters, fundamental rights and public liberties and requires an absolute majority of the lower chamber (Congress) in a final vote on the whole bill. Ordinary (non-organic) laws only require a simple majority.

9 An equality plan is a set of measures to advance women's status undertaken by several ministries under the initiative of the Institute of Women. Socialist governments established two equality plans: the first plan, to be applied between 1988 and 1990 (Instituto de la Mujer 1988); and the second plan, to be applied between 1993 and 1995 (Instituto de la Mujer 1993). The third equality plan is going to be implemented between 1997 and 2000.
10 *Diario de Sesiones del Congreso de los Diputados, Comisión de Justicia e Interior*, VI Legislatura, 6 October 1998: 15205.
11 *Diario de Sesiones del Senado, Comisión de Justicia*, VI Legislatura, 15 March 1999: 7.
12 *Diario de Sesiones del Senado, Pleno*, VI Legislatura, 24 March 1999: 5888.
13 In this case, sexual blackmail perpetrated by superiors is punished with imprisonment of six months to a year, and indirect harassment caused by a hostile environment with imprisonment of 12 to 24 weekends, or with a fine of 36,000 to 18,000,000 pesetas (approximately £130 to £66,000).
14 The unemployment rate is the proportion of the registered unemployed out of the active population (the employed and the unemployed).
15 As said, the exception to this rule is the conservative party. Some sectors of it (including the directive team of the Institute of Women and other policymakers in the policy area of gender equality) have, since the mid- or late 1990s, been in favour of the official prohibition of sexual harassment. Nevertheless, this change of position was probably not the effect of the implementation of the previous reforms but a product of international influences.
16 To analyse the position of employers' organisations towards sexual harassment, I have consulted the periodical publications of the main employers confederations: the *Confederación Española de Organizaciones Empresariales*; and *Confederación Española de la Pequeña y Mediana Empresa*. I have analysed all issues of the *Boletín de CEOE* (since January 1993 *Noticias de CEOE*) and of *El Empresario: Revista de la Confederación Española de la Pequeña y Mediana Empresa* from 1985 to 1996 (both years included) without finding any piece of news or article related to sexual harassment.
17 Generally speaking, two types of people are employed by the state: *funcionarios* (career civil servants) and *personal* laboral (lower-executive grades). The professional status and working conditions of the former are regulated by civil service acts, and those of the latter by collective agreements.
18 This statement is based on a study of the daily edition of the main nationally based newspaper *El País* from 1985 to 2000.

References

Bacchi, C.L. (1999) *Women, Policy and Politics: The Construction of Policy Problems*, London: Sage.
Barreto, P. (1999) 'Intervención asistencial especializada' in *Violencia de Género: Experiencias del Centro Mujer 24 Horas de Valencia, 1997*, Valencia: Generalitat Valenciana.
Calle, M., González, C. and Núñez, J.A. (1988) *Discriminación y acoso sexual a la mujer en el trabajo*, Madrid: Fundación Largo Caballero.
Carter, V.A. (1992) 'Working on dignity: EC initiatives on sexual harassment in the workplace' *Northwestern Journal of International Law and Business*, 12: 431–460.
Centro de Investigaciones Sociológicas (September 1994) Study 2133.
Centro de Investigaciones Sociológicas (December 1995–January 1996) Study 2200.

Comisiones Obreras and Unión General de Trabajadores (1997) 'Propuesta para una negociación interconfederal sobre la igualdad de oportunidades entre los sexos', November, unpublished document.

De la Fuente, D. (ed.) (1998a) *Análisis de la Negociación Colectiva de la Comunidad de Madrid desde la Perspectiva de Género*, Madrid: Dirección General de la Mujer de la Comunidad de Madrid.

De la Fuente, D. (ed.) (1998b) *Análisis de la Negociación Colectiva de la Comunidad Foral de Navarra desde la Perspectiva de Género*, Pamplona: Instituto Navarro de la Mujer.

Del Rey, S. (1997) 'Acoso sexual y relación laboral' in Instituto de la Mujer (ed.) *La Igualdad de Oportunidades en el Ámbito Laboral*, 117–154, Madrid: Instituto de la Mujer.

Delgado-Iribarren, M. (ed.) (1996) *Ley Orgánica del Código Penal: Trabajos Parlamentarios*, Madrid: Cortes Generales.

Dery, D. (1984) *Problem Definition in Policy Analysis*, Lawrence, AR: University Press of Arkansas.

Diario de Sesiones del Congreso de los Diputados (1988) *Comisión de Política Social y de Empleo*, III Legislatura, 16 November: 12795–12817.

Diario de Sesiones del Senado (1989) III Legislatura, 22 February: 5101–5107.

Elman, A. (1996) *Sexual Subordination and State Intervention: Comparing Sweden and the United States*, Providence, RI: Berghahn.

Escudero, R. (1993) 'El acoso sexual en el trabajo', *Relaciones Laborales*, 24: 468–479.

Estudios de Mercado EMER (1994) 'Resumen del Estudio sobre Acoso Sexual de la Mujer en el Trabajo', for the Institut de la Dona de la Comunidad Valenciana, unpublished report.

Fitzgerald, L.F. (1993) 'Sexual harassment: violence against women in the workplace', *American Psychologist*, 48 (10): 1070–1076.

Husbands, R. (1993) 'Análisis internacional de las leyes que sancionan el acoso sexual', *Revista Internacional del Trabajo*, 112 (1): 109–137.

INNER (1987) 'El acoso sexual en el puesto de trabajo', unpublished report.

Instituto de la Mujer (1988) *Primer Plan para la Igualdad de Oportunidades de las Mujeres, 1988–1990*, Madrid: Instituto de la Mujer.

Instituto de la Mujer (1993) *Segundo Plan para la Igualdad de Oportunidades de las Mujeres, 1993–1995*, Madrid: Instituto de la Mujer.

Instituto de la Mujer (1997) *Tercer Plan para la Igualdad de Oportunidades de las Mujeres, 1997–2000*, Madrid: Instituto de la Mujer.

Instituto de la Mujer (2000) *Las Mujeres en Cifras 2000*, available on 31 May 2000 at: http://www.mtas.es/mujer/mcifras/delmes.htm.

Kingdom, J. (1984) *Agendas, Alternatives, and Public Policies*, Glenview, IL: Scott, Forest & Company.

Lousada, F. (1998) 'Acoso sexual' in Instituto de la Mujer (ed.) *Hacia la Igualdad Laboral entre Hombres y Mujeres*, 83–99, Madrid: Instituto de la Mujer.

Martín, E. and Martín, M. (1999) *Las Violencias Cotidianas cuando Las Víctimas Son las Mujeres*, Madrid: Instituto de la Mujer.

Mazur, A.G. (1993) 'The formation of sexual harassment policy in France: another case of French exceptionalism?', *French Politics and Society*, 11 (2): 11–32.

Mazur, A.G. (1996) 'The interplay: the formation of sexual harassment legislation in France and EU policy initiatives' in R. Amy Elman (ed.) *Sexual Politics and the European Union: The New Feminist Challenge*, 35–49. Providence, RI: Berghahn.

Outshoorn, J. (1996) 'The meaning of "woman" in abortion policy: a comparative approach' paper presented at the 1996 Annual Meeting of the American Political Science Association, San Francisco, 29 August–1 September.

Pérez, M.T. (1995) 'Informe General 1995: Nivel de Aplicación del Derecho Comunitario en Materia de Igualdad', unpublished report.

Pernas, B., Román, M., Olza, J. and Naredo, M. (2000) *La Dignidad Quebrada: Las Raíces del Acoso Sexual en el Trabajo*, Madrid: Los Libros de la Catarata.

Ruiz, A.M. (1999) 'Evolución y actitudes del AP-PP hacia la participación femenina en el mercado de trabajo: discusión de algunas hipótesis explicativas' in Margarita Ortega, Cristina Sánchez and Celia Valiente (eds) *Género y ciudadanía: revisiones desde el ámbito privado*, 449–468, Madrid: Universidad Autónoma de Madrid.

Sánchez, E. and Larrauri, E. (1999) *El Nuevo Delito de Acoso Sexual y su Sanción Administrativa en el Ámbito Laboral*, Valencia: Tirant Lo Blanch.

Smith, A.C. (1996) 'National identity and sexual harassment', paper presented at the Tenth International Conference of Europeanists, Chicago, 14–16 March.

Stetson, D.M. (1991) *Women's Rights in the U.S.A.: Gender Debates & Gender Roles*, Belmont, CA: Wadsworth.

Stockdale, J.E. (1991) 'Sexual harassment at work' in Jenny Firth-Cozens and Michael A. West (eds) *Women and Work: Psychological and Organizational Perspectives*, 53–65, Milton Keynes: Open University Press.

Timmerman, G. and Bajema, C. (1999) 'Sexual harassment in northwest Europe: a cross-cultural comparison', *European Journal of Women's Studies*, 6: 419–439.

Toharia, J.J. (1994) *Actitudes de los Españoles ante la Administración de Justicia*, Madrid: Centro de Investigaciones Sociológicas.

Torns, T., Borràs, V. and Romero, A. (1999) 'El acoso sexual en el mundo laboral: un indicador patriarcal', *Sociología del Trabajo*, 36: 57–77.

Unión General de Trabajadores-Departamento de la Mujer (1994) *Guía Sindical sobre Acoso Sexual en el Trabajo*, Madrid: UGT-Departamento de la Mujer.

Valiente, C. (1998) 'Sexual harassment in the workplace: equality policies in post-authoritarian Spain' in T. Carver and V. Mottier (eds) *Politics of Sexuality: Identity, Gender, Citizenship*, 169–179, London and New York: Routledge.

5 Combating violence against women

Celia Valiente

Introduction

Violence against women is a phenomenon that has increasingly preoccupied national and international authorities because of its lasting scars on victims and, in the case of domestic violence, on the children of the household and even on the perpetrators. The United Nations has defined violence against women as 'any act of sexist violence that may result in physical, sexual or psychological harm, including threats, coercion or arbitrary prevention of freedom, whether this happens in public or in private life' (UN 1996). In the last three decades national public policies combating violence against women have been similar in Spain to those of other

Figure 5.1 Against rape: justice for women. Demonstration by the Coordinadora Feminista, 17 September 1977.

European Union member states. Measures have mainly been of two types: legal reforms, in order to make violent actions against women unlawful and punishable by law; and services for victims of violence, for instance refuges for battered women.

Such measures are good examples of how women's advocates have engendered social policy and criminal law. When domestic violence was not viewed through the lens of gender, it was considered a private family matter. In practice, men were free to commit acts on their spouses, which, if they had been committed on other men or women, would have landed them in prison. Women's policy advocates and the victims of violence themselves were the ones to persuade policy-makers and the public that they ought to view domestic violence as a consequence of the subordination of women in society. It became illegitimate, both in discourse and in law, to treat violence against women as if it were inevitable or unstoppable.

In Spain, however, such policies were formulated and implemented with some delay in comparison with other Western countries, due in part to the way the Franco regime buttressed male authority and tried to teach women to be submissive as part of a traditional and highly regulated gender order.

As in many other industrial countries, Spanish policies against violence have been only partially successful in the last two decades, the cause being problems of implementation, which as this chapter argues, can be partially explained by the specific characteristics of this difficult field. Those responsible for the implementation of most policies against violence against women are a variety of public-service professionals and 'street-level bureaucrats' (to use Lipsky's (1980) term), judges, defence and prosecution lawyers, police officers, hospital staff, forensic surgeons and social workers, to name just a few. All these public servants deal directly with 'clients' (whether the alleged perpetrators of violence or their victims) and are thereby in a position to jeopardise the implementation of most policies against violence against women quite easily. They have a high degree of discretion and autonomy in performing their job as they are not subjected to strict supervision by middle or senior managers in the institutions in which they work.

The first section of this chapter sets out the background to the problem: the contours of the problem, the legal position and law reforms, the attempt to gauge the prevalence of violence in numerical terms and the services that have been instituted in response to the problem. The second section contains an analysis of the peculiarities of this policy area that have hindered the implementation of most of the policies in Spain as in other countries. The final section focuses on the role played by different social and political actors (chiefly feminists in government posts, civil servants and public-sector officials) involved in the policy-making process in Spain since 1975.[1]

The problem of violence against women in Spain

A broad definition of the phenomenon of violence against women includes 'any act of verbal or physical force, coercion or life-threatening deprivation directed at an individual woman or girl that causes physical or psychological harm, humiliation or arbitrary deprivation of liberty and that perpetuates female subordination' (Heise *et al.* 1994: 1165). For reasons of space, this chapter focuses on the study of policies directed at curbing or punishing violent behaviour against adult women only, in cases of rape and other forms of sexual attack, and in cases of domestic violence perpetrated in the family sphere. The main policies for these types of violence are chiefly legal reforms and services for female victims of violence. Other violent behaviour, such as forced prostitution, sexual harassment at work, genital mutilation and abuse of female children are not considered in this chapter.

Law reform

A series of legal reforms introduced the most important policies against violence against women in Spain. In the Penal Code, the different violent acts perpetrated against women are defined as either misdemeanours or crimes, and each of them is assigned a punishment commensurate with its gravity. Up to 1989 sexual attacks against women were still listed under the heading 'crimes against purity', with most attacks against *adult* women other than rape still called 'indecent abuses'. The terminology itself was a telling aspect of the legal definition of such attacks, because it reflected the fact that at the time it was formulated, perpetrators were considered to have offended against the purity, decency or chastity of women, rather than against women's freedom to decide whether to engage or not in sexual relations.[2] Besides, rape was defined in a very restricted way, because it referred only to heterosexual vaginal coitus, and not to anal or oral coitus, and because it was perceived that only men could rape women. Moreover, in all cases of sexual attacks against women, including rape, if the victim 'forgave' the perpetrator, no prosecution could take place. Furthermore, as divorce was not established in Spain until 1981,[3] if a woman was married to the perpetrator of violent acts against her, she could not obtain a divorce, remaining legally married to (or legally separated from) the violent husband.

By the 1980s the concept of forgiveness had become politically indefensible and was legally under challenge. In the key reform of the Penal Code of 1983 (Organic Law 8 of June 25), rape became a public offence. It established that even if rape victims forgave the perpetrators, suspects would still be charged and brought to court (though not for other types of sexual attacks). The consequences of a rape resulting in pregnancy were also particularly humiliating for women until the introduction of the abortion law of 1985. Before 1985 abortion in all circumstances was a crime, penalised in most cases with a prison sentence ranging from six months to six years for the woman, and longer for the abortion practitioners. So even if a woman became pregnant as the result of rape she was legally obliged to continue with the pregnancy. The Organic Law 9/1985 of 5 July, allows abortion in three circumstances: where a woman has been raped, when a pregnancy seriously endangers the life of the woman and when the foetus has malformations.

A further crucial reform of the Penal Code regarding violence against women took place in 1989 when Organic Law 3/1989 of 21 June, was passed, which instituted the kinds of changes that had already taken place in other countries. Sexual attacks were no longer called 'offences against purity' but 'offences against sexual freedom'. By the same token, some sexual attacks different from rape were no longer called indecent abuses but sexual aggressions, and the concept of rape was expanded to include not only vaginal but also anal and oral coitus. Nevertheless, penetration with the penis was required in order to legally define an assault as rape, a point that was hotly contested as it could be deduced that penetration with other objects might not be considered a rape. In addition, it was illegal for men to rape women or men, but only for women to rape men (Bustos 1991: 115; Cabo 1993: 261). Rape, like homicide, was to be punished with a prison sentence ranging from 12 to 20 years, while 'sexual aggressions' short of rape were liable for severe sentences of six months to 12 years imprisonment. In both cases the perpetrator had to compensate the victim financially, although it is thought that this sum of money was only very rarely paid.

In other aspects the law reflected the position of feminist policy advocates in so far as it defined rape and other sexual aggressions as crimes independently of the marital or professional status of victims; in other words, even if the perpetrator was the victim's husband, or if she worked as a prostitute (Bustos 1991: 115). Additionally, the reformed article 425 of the 1989 Penal Code classified habitual physical domestic violence against women perpetrated by husbands or cohabiting partners as a crime, not as a misdemeanour, upgrading it from its former lower status and punishing it with a period of imprisonment ranging from one to six months. 'Habitual' here means violence that has been perpetrated at least three times (Bustos 1991: 65; Cabo 1993: 229). The controversial legal effect of 'forgiveness' by any victim of an offence against sexual freedom was abolished, so that forgiveness whether sought or offered can no longer lead to any prosecution of the defendant being dropped or conviction quashed.

The 1989 reform also contained new measures to combat rape and violence against women in a particularly vulnerable situation, namely in prisons. Prison-service workers, officers or guards who take advantage of the power and influence conferred by their jobs to abuse their clients or request sexual favours of them or their relatives are to be punished more severely than before (López 1992: 317–323).

Another important legal reform regarding violence against women took place in 1995 (Law 10/1995 of 23 November) when a fully revised Penal Code was passed, as this was long overdue (the existing Code was only an amended version of the nineteenth-century text). The word 'rape' disappeared from the Penal Code and was replaced by 'sexual aggressions'. The definition of what was formally called 'rape' was again expanded, to include penetration with objects. This aggression is subject to a lower maximum number of years of imprisonment, 12 instead of 20. In another revision, group sexual aggressions are now explicitly defined, namely as acts committed by three or more people, punishable by a longer sentence. The punishment of repeated physical domestic violence was increased (from a period of imprisonment which ranged from one to six months to a period which ranges from six months to three years). In practice it can be surmised that the most important change was the move towards public prosecutions in cases of sexual aggressions, sexual abuses or sexual harassment whereas before a complaint by the victim was required before initiating proceedings. This meant that the decision to prosecute was taken out of the hands of the victim, which was designed to lessen the burden of responsibility on the victim and the risk of threats by perpetrators and their allies.

While the previous reforms were carried out during the last years of the socialist government, it is interesting to note that the new conservative government which took office in 1996 also came under pressure to respond to the problem of domestic violence, when a surge of violent cases caught the attention of the media (see *El País*, 26 December 1997, 7 January 1998, 8 February 1998: 22) and led to a broad public debate, demonstrations and calls for action. On 30 April 1998, the Spanish cabinet approved an action plan against domestic violence drawn up by the Institute of Women (Instituto de la Mujer 1998). This action plan contains proposals for measures to combat violence against women in the fields of prevention, education, support services for victims, health, legal reforms and research.

Legal reforms developing the action plan against domestic violence were enacted a year later. In June 1999 the Penal Code of 1995 and the law of criminal indictment were once again modified (Organic Law 14/1999 of 9 June) in order to include a newly defined offence of 'repeated psychological violence' in the home (up till then only physical violence had been defined). The possibility of new injunctions against aggressors was established, forbidding him to approach the victim, to communicate with her, or to live close to her. The unusual feature of this last measure is that it is one of the rare instances in which we find the public authorities attempting to prevent the perpetration of violence, rather than intervening after the event.

These reforms also stipulated that judges should not impose fines on violent attackers if such a financial sanction would have the effect of damaging the victim's or her family's financial situation as well. It should be borne in mind that the most common regime for marital assets in Spain is shared assets in which each spouse owns half of all properties and income obtained by any of the two spouses during their marriage. When in this situation a violent husband has a fine imposed on him, he normally pays it out of shared assets, half of which belong to his wife, thereby damaging the financial position of his spouse, who herself might have been the victim of violence.

The prevalence of violence against women

The next step after passing such law reforms is the collection of statistics of reported cases of violent attacks on women. Statistics of this type, for instance in the case of domestic violence, hardly existed in Spain until 1983, and started with feminists urging the police and also the civil guard, who work chiefly in rural areas, to collect data of reported cases of aggression in which victims have been women (Gutiérrez 1990: 129). This generated some data, but only of reported cases. The judiciary was also urged to collect data regarding sentences passed in cases of violence against women (Gutiérrez 1989: 9), and the same was asked of the staff who work in social services and in refuges for battered women (Spanish Senate 1989: 12185–12187). But until late in the 1990s all these statistics were still incomplete and hardly comparable (Defensor del Pueblo 1998). As in many other countries (Kornblit 1994: 1181), under-reporting is a common phenomenon in Spain, and estimates of the real number of cases were only tentative until 2002. Furthermore, there were few studies on the prevalence of violence against women available to the general public in Spain before the analysis of the major survey commissioned by the Women's Institute was published in 2002. The following account therefore puts together a variety of sources to gauge the prevalence of violence against women.

Fragmentary data show that violence against women is a widespread phenomenon. For instance, in 1990, almost three out of ten (29 per cent) adult Spaniards of both sexes knew of cases of domestic violence against women (Cruz and Cobo 1991: 107–108). It was in the last days of 1999 that the public was first made officially aware of the extent of the problem. In a report to Congress (the lower Chamber of Parliament), the government stated that there had been 6527 reported cases of sexual aggression and that the number of reported cases of domestic violence had been 24,985 in the previous year (*El País* 27 December 1999: 34). Then the findings of the government's first commissioned survey were published in 2000, indicating that no less than 14 per cent of the adult female population, one in seven, had been a victim of physical or psychological domestic violence (*El País* 4 February 2000: 35).

In a major analysis of this survey, published two years later, some useful definitions were set out. Women were defined as living in 'an objective situation of violence' when interviewees answered 'frequently' or 'sometimes' to 26 different questions on aspects of the marital life and behaviour of spouses. These were then grouped into four types: physical violence, psychological 'devaluative' violence ('putting down'), psychological control violence and sexual violence. Questions were classified as 'strong' or 'weak' indicators of each of these types (Alberdi and Matas 2002: 126, 132). These authors expressly made a separation between strong and weak objective situations of violence, and individual women's awareness of being victims, because many did not recognise themselves as such (Alberdi and Matas 2002: 133). On this basis they reached the figure of 14.2 per cent of women responding affirmatively to more than one of the 13 strong indicators of objective violence and concluded that it represented 2,090,767 women, i.e. over two million women in all (for 1999) (Alberdi and Matas 2002: 135). Most of this violence occurred in the family or household environment and in 74 per cent of cases the aggressor was a spouse, partner or boyfriend, and calculated that one-and-a-half million women were to be found in a violent personal relationship (Alberdi and Matas 2002: 138).

As for women who have been killed by their spouse or partner, the figures vary considerably, which is in itself worrying, ranging from 42 per year during 1999–2001 (Ministry of the Interior) to 68, 77 and 69 for those same three years, according to Themis, the Association of Women Lawyers (Alberdi and Matas 2002: 117). While an analysis of the causes of such violence is beyond the scope of this chapter, commentators believe that one of the factors in this rise of domestic violence in the later nineties is the instigation of divorce proceedings. Many of the murdered women were in the process of obtaining a legal separation or divorce from their spouses. According to Enriqueta Chicano, president of the Federation of Progressive Women, 95 per cent of incidents of domestic violence reported to the police occurrs during these two processes (*El País* 12 March 2000).

Services for victims

Let us take a brief look at services for victims of violence. In this sphere, we note a less than adequate response on the part of the authorities, whether local, regional or central, given the pressing nature of the problem. The most readily available type of service for victims of violence is nothing more than information points or help lines about rights and the steps that women can take to protect themselves. Of course information and awareness are a crucial first step because only when women become aware of their legal right to freedom from physical assault can they defend themselves efficiently and then glean information about which social services and other resources are available for them. The first step that the Institute of Women took in the 1980s was to set up and administer 11 women's rights information centres in different cities, where anyone can get information about all aspects of women's rights in general by enquiring in person, by phone or by mail.[4] By 1991, a free phone line had been set up, mainly to reach women living in small towns and villages who could not get to the centres.

In addition to general information services, the Institute of Women organised several publicity campaigns in the early 1980s to raise both the public's and women's awareness that inter-personal violence was not to be tolerated (Gutiérrez 1990: 125; Threlfall 1985: 63). One such awareness drive in more recent years was organised by a consortium consisting of the Spanish Confederation of Neighbours Associations, the Institute of Women, the Ministry of Labour and Social Affairs, and the Ministry of the Interior during 1998. It featured dramatic pictures of battered women accompanied by a bold statement and call to action: 'If he beats you, he doesn't love you. Love yourself! File a complaint against him!' (*El País* 14 October 1998: 31).

But of course victims need more than just awareness and the courage to report an aggressor to the police, and this is where the inadequate provision of support services really lets women victims down. The figures on the number of centres also vary considerably, partly due to the variety of organisations that run them. By 1991 there were still only 31 publicly funded refuges for battered women to escape to, rising to 38 in 1995, running alongside some 13 non-governmental ones, such as those run by non-profit women's organisations (Instituto de la Mujer 1994: 107). Another publication by the same source claims they had 81 on their database by the end of 1992, but these might not all be up and running at the same time (Instituto de la Mujer 1993: 58). One of the problems is that as the Autonomous Communities have responsibility for social services, the initiative has been left to them much of the time, and that has meant patchy geographical coverage, so that there is a very uneven access for women. For instance, the Association of Centres to Help Victims of Sexual Aggressions (CAVAS) brings together 11 centres that provide therapeutic services as well as lawyers who will take up individual women's cases, and see them through police and court proceedings. But the 11 are not well spread out, according to CAVAS's President. Andalucía, governed by the PSOE, runs only one centre in Seville, while the conservative government of the thinly populated Castillia-León region has three. Galicia and the Canary Islands have none at all (Alarcón 2001). Earlier research found only two centres had ever existed in Catalonia, though there was a plan for a third back in 1994 (Threlfall 1996). All in all, provision is currently less comprehensive in Spain than in other countries, as happens with social services in general. A similar conclusion was reached by the Defender of the People (an independent institution charged with protecting citizens against abuse of power by state authorities), who reported that while the legal framework was, on paper, fairly complete in Spain, the support services for victims were still clearly insufficient (Defensor del Pueblo 1998).

Nonetheless, the most supportive kind of service for victims of domestic violence are the refuges where they can actually stay with their children for a period of time (Instituto de la Mujer 1986: 22; Scanlon 1990: 99). The first such refuges were set up in 1984, and by 1997, 129 refuges were said to be functioning in Spain (Instituto de la Mujer 1997: 117).[5] So by the late 1990s, there was one refuge for every 302,000 inhabitants in Spain. While this may appear adequate at first sight, it is a much lower proportion than that recommended in 1997 in a resolution of the European Parliament: one shelter for every 100,000 inhabitants. Furthermore, the supply of Spanish refuges, as with the legal-advice centres, is geographically uneven, and only one region (Castilla y León) has the appropriate number of shelters in relation to its population (Defensor del Pueblo 1998), a problem which is partly related to their being administered either by the central administration, local and regional governments, or voluntary organisations.

Spanish refuges in the main only provide a short-term safe haven with accommodation for women and children and have a limited number of places. While living there, women are offered other services ranging from legal advice to psychological support and vocational training, with the aim of helping them to initiate a new type of life away from their aggressors. However, given the near-absence of public housing and the steep rise in rents and housing costs in Spain, there is little chance of victims being able to move into new low-rent accommodation. In short, victims fleeing their homes are left to their own devices with regard to future living arrangements. Tina Alarcón, the President of CAVAS, confirmed that the most common housing 'solution' for such women was, in her experience, for the woman and her children to be taken in by her parents.

Other ways in which women's rights' advocates approached the problem of violence against women is by involving the police force and the Civil Guard. Some of the first measures were to organise training courses for police officers to improve their attitude towards such violence, as many still considered it a private matter. A bolder move is that for whole police stations or whole departments within them to be devoted to dealing with women victims of violence. In 1988 a police station devoted exclusively to such cases, and staffed only by policewomen, was opened in Barcelona. Other stations set up specialised units, called women's services units. These numbered 16 by 1998 with a further nine units set to open in different cities by the end of that year. The Civil Guard, which had a reputation for being the most traditionally 'macho' and cruel of the repressive forces, was running similar services for women in 15 of Spain's 52 provinces by 1998, using the term Women and Minors Teams (*El País* 16 March 1998:

31). Some 216 police officers and staff and 56 civil guards were devoted to these services by then, which represented quite a change from their usual duties (*El País* 21 December 1999: 34).

While the forces of law and order submitted to training and to changing their patterns of service delivery, there was one crucial group of actors in the drama of domestic violence who seemed to escape any form of treatment or training, and these were the male transgressors themselves. In contrast with other countries, there are very few programmes for male perpetrators of violence against women: only some treatments in prisons for rapists and sexual abusers, but virtually none for batterers.

In sum, it would be incorrect to say that nothing had changed and that Spain remained anchored to a gender system where women were eternally subordinate to aggressive, controlling men who literally got away with murder, as they used to do. There is no doubt that the expectations of justice, fairness and equality that the new Constitution raised to be its supreme national values also spread to the domestic arena, undermining the male 'head of the household's right to threaten and beat with impunity. Aided by feminist activists, a variety of legal reforms were passed to protect women and support services developed to combat violence against women by helping them to prevent its recurrence and even to flee from it. As with so many deep-seated social problems, the solutions have been inadequate or patchy in their coverage, but no one so far has doubted their worth. In particular it is notable that there was no backlash on the part of the conservative government. No refuges were closed nor were services noticeably cut back. But the level of violence rose and the outcry over the spate of killings of women around the turn of the millennium was strong enough to make the Partido Popular engage more fully with the issue. It is to the detail of policy conception and policy implementation that we now turn.

Violence against women as a policy area

Jane Caputi (1992: 204–205) is one of several authors to conceptualise violent acts against women as necessary means for maintaining patriarchy, the dominance of women by men that exists in virtually all societies. If they are right, then it follows that violence against women will be a permanent feature of our societies until they cease to be patriarchal – in other words a radical transformation would have to take place before this sort of violence could be eradicated. Therefore it can be argued that policies combating violence against women are bound to be inefficient because they do not substantially undermine the source of the phenomenon of violence against women: male domination. R. Amy Elman and Maud L. Eduards (1991: 420), while examining the assistance that battered women receive in Sweden, conclude that such assistance is basically insufficient, despite not being negligible. It is so, in their view, chiefly because in the area of gender equality policy-making, the notion of 'progress in women's conditions is defined exclusively in terms of gainful employment and shared parenthood rather than in terms of sexuality'. They claim that this type of understanding of what constitutes 'improvement' of women's status systematically deviates policy-makers' attention away from the essence of the phenomenon of violence against women.

Disagreeing with both Caputi, and Elman and Edwards's propositions, this chapter suggests that in most western countries most policies against violence against women have been difficult to formulate and implement not because of the presumed necessity of violence as a means to maintain patriarchal domination, or because of policy-makers' attachment to a restricted definition of improvement in women's lives, but because of some very distinct characteristics of this policy area, understood in terms of problem definition, policy formulation, and especially policy implementation.

Looking first at problem definition, we argue it is a crucial stage in the policy-making process because for a policy to exist a situation must be conceptualised as a 'problem', about which the authorities and officialdom in general are willing to do something. In all countries, it has been very hard for feminists and public administrators to get violent behaviour against women to be defined as a general social problem, because they have to argue against those (among the general population and the political elite) who believe that no one could seriously think violence was something that affected all of society, and that it really is only about isolated episodes of violence committed by deviant or mentally disturbed men who constitute the margins of society. So these new problem-definers had to break up the deeply embedded assumption that violence against women belongs to the sphere of individual privacy, a realm where the state must refrain from intervening (Connors 1989: 49). Finally, the problem-definers also had to disarticulate the double argument that violence is a normal – if regrettable – means to solve disputes and disagreements among people, that is an ordinary component in human relations, and therefore that violent behaviour against women is not really a social problem but 'just one of those things'.

In addition to this set of issues around problem definition and policy formulation, it is argued here that even greater obstacles for establishing effective policies against violence against women appear at the later implementation level. The barrier that implementation represents is also underscored by other scholars. For example, Jill Radford (1992: 255), examining the treatment of domestic killings by the legal system in England, claims that 'discretion dominates every stage of the process – from the decision to act on reports of violence in the first place to the appropriate punishment for the crime at the final stages'.

The Spanish case arguably confirms Radford's proposition, since the main problem at the implementation stage, which has frequently become an insurmountable obstacle, has been the enormous number of 'street-level bureaucrats' (to use the term coined by Lipsky in 1971 and developed in 1976) who hold disparate views on the same problem, preventing a consistent, or even a coherent, response. In the UK, 'street-level bureaucrats' are probably better known as front-line workers, those public officials or civil servants who interact directly with members of the public, the citizenry, or 'clients' as they are also termed. Lipsky's early research led him to believe that 'certain conditions in the environment of these bureaucracies' make them 'inherently incapable of to contemporary demands for improved and more sympathetic service to some clients' (Lipsky 1976: 208–210). In other words that there was an embedded tendency for the quality of the interactions with clients to deteriorate or at least be perceived negatively by the latter. His and Radford's view was also that these front-line workers 'have considerable discretion in determining the nature, amount, and quality of the benefits and sanctions provided by their agencies' (Lipsky 1980: 3). Several reasons account for this high degree of discretion, among others that the street-level bureaucrats and front-line public service workers are often professionals or professionalised career services. They are expected to use their own knowledge, judgment and *savoir-faire* to solve problems that are quite complex and not easily solved by the simple implementation of routinised procedures. In addition, the population expect from such civil servants and public-service workers not only impartiality but also flexibility and responsiveness to unique circumstances. Furthermore, the number of rules that street-level bureaucrats have to follow, at least in theory, is almost infinite and constantly changing. No wonder, then, that such front-line workers adhere only to the most basic of the rules and exercise discretion in the remaining aspects of their work, without being *de facto* closely supervised by anybody above them. Moreover, street-level bureaucrats' priorities can be different from the goals of the higher-ranking managers of the institutions and agencies appointed to deal with the problem.

As a result, although the basic guidelines of any policy are set up by legislators, or by policy-makers and high-level public administrators, street-level workers can actually modify and distort such basic guidelines in accordance with their own priorities and views. Finally, civil-service provisions, originally established to guarantee non-arbitrary hiring and promotion, actually confer a high degree of autonomy to civil servants, since it is very costly for their superiors to fire them or to reduce their rank (Lipsky 1980: 13–24).

The numerous front-line workers involved in policies against violence against women can, in consequence, easily obstruct the implementation process, since they enjoy a high degree of discretion. It is important to remember that in Spain the main policies against violence against women have been legal reforms, precisely the kind of measure that involves the highest number of actors for its implementation. An example might be useful to illustrate this point. In Spain, repeated domestic violence against women committed by their husbands or cohabiting partners is defined by the Penal Code since 1989 as a crime, and is punishable accordingly. For this law to be applied in practice, the police and civil guards have to know it, and be willing to receive and adequately handle the complaints. Moreover, personnel who work in health centres and/or forensic surgeons have to be prepared to examine the victims rapidly. If both health centre personnel and/or forensic surgeons perform their tasks with some tardiness, the injuries may have partially or totally healed, thereby depriving the victims of violence of some important incriminating evidence.

In addition, it could be the case that victims of domestic violence have to leave the family home, where violent acts are repeatedly committed against them. If victims do not have enough economic resources to afford other accommodation, and have no relatives who can lodge them, they might have to go to a refuge, if vacancies exist. In some cases refuges are full, and their personnel (or social workers who work for state agencies) have to decide rapidly which potential clients are to be given preference, and which others have to be dismissed (or sent to other social services providing accommodation as a last resort). As for the legal system, judges and prosecutors first investigate the cases, and then the trial of the alleged perpetrator is held. Judges and prosecutors have to know the special characteristics of the offence of repeated domestic violence, among others that it normally takes place in the home without witnesses except for the victims themselves, or their children, and that the evidence, such as injuries, might have already disappeared.

Due to these and other characteristics of domestic assaults, prosecution lawyers and judges actually have to be willing to pursue cases of domestic violence more zealously than others and actively seek out the evidence in order to convict the offender. This suggests a complex operation of co-ordination in order for all the actors to perform their tasks adequately in order to apply the 1989 legal reform effectively in its explicit goal of protecting victims of domestic violence. Such co-ordination is difficult to attain for multiple reasons, some of which are illustrated in the following section, which examines the role played by different social and political actors in the policy-making process related to measures against violence against women in Spain since 1975.

Social and political actors in the policy area of violence against women

Generally speaking, in Spain the issue of violence against women was not a priority for activists in the women's movement up to the late 1970s or early 1980s, when some feminists 'discovered' the problem of violence against women, by stumbling upon it almost by accident. For instance, feminists from the Separated and Divorced Women's Association, who provided counselling and legal advice to women wanting to initiate separation and/or divorce proceedings, found that many of their clients' main motive was to escape from a relationship containing high levels of domestic violence. At the same time, other activists working in health centres as physicians or psychologists were shocked by the number of female victims of violence who turned to these centres for help. Finding that these came from all kinds of social and class backgrounds, they began to suspect that the number of victims who did not ask for help must be very high, taking into account women's general lack of awareness of their rights, and their fear of being even more violently treated by their aggressors if they dared to report their case (Threlfall 1985: 62–63).

The next step taken by feminists was to open the eyes of state officials and name the problem to the public in general, so as to reduce the evidently excessive tolerance towards violence against women. They also demanded that policy-makers intervene, organising services for the relief and help of the victims, and reforming the legal system in order to effectively protect women against aggressors. It should be borne in mind that in those years only very few figures were available to indicate the number of violent assaults on women and not one reliable source existed to reflect levels of domestic violence. So at the beginning it was extremely hard for feminists to argue convincingly to policy-makers that violence against women was a serious social problem – not to say a matter of life or death for victims – deserving of the authorities' attention and corrective action.

One of the first tactics tried by the feminist groups' to call attention to the magnitude of the phenomenon of violence against women was to hold sporadic but highly visible demonstrations, generally straight after a violent assault, often a case of rape, had taken place somewhere in the country. Sometimes it was the members of a neighbourhood association, or a political party or trade union, which took the lead. These demonstrations were quite successful in bringing out people who were not normally particularly active politically, but who felt moved by the violence perpetrated on women who lived locally. This was followed in 1982 by the initiative of the women who were providing direct assistance to the victims – the social workers, psychologists and lawyers – to set up the Commission to Investigate the Ill-treatment of Women. They collected as much data as they could and used it as evidence to put pressure on the authorities to formulate a specific new response as well as to use the instruments already in their power. Their first target was to change the attitude of the police (Gutiérrez 1990: 131). The Ministry of the Interior which has authority over the police and the civil guard was requested to order police officers to comply with their obligation to register all complaints received of acts of violence against women and to report back. Commission activists also urged the Ministry of the Interior to order police stations to keep records so that statistics could be compiled (Gutiérrez 1990: 124; Threlfall 1985: 62, 1996: 133).

In this way certain grass-roots feminist organisations began to 'specialise' in the issue of violence against women from the mid-1980s, such as the Association of Assistance to Raped Women and the Commission Against Aggression. At the same time, the official Institute of Women, then headed by socialist-feminists, took up violence against women as one of its concerns, according to one of its Directors (Gutiérrez 1990: 130). By the mid-1980s, then, both institutional gender-policy advocates and grass-roots feminists were already active, defining the different dimensions of the problem and requiring responses from higher authorities. They soon caught the attention of no less an august body than the Senate, which set up a sub-committee to investigate the ill-treatment of women on 5 November 1986 and to liaise with the Defender of the People and the human rights committee of the Senate. It was to collect and analyse information about domestic violence against women in Spain, and give advice to the Ministries of Interior, of Justice and of Education about potential measures to be taken (Gutiérrez 1990: 124).[6] Reporting in Spring 1989, its understanding of the issue and recommendations closely reflected the feminist view and were well received by them (Spanish Senate 1989).

Despite such early successes in raising awareness and getting the attention of major institutions, feminist-policy advocates found that getting the new policies fully implemented proved to be much more of a hurdle than anticipated. They found that constant pressure had to be exercised on the administration and civil service for programmes to become more than rhetorical declarations. For instance, the CAVAS President complained that the new law allowing banishment of abusers from their home was surrounded by exceptions that made it ineffective and too difficult to apply, and that the plan to compensate victims of violence made it so complicated to apply for the benefits that it was not worth it (Alarcón 2001). So they concentrated their lobbying efforts on the police and civil guard, personnel of health centres and members of the judicial system.

With regard to the behaviour of the police and civil guard, while today an increasing number of agents perform their duties adequately in treating victims of violence, in the recent past feminists regularly complained about the insufficient protection given by the police and civil guard to women, especially in cases of domestic violence. Sometimes they responded too late to a call for help when violent aggression against women was involved (Cova and Arozena 1985: 36). Still today they often do not give proper protection to women who have repeatedly been victims of violent attacks, so that women end up being severely injured or killed. According to the 1998 report on domestic violence made by the Defender of the People (Defensor del Pueblo 1998), 89 out of the 91 women killed by their partners in 1997 had filed complaints on domestic violence against their aggressors. The *Asociación de Mujeres Juristas Themis* (1999) accuses the Spanish state of bearing the ultimate responsibility for their deaths.

Policy activists also denounced that when some women go to the police station to report a violent attack against them, the police (or civil guards in the rural areas) still continued to try to convince victims not to sign a complaint 'for their own sake', and also acted as mediators in efforts to reconcile the two partners. In other cases officers did not inform female victims that they had the right to be seen by a policewoman or female civil guard if they were victims of violent assaults. Furthermore, when victims of violence are women prostitutes, the police and civil guards are considered to perform their duties much less diligently than in the case of other types of working women.

Activists consider that one of the reasons to explain the lack of police and civil-guard interest and even lapses in professionalism in cases of violent assaults of women, especially if they are committed in the home, lies in their professional and cultural bias. A significant number of police officers still think that they should not be dealing with such cases, believing them to belong to a person's private life in which the state should not intervene or, at best, in which they could intervene if they had adequate means to do so. Others in turn simply disbelieve some women's accounts of the episode, and still others still think that some women 'were asking for it'. The point is that police officers' and civil guards' attitudes are significant because they can easily translate their ambivalence into inaction or omission. As has been shown, it is the street-level or front-line workers who have a high degree of discretion in dealing with such cases of need. In fact the police are central to such a view since it is they who make the daily decisions on 'who to arrest and whose behaviour to overlook' (Lipsky 1980: 13).

To overcome such attitudes of indifference and improve weak performance, feminist-policy activists demanded that the authorities supervise their subordinates more closely in order to make them more pro-active in the field of violence against women. As a result there is evidence from the second half of the 1980s that Chiefs of Police sent clear instructions to police stations explaining the law that criminalises violence against women, ordering them to be diligent in the performance of their duties in this matter and to be rigorous in collecting the statistics (Ministerio del Interior and Instituto de la Mujer 1991: 110). Using a different approach, training of police officers has been targeted and tailor-made courses devised with feminist input delivered to the police and civil guard (Threlfall 1985: 162–163; Instituto de la Mujer 1986: 15–16; Gutiérrez 1990: 129).

After almost two decades of feminist mobilisation, the situation is hardly satisfactory, as the figures in the first part of the chapter reveal. Granted, some female victims of violence have been given adequate attention by policewomen (or by policemen knowledgeable about the issue); some victims have been truly protected from their aggressors; and statistics have been collected. Nevertheless, these cases are still not the majority. Therefore, there is still a lot of work to be done with the police and the civil guard in this area.

Turning now to the performance of health-services personnel, feminists insistently denounced that these front-line workers quite often fail to examine the victims early enough after the assault, that examinations are somewhat cursory – not as exhaustive as they are supposed to be – and the privacy and intimacy of the victim is quite often insufficiently respected in the course of them (Gutiérrez 1989: 26–27). Feminists then put pressure on the competent authorities to order such professionals to be more diligent, and it is thought that some professionals became more responsive to the needs of women victims, but claim they are not the majority. So once again we see how crucial the behaviour of health services are for the effectiveness of any policy to combat violence. As Heise *et al.* (1994: 1172) noted, they are crucial actors, because 'as one of the few institutions that see women throughout their lives, the health sector is particularly well placed to identify and refer victims to available services'.

The third area of feminists' concern about the pitfalls in the implementation of policies against violence against women is the functioning of the judiciary – some even considered it to be the biggest obstacle for successful implementation of measures against perpetrators of violence against women (Threlfall 1985: 61; Gutiérrez 1989: 42–43; *Asociación de Mujeres Juristas Themis* 1999). There have been insistent complaints about the delays and superficiality of the examination of the victim conducted by forensic surgeons (*Asociación Española de Mujeres Separadas y Divorciadas* 1985: 23; Gutiérrez 1989: 25–26). Worse still, the alarm has been raised about the high number of cases of violent attacks, especially domestic cases, which get classified as a misdemeanor instead of as a crime by lower-court judges and therefore get lighter sentences at the subsequent trial. The trial stage of cases of violence against women is also fraught with biases against the woman, which obstruct the explicit aim of the law, which is to protect victims and punish perpetrators.

Where rape trials are concerned, the research on bias in judicial procedures is well known. Research by Allison and Wrightsman (1993: 171–194), on rape trials in the United States context, and by Sue Lees (1992), on murder trials in Great Britain, has shown that on many occasions it is the victim who is in effect put on trial. She frequently has to answer questions relating to her lifestyle and past sexual experience. Women who wear certain types of clothes, go out alone at night, frequent bars, have no stable partner or no permanent residence are conceptualised as promiscuous and believed to put themselves in danger of abuse and even to indirectly induce men to behave violently. In Spain, feminists have forcefully demanded judges, prosecutors and lawyers *not* to investigate the private life of victims unless it is *strictly* necessary, since it should not be the private life of the victim that is scrutinised in lieu of the alleged perpetrator (Instituto de la Mujer 1985: 71–72).

Fortunately, this issue has been heard and received a considered response. A 1990 decision of the Supreme Court of Justice declared that the sexual life of a victim of rape previous to the rape's occurrence is irrelevant in the trial (*El País* 5 November 1990: 29). But not all investigating magistrates, judges, prosecutors and lawyers are persuaded of such jurisprudence and follow their own prejudices in continuing to investigate the previous sexual life of the victim, even where this is not needed to resolve the case, according to anectotal evidence from specialists. From very early on, the feminist movement complained that prosecutors frequently lack diligence in the investigation of violent offences against women at the stage of accumulating incriminating evidence where a case requires further proof before going to trial, and subsequently drop the charges against the defendants (Baiges 1985: 11; Cova and Arozena 1985: 36; *Asociación de Mujeres Juristas Themis* 1999). This sorry state of affairs has continued in spite of repeated injunctions from the state attorney-general that violent crimes against women should be prosecuted more actively (*El País* 17 October 1998).

Another battle-front for women's policy advocates is the dubious investigation during the trial of the victim's reactions, especially in cases of rape. The Penal Code is silent on this matter, but in Spain, as in many other countries, during a trial there is a widespread onus on rape victims to have to demonstrate that they had very actively resisted their aggressors. Such a *de facto* requirement is inconsistent, since victims of other crimes – robbery, for instance – do not have to prove that they had put up a resistance to the thief. When judgments continued to refer to the high degree of resistance of rape victims, the Supreme Court confirmed in 1987 that rape victims do not have to prove that they have 'heroically' resisted the rapist. It was enough if they could show that they had been intimidated or threatened, such as with a knife (*El País* 8 October 1987: 29). While legal authorities have made clear how rape trials should be conducted in theory, feminists claim that in many trials the victim is still asked to prove that her degree of resistance to rapists was high. This *de facto* requirement leads to an investigation of the degree of the resistance, during which victims have had to answer humiliating and embarrassing questions. For instance, in 1989 a victim was asked if on the day of the rape she wore underpants. The presiding judge claimed the question was necessary in order to evaluate how the alleged rapist had acted (and the victim resisted), bearing in mind that he had a knife in one hand and with the other had to undress the victim, a task which would have been facilitated or obstructed depending on the victim's degree of resistance (*El País* 27 June 1989: 24, 28 June 1989: 31).

Where the nature of punishments is concerned, women's policy advocates were the first to denounce the unfairness of a number of sentences that used to be passed on perpetrators, particularly in cases of domestic violence between husband and wife. An outstanding example was where the guilty party was sentenced to *house arrest*, evidently a wholly counterproductive punishment (Baiges 1985: 10) since it was the victim who got punished by having her aggressor condemned to be under her nose day and night – a provocation likely to lead to further violence.

In time, feminists found several allies to back their claims on the judiciary. A minority sector of judges and prosecutors has supported them by pressing charges and by reaching their sentencing decisions using criteria that sometimes went beyond the letter of law. For instance, in one case the judge considered that a woman had been raped in a case of anal coitus, at a time when, in strict legal terms, rape could only take place in cases of vaginal coitus (*El País* 19 January 1989: 32). Feminists and their allies also put pressure on highly placed policy-makers to draw up guidelines to make the judicial system a more efficient mechanism to punish violent attacks. The Attorney-General, who is allowed to instruct investigating magistrates on how to act, took the important initiative in 1984 of sending circulars to prosecuting magistrates calling on them to be more diligent and to act faster in investigating cases of ill-treatment of women and to take great care to ensure that trials were conducted in the proper manner and guarantees of fairness. The Attorney-General again saw fit to send a formal 'Instruction' to all courts and investigating magistrates reminding them of their duty to put an end to such behaviour, to gather the evidence that the victims might not have been able to put together themselves, and to give exemplary sentences to indicate how seriously they were taking the problem and to collect annual figures. The former director of the Women's Institute termed the Attorney-General's attitude 'belligerent' (Gutiérrez 1990: 134–135).

As a result of these and other efforts, some trials now take place without irregularities, but not all of them. It should be stressed that judges and prosecutors are also, in their own way, Lipsky's 'street-level bureaucrats', with a high degree of autonomy, and rather emblematically so since they are the ones to decide who shall receive a suspended sentence and who shall receive the maximum punishment. While the Attorney-General's Office can dictate mandatory instructions about how prosecutors have to perform their duties, they cannot instruct the judges, who are independent. No one has the authority to instruct them how to behave. Of course, they instruct juries and pass sentence in accordance with the constitution and Spanish law, but the law is their only guide (Gutiérrez 1989: 9–11).

Conclusion

This chapter described the main policies against violence against women established in Spain after 1975. It argued that even though difficulties arise when policies against violence against women are formulated, by far the most problematic stage, littered with sometimes unsurmountable obstacles, was the implementation phase. The reasons for this were complex and went beyond the question of men's need for violence as a means of

maintaining domination over women, in order to perpetuate patriarchy or
the gender order. Neither was this due to any bias in the solutions advocated by policy-making communities or feminist advocates to remedy
women's oppression – such as when they see the improvement of women's
condition mainly in terms of increased access to waged labour outside the
home – even though this does tend to turn attention away from the phenomenon of violence against women, as several scholars have argued.

Instead, the constraints found in the implementation stage of policies
against violence against women arise chiefly because implementation is
dependent on a high number of professionals, officials and civil servants
(Lipsky's 'street-level bureaucrats') who have to deal directly with the
'clients', the affected citizens. In the field of violence against women, these
included judges, prosecutors, lawyers, forensic surgeons, doctors, nurses
and psychologists, police officers and civil guards, among others. These are
the professions that enjoy a high degree of discretion and autonomy when
performing their duties. They are also, sadly, in a position to jeopardise
the implementation of any programme against violence against women, a
realisation that has somewhat dampened the optimism of feminists eager
for effective preventive and remedial action. For a policy to be implemented properly, concerted, single-minded action from all these people is
necessary, something that is difficult to organise, not least because each
profession has its own priorities and ways of working.

In addition, since violence against women is perpetrated in all parts of a
country, the implementation of policies to counteract it should by definition occur in a very decentralised way. Consequently, successful implementation in any single village, town or city depends on all these front-line
professionals commanding a clear understanding of the complex questions
involved in gender-based violence and being correctly trained to assist the
victims. Furthermore, when so many actors are involved, the question of
who does what tends to remain permanently undefined or in process of
being renegotiated. The interviews conducted as part of the research for
this chapter showed up both persistent responsibility gaps as well as
responsibility overlaps among several actors, for instance between staff
working in health centres and forensic surgeons.

For at least three decades feminists of all countries have publicly
claimed that women live in a violent world. An increasing number believes
that effective resistance requires a combination of women's own action
with state institutional action (Heise *et al.* 1994: 1174). This chapter shows
just how problematical the latter can be. Feminists need to put pressure on
the behaviour of institutional actors not only to get them to continue to
develop new measures against violence, but also to ensure that they implement existing measures much more effectively. Furthermore, there is a dis-
cernible tension and contradiction between the high degree of autonomy
of front-line workers and professionals and the scattered nature of the
sites where correct policy implementation should take place. This can be

quite frustrating for feminist-policy advocates, who find they need to influence not only the top echelons of a variety of professional and semi-professional bodies but also, ideally, every single professional in the field and their line-managers into the bargain – clearly a Herculean task. It is no wonder that women's-movement activists often feel that they have to fight on so many fronts at the same time and that battles are fought but never clearly won.

One of the implications of this study is that if the current institutional dynamics of counteracting violence have been captured accurately, then direct provision of help by feminist organisations to victims of violence may prove to be crucial and even invaluable in the years to come. Ironically, setting up feminist-inspired services for victims can sometimes prove an easier task than lobbying the administration and the professionals, since the former can make exclusive use of feminist professionals who understand the problem with the help of a few well-placed sympathetic contacts. In other words, by running a rape crisis centre themselves (with funding), feminists can bypass the stage of first having to convince a large number of professionals of the wider merits of public-service delivery in this area. Indeed this has been precisely the strategy pursued by certain women's advocates in Spain in the last two decades. Not only has the supply of direct assistance to victims of violence (or other groups) been maintained, it has even flourished in the last few years. The drawbacks of this strategy are also evident, since human and material resources for the feminists to 'go it alone' are bound to be insufficient, and only the police and the courts can prosecute and put an assailant behind bars. However, it does raise issues about 'mainstreaming', a popular feminist strategy which seeks to ensure that administrative authorities take on the burden of implementation of gender strategies and services.

In any case, there is no doubt that the main policies against violence against women of the last two decades in Spain could be substantially ameliorated in the near future with the help of an increase in mainstream social services. Such a scenario can also be optimistically envisaged if one considers that violence against women, together with abortion, are still major unifying and motivating causes for all branches of Spanish feminist activism. There is also a public consensus over violence, specifically that the number of victims is quite unacceptably high – an outrage for a society that takes pride in having achieved European levels of modernity and civilised behaviour.

Notes

1 This chapter is largely based on an analysis of secondary literature, legislation, published and unpublished political documents, and 17 in-depth personal interviews with social and political actors active in the policy area of violence against women: four members of women's organisations; a judge; a police agent; three civil guards (police agents mainly for the rural areas); a social worker; two

members of the personnel who work in a battered women's refuge; a female victim of violence (rape); a forensic surgeon; a physician specialist in the examination of female victims of violence; and two lawyers specialising in gender equality legal measures. All interviews were conducted in the city of Madrid in March 1995. In order to maintain the anonymity of the interviewed, their names do not appear in this chapter. The first findings about policies against violence against women in Spain were published in Valiente (1996).

2 This type of terminology also enjoyed certain currency in other Roman-law countries. For instance, in Italy, sexual violence was listed in the Penal Code under title 'crimes against public morality and right living' (Addis 1989: 2). In France, sexual assaults were prosecuted according to an article of the Penal Code which dealt with 'assaults on morals' (Stetson 1987: 163).

3 Divorce had also existed during the Second Republic (1931–1936), but it was abolished by the subsequent dictatorship.

4 Three of these information centres had already been set up under the UCD government by the former Subdirección General de la Mujer, part of the Ministry of Culture, and the PSOE-led Women's Institute inherited them and increased their number.

5 The first battered women's refuges were set up in 1971 in the UK (Connors 1989: 34) and in 1974 in the USA (Stout 1992: 134).

6 The sub-committee was headed by a woman senator from the PSOE, and included two male PSOE senators, a male senator from the conservative party (Partido Popular) and a male senator from the mixed group.

References

Addis, Elisabetta (1989) 'What women should ask of the law: Italian feminist debate on the legal system and sexual violence', Harvard University Center for European Studies Working Paper Series Number 18.

Alarcón, Tina (2001) Interview given to Monica Threlfall in February.

Alberdi, I. and Matas, N. (2002) *La violencia doméstica: Informe sobre los malos tratos en España*, Barcelona: Fundación La Caixa.

Allison, Julie A. and Wrightsman, Lawrence S. (1993) *Rape: the Misunderstood Crime*, Newbury Park, CA: Sage.

Asociación Española de Mujeres Separadas y Divorciadas (1985) 'Pago de emplazamientos a funcionarios de justicia' in Instituto de la Mujer (ed.) *Primeras jornadas: aplicación del Derecho y la mujer*, 21–23 Madrid: Instituto de la Mujer.

Asociación de Mujeres Juristas Themis (1999) *Respuesta penal a la violencia familiar*, Madrid: *Asociación de Mujeres Juristas Themis* and *Consejo de la Mujer de la Comunidad de Madrid*.

Baiges, Mayte (1985) 'Introducción' in Instituto de la Mujer (ed.) *Primeras jornadas: aplicación del Derecho y la mujer*, 9–12, Madrid: Instituto de la Mujer.

Bustos, Juan (1991) *Manual de Derecho Penal: parte especial*, Barcelona: Ariel.

Cabo, Manuel (ed.) (1993) *Manual de Derecho Penal (parte especial) I*, Madrid: Editoriales de Derecho Reunidas.

Caputi, Jane (1992) 'Advertising femicide: lethal violence against women in pornography and gorenography' in Jill Radford and Diana E.H. Russell (eds) *Femicide: the Politics of Woman Killing*, 203–221. New York: Twayne.

Connors, Jane Frances (1989) *Violence Against Women in the Family*, New York: United Nations Office at Vienna, Center for Social Development and Humanitarian Affairs.

Cova, Luz M. and Soledad, Arozena (1985) 'Aplicación del Derecho' in Instituto de la Mujer (ed.) *Primeras jornadas: aplicación del Derecho y la mujer*, 35–37, Madrid: Instituto de la Mujer.

Cruz, Pepa and Cobo, Rosa (1991) *Las mujeres españolas: Lo privado y lo público*, Madrid: Centro de Investigaciones Sociológicas.

Defensor del Pueblo (1998) 'Informe sobre la violencia doméstica contra las mujeres' (unpublished report).

Elman, R. Amy and Eduards, Maud L. (1991) 'Unprotected by the Swedish welfare state: a survey of battered women and the assistance they received', Women's Studies International Forum, 14 (5): 413–421.

Gutiérrez, Purificación (1989) 'La administración de la justicia ante el problema de los "malos tratos" en el ámbito doméstico' (unpublished paper).

Gutiérrez, Purificación (1990) 'Violencia doméstica: respuesta legal e institucional' in Virginia Maquieira and Cristina Sánchez (eds) *Violencia y sociedad patriarcal*, 123–136, Madrid: Pablo Iglesias.

Heise, Lori L., Raikes, Alanagh, Watts, Charlotte H. and Zwi, Anthony B. (1994) 'Violence against women: a neglected public health issue in less developed countries', *Social Science Medicine*, 39 (9): 1165–1179.

Instituto de la Mujer (1985) 'Conclusiones de las primeras jornadas de aplicación del Derecho en relación a la mujer' in Instituto de la Mujer (ed.) *Primeras jornadas: aplicación del Derecho y la mujer*, 69–75, Madrid: Instituto de la Mujer.

Instituto de la Mujer (1986) *El Instituto de la Mujer 1983–1986*, Madrid: Instituto de la Mujer.

Instituto de la Mujer (1993) *Memoria 1992*, Madrid: Ministry of Social Affairs.

Instituto de la Mujer (1994) *La mujer en cifras: una década, 1982–1992*, Madrid: Instituto de la Mujer.

Instituto de la Mujer (1997). *Las mujeres en cifras 1997*, Madrid: Instituto de la Mujer.

Instituto de la Mujer (1998) *Plan de Acción contra la violencia doméstica*, Madrid: Instituto de la Mujer.

Kornblit, Ana Lia (1994) 'Domestic violence – an emerging health issue', *Social Science Medicine*, 39 (9): 1181–1188.

Lees, Sue (1992) 'Naggers, whores, and libbers: provoking men to kill' in Jill Radford and Diana E.H. Russell (eds) *Femicide: the Politics of Woman Killing*, 267–288, New York: Twayne.

Lipsky, M. (1976) 'Towards a theory of street-level bureaucracy' in W.D. Hawley *et al.* (eds) *Theoretical Perspectives on Urban Policy*, Englewood Cliffs, NJ: Prentice Hall.

Lipsky, Michael (1980) *Street-Level Bureaucrats*, New York: Russell Sage Foundation.

López, Jacobo (1992) *Manual de Derecho Penal: parte especial III*, Madrid: Akal.

Ministerio del Interior and Instituto de la Mujer (1991) *Violencia contra la mujer*, Madrid: Ministerio del Interior.

Radford, Jill (1992) 'Womanslaughter: a license to kill? The killing of Jane Asher' in Jill Radford and Diana E.H. Russell (eds) *Femicide: the Politics of Woman Killing*, 253–266, New York: Twayne.

Rodríguez, Luis, Alvarez, Francisco J. and Gómez, Pilar (1988) *La justicia ante la libertad sexual de las mujeres*, Madrid: Instituto de la Mujer.

Scanlon, Geraldine M. (1990) 'El movimiento feminista en España, 1900–1985: logros y dificultades' in Judith Astelarra (ed.) *Participación política de las mujeres*, 83–100, Madrid: Centro de Investigaciones Sociológicas and Siglo XXI.

Spanish Senate (1989) 'Informe de la Comisión de Relaciones con el Defensor del Pueblo y de los Derechos Humanos encargada del estudio de la mujer mal-tratada', *Boletín de las Cortes Generales*, Senado 12 May, No. 313: 12182–12211.

Stetson, Dorothy McBride (1987) *Women's Rights in France*, Westport, CT: Greenwood Press.

Stout, Karen (1992) ' "Intimate femicide": effect on legislation and social services' in Jill Radford and Diana E.H. Russell (eds) *Femicide: the Politics of Woman Killing*, 133–140, New York: Twayne.

Threlfall, Monica (1985) 'The Women's Movement in Spain', *New Left Review*, 151: 44–73.

Threlfall, M. (1996) 'Feminist politics and social transformation in Spain' in M. Threlfall (ed.) *Mapping the Women's Movement: Feminist Politics and Social Transformation in the North*, London: Verso.

Threlfall, Monica (1998) 'State feminism or party feminism? Feminist politics and the Spanish Institute of Women', *European Journal of Women's Studies*, 5: 69–93.

United Nations (1996) *The Beijing Declaration and Platform for Action*, Fourth World Conference on Women, Beijing, 14–15 September 1995, Department of Public Information, United Nations, New York.

Valiente, Celia (1995) 'The power of persuasion: the Instituto de la Mujer in Spain' in Dorothy McBride Stetson and Amy G. Mazur (eds) *Comparative State Feminism*, Newbury Park, CA: Sage.

Valiente, Celia (1996) 'Partial achievements of central-state public policies against violence against women in post-authoritarian Spain (1975–1995)' in C. Corrin (ed.) *Women in a Violent World: Feminist Analyses and Resistance Across 'Europe'*, 166–185, Edinburgh: Edinburgh University Press.

6 Towards parity representation in party politics

Monica Threlfall

In the space of two decades, Spanish women radically repositioned themselves with regards to the political system. At the beginning of the transition to democracy, they were typecast as a conservative bloc,[1] a concern for the forces of democracy who feared their political passivity and tendency to make last-minute voting decisions or abstain altogether. Within a few years, this biased image had been dispelled. By the end of the millennium they had not only entered the political system, directed policy-making in a number of spheres, succeeded to elective office and gained many public appointments, but were also demanding full parity of representation with men. If in 1977 women's hopes centred on scrambling out of the ditch of political exclusion, twenty years later a 28 per cent participation rate in the main legislative chamber of Parliament – comfortably above the European Union average – was no longer a cause for special celebration. By the start of the twenty-first century the political class believed the presence of women in leading posts to be essential to a party's credibility with the electorate, and women presided over both chambers of Parliament. How were Spanish women able to catch up so quickly and overtake their counterparts in many other countries to end up ranking twelfth in the world?

This chapter traces the trajectory of women's participation in political decision-making, focusing on party politics in the three main democratic parties and on elective office, rather than other spheres of politics and representation. Secondly, it seeks to identify the key turning points in the trend towards greater participation, arguing that these coincide with the adoption by the PSOE of gender quotas for candidates, followed by the policy of parity democracy, and that after this the trend in other parties also rose. Thirdly, the chapter uses this evidence to shed light on the reasons for the rise of women in party politics. Although in theory a structural explanation could be found in Spain's social and economic modernisation, this is discarded because of the differences in participation between one European state and another at a similar level of development. The conditioning influence of the electoral systems is also discussed for the Spanish case, taking into account proportional representation for the national and regional assemblies and the plurality system for the upper house, but is found to have insufficient explanatory power for a number of reasons.

The chapter then looks at institutional party-political explanations and proposes that increases in women's representation in Spain have depended largely on the adoption of new constitutional provisions regarding gender quotas and parity within one party, the PSOE, that unleashed a series of gender re-balancing exercises. It further argues that a key factor for the success of party statutory reform as a way of increasing women's presence in elected posts is its efficient implementation, in the manner of a national law. The chapter analyses why the realisation of intra-party reform was effective in the case of the PSOE, identifying the phenomenon of 'enlightened elitism' in top echelons of the party as one reason – namely a collection of persons who led by example and enjoyed sufficient power and persuasiveness to ensure the implementation of the new parity 'law' at regional and at local levels. A second, supporting reason is the politico-organisational conjuncture that the PSOE found itself in, namely its need for renewal in the face of political sclerosis. This led it to adopt women's representation as an instrument to promote its own renewal. In addition, when examining the extent and level of implementation of the party's reformed statutes on gender representation, the chapter discusses whether women participating in institutional politics only find a space to operate at the margins and in the lower echelons of power, and whether the Spanish case illustrates or belies this commonly held view. In its conclusions, it emphasises the decisive impact made by the adoption of a quota of women candidates and of gender parity made on the PSOE and other parties, and asks how far women's progress is, paradoxically, the result of strong top-down political leadership, and a form of 'enlightened elitism' that perceived women's increased representation as a cause – a cause that would hopefully aid the internal renewal of the party's leadership, membership and voter base.

Some necessary limitations to the scope of the chapter should be pointed out. Firstly, given Spain's socio-economic and political diversity and its strong structures of devolved self-government (the Autonomous Communities – ACs), a regionally based analysis would have steered us away from the treating women as a nationwide bloc. But sub-national governance is quite heterogeneous in its powers and patterns of political behaviour: some ACs consist only of one province with a single large town, yet elect representatives to local, regional and national assemblies, just as the larger ones do. Large population variance means that they are difficult to compare with each other or contrast with the national level. Instead, the chapter compares three institutional tiers – local, regional and national – of public and party governance. A second necessary choice was to discard the hope of covering all nationwide, nationalist and regionalist parties in equal depth. A focus on the PSOE is rewarding because, being something of a pioneer in this field, it has undertaken greater gender monitoring and published more detailed data than other parties.

The PSOE and gender representation issues

Formed in 1879, the PSOE became a classic social-democratic, mass-membership party with a well-developed internal structure of local groups and provincial and regional organisations. It played prominent roles in the Second Republican governments (1931–1936) and in the Civil War (1936–1939). Despite the disruptions of the Civil War and near dismemberment during the Francoist repression (see Gillespie 1989), it maintained its traditional federal structure, with each federation electing members to a Federal Committee (*Comité Federal*), which is the highest decision-making body according to party statutes. At the same time, delegates to the party conference from all over the country elect a Federal Executive Commission (*Comisión Ejecutiva Federal*) that is responsible for implementing policy between conferences and is subject to approval from the Federal Committee. In practice, the Executive Commission is the most powerful political organ and tends to decide on policy as well as organise its implementation.

But even though many political initiatives tends to flow downwards from the top, it would be a mistake to think of the PSOE as a monolithic structure freely run by a small elite located at 'the top', because the party's regional federations are powerful,[2] and their power has grown with that of the autonomous regions. Party federations take the credit for any success in the autonomy elections that will take the party into the regional government, either single-handedly or in coalition. The bigger the AC and the larger the PSOE's electoral dominance of it, the greater will the party federation's influence on the Federal Executive Committee be, as has been the case for Andalucía. During the period studied, any socialist president of an AC was likely to be elected on to the party executive. And despite the *de facto* political or ideological sway that a leader as successful as Felipe González might have held, the PSOE's internal structures, committee meetings, regional and federal congresses take forward party life in accordance with statutes and procedures.

In the early days of debate about the lack of visibility of women in party politics in the late 1970s and early 1980s, the argument among members of leftist parties was that they had too few women members for these to expect to reach leadership posts except in a handful of cases. In some internal debates it was envisaged that there would be, at most, a similar proportion of women leaders as there were women members, and probably less given women's ongoing responsibilities in the home. This view at first seemed acceptable to party feminists, but after a while it struck them as a constraint. Why should a 10 per cent female membership rate mean that only one woman among ten leaders was enough? The proportionality argument could be undermined if the 'quality' of the women members was greater than that of the men (Threlfall 1979). A study had shown that women affiliates were younger and better educated than male members, tended to be employees rather than shy homemakers, often had relevant experience as professionals[3] and, lastly, tended not to be dormant members who never came to meetings.[4] Arguably, PSOE women were therefore more highly qualified in potential leadership skills than the average party member, over half of whom were manual workers.[5] All this suggested that the proportion of women with political responsibilities could be higher than the proportion of women rank-and-file members. The feeling of being under-represented at leadership levels would not go away.

By 1982 only three women, less than 3 per cent of the total, had become elected onto the PSOE's Federal Committee by the regional federations and a further three women had reached the Federal Executive Commission (12.5 per cent of 24 members). If the Executive was divided into its two tiers of responsibility, only one woman was left at the top.[6] The situation remained the same in 1985–1986 (IDES 1988: 61). Party feminists argued that a subtle mechanism of political discrimination operated against the selection of women for such positions, but even sympathetic male leaders responded that there were simply too few good women available. It was true that at 12 per cent, proportionality between the female membership and their presence on the Executive Commission had been reached, but there was the fundamental question of gender representation to be addressed. Spanish feminists were not alone in thinking this: feminist party caucuses in many social-democratic parties had been demanding better representation on principle. The outcome was that member parties of the Socialist International (the world-wide organisation of social-democratic and democratic-socialist parties) decided that the principle of balanced representation of the genders counted for more than the issue of the alleged unavailability of suitable women (Socialist International Women 1995). It would simply take too long for a similar proportion of women and men to be elected spontaneously in member parties, they recognised, so member parties would take steps to make it happen as a matter of principle, by deciding that a specified proportion of candidates for public and party posts would be reserved for women as part of a quota system. According to Squires (1996: 81, 87), moving to a quota system signifies a departure from the traditional liberal understanding of representation towards an endorsement of a 'microcosm conception of representation' in which there is fair group presence.[7]

The PSOE had retreated from the view that leaders simply reflect the composition of the party – which they never did anyway, being at the time mainly composed of working-class members but led by white-collar or professional middle classes – and now espoused the belief that the leadership should reflect not just class interests, but wider society. In fact the PSOE even accepted that in the course of this change-over women might become over-represented in party leadership in relation to their presence among the membership. When its 31st Conference in 1988 adopted a 25 per cent quota for women, there was less than that proportion of women among the members. At its 33rd Conference in 1994 it adopted the principle of gender parity representation: there was to be no more than 60 per cent of either men or women in party and elective posts. By its 1997 conference, this had been written into party statutes.

The full story of why and how an overwhelmingly male party was persuaded to take these drastic measures is still to be written and the impact of the changes on the daily political practice of the party has hardly been researched at all. Building on Threlfall (1997), in which the PSOE feminists' strategy was analysed, this chapter attempts to fill some of the gap, firstly by analysing the numerical evidence for a shift in the gender balance of political participation and secondly by discussing the speed with which Spanish women have broken into politics in terms of their presence in the main nationwide parties.

The gender balance in top party posts

The PSOE's 34th Conference in 1997 implemented the 40/60 gender parity mechanism for the election of the Federal (Spain-wide) Executive Committee (FEC). Fourteen women out of 33 members (42 per cent) became part of the FEC. Felipe González, as outgoing General Secretary of the party and Joaquín Almunia, his replacement, fully backed the measure. When the Federations held their regional conferences in the ensuing months, they followed suit. The example set at the top was undoubtedly influential, and can be seen as an example of the top-down flow of a principled idea.

It is also worth going in some detail about how the Federal Executive Commission is elected. It is traditionally a negotiated list agreed by and with the incoming leader rather than a competitive election of individuals. The candidate leader will put together his (it has always been a man) dream list of FEC members, then consult with the powerbrokers who are the leaders of the political tendencies, the federations and the parliamentary party. The inclusion of women in a leader's candidate list is both facilitated by his freedom to select preferred women, and constrained by the need to balance political and regional considerations, which will mean some candidates fall off the list. One mechanism to aid negotiations is that the FEC has two tiers, the upper for the policy portfolio posts, the lower for ordinary members. In 1997, the outcome of these negotiations was that the women (79 per cent) were overwhelmingly to be found among the lower tier of the FEC posts with no specific policy responsibilities. Only three women joined the upper tier, thereby becoming 'federal spokespersons', leading the Secretariats of 'Social Movements', 'Social Welfare' and 'Participation of Women'. As these were typical 'feminised' posts,

González was seen to formally comply with the parity policy while not entrusting a key policy position to a woman.

Therefore, while there was a clear surge in the presence of women in party leadership posts after 1997, the move was actually implemented in a cautious way that did not take the PSOE's reins of power away from male incumbents. The top four political posts (PSOE President, Secretary-General, Deputy Secretary-General and Secretary of Organisation) remained firmly in the hands of men. At federation level, among the 84 very top posts (four each) in the PSOE's 21 regional and nationality federations, there were still only ten women (12 per cent). Furthermore, these ten women became prominent only in small or politically less prominent federations, with the exception of Madrid. They became President of the Madrid, Cantabria and the Balearics federations; Secretary-General in Murcia and 'America' (emigrants in Latin and North America); Deputy Secretary-General in Castilla-La Mancha and Navarre; and Secretary of Organisation in Extremadura, La Rioja and 'Europe' (emigrants). The pattern was repeated at provincial level, with only 13 women (11 per cent) reaching one of the four most powerful posts in each of the 30 provincial party organisations.[8]

As the gender balance rule does not apply to specific named posts, only the Executive Committee as a whole, it is not surprising that women did not immediately scale the peaks of PSOE leadership or cause the elite of top males to lose power. Nonetheless, the gender distribution of post-holding throughout the PSOE, presented in Table 6.1, reveals an unexpected dynamic. In column (a) the proportion of women is governed by the binding congress decision on parity of the previous year (1997), and this would explain a certain similarity in the proportion of women at the three levels (42–37–39 per cent). A five-point lag is evident for the regional level, but this can be explained away by the fact that two regions held their conferences before the parity decision had been taken and consequently had fewer women, bringing the average down to 37 per cent. Columns (b), (c) and (d), on the other hand are a reflection of more spontaneous party dynamics (within the 40 per cent quota constraint) and here the pattern is clear: women are still quota-fillers, included in the leadership on account of a political rule, but pushed into the lower tiers of it at all three geographical levels (79 per cent, 58 per cent, 62 per cent).

This dynamic repeats itself at all three levels, leading to similarities between them. Such similarities show, unusually, that the gender distribution of political power in the PSOE is not a reflection of the trend observed for other countries whereby the furthest from the centre of power, the more women are to be found (Randall 1987). How can this be? In Spain, regional and provincial party structures are also power centres in their own right, controlling several important spheres of political life in the Autonomous Communities. These are, firstly, decisions taken regarding party election strategies and candidates; secondly, the party's contribution

Table 6.1 Women in leadership positions in the PSOE in 1998

	(a) All posts	(b) Lower tier of 'orators' (vocals)	(c) Upper tier with portfolios	(d) Four posts with most power
Federal Executive Commission	14 of 33 (42%)	11 of 20 (55%)	3 of 13 (23%)	0 of 4 (0%)
Federal Committee	75 of 234 (32%)	41 of 144[a] (28.5%)	20 of 49[b] (41%)	–
Regional and Nationality Executive Commissions	232 of 628 (37%)	134 (58%)	98 (42%)	10 of 84 (12%)
30 Provincial Executive Commissions[c]	386 of 988 (39%)	241 (62%)	145 (38%)	13 of 120 (16%)

Source: Own calculations using data in Secretaría de Participación de la Mujer (1998).

Notes

a Elected by the regional federations;

b elected by Conference;

c excluding Cataluña, Galicia, País Valenciano, Canarias and Balearics because party structures there are not based on provincial boundaries, having smaller units instead – total numbers including these island and district councils is 608 of 1610, i.e. nearly 38%.

to, and even control of, the running of regional governments, city councils in provincial capitals and mayors of towns and villages; and, thirdly, internal party-political processes and policy via the delegates sent to regional and federal conferences and to the Federal Committee. Arguably, in these decentralised power centres male leaderships are more reluctant to hand over a full share of real power to women, as opposed to 'just' 40 per cent of posts.

Consequently, one finds that most of the women rising to a regional leadership post do not get a policy portfolio at all. They are brought in as lower-tier junior members ('orators' or *vocales*). On the other hand, it could be said that for a woman with little political experience who gets to stand for a local leadership position relatively soon after becoming active in the party, the fact of being in the lower tier with no portfolio, or in the upper tier with a 'feminised' portfolio that is nonetheless interesting, can be a satisfying opportunity for political training. Rather than the post-holders, it is the feminist strategists in the party who grumble.

Looking at the question of the jobs women tend to be given once they do reach a top post, one finds that the PSOE conforms to type, giving them the 'soft' portfolios (called the 'reproductive ministries' by Henig and Henig 2001: 102). The largest number of those with a portfolio had responsibility for 'participation of women' (predictably) followed by 'social welfare', 'environment', 'social movements', 'political education' and 'education, culture and youth', the full roll-call of feminised areas of interest. Again, the geographical levels are similar: at provincial level, where the number of women in the provincial executives rose to 39 per cent from 25 per cent before the historic parity decision, they are concentrated in exactly the same areas.[9] Nonetheless, it could also be argued that the PSOE system offers women a less brutal entry into political leadership than the one they would have had if there had been no quota and they had had to do battle with male gatekeepers armed with unfettered prejudices. And whatever was predicted about the quota arousing male resentment and making matters worse, in Spain there has so far been no evidence of a concerted backlash against it. The conclusion that can be drawn from this is that, for the time being, *second order positions of power, but with future prospects, appear to be the price of women's rather sudden political inclusion.*

Let us look now at the situation regarding top party posts in the other main nationwide parties, the Partido Popular (People's Party) and the Izquierda Unida (United Left alliance) in which the PCE (Communist Party) was the main component. From Table 6.2, one can see most strikingly that women in the Partido Popular have not reached leadership positions to the same extent as in the PSOE. The very large 94-member National Executive Committee of the PP only included 20 women, and among these, only two made it to the top tier of executive portfolio posts. Only the vast National Board had more women on it, reaching a quarter of

Table 6.2 Gender composition of the Partido Popular leadership

Partido Popular organs	Total women	Women area co-ordinators on NEC	Women in portfolio tier	Two posts with most power, of which >>	Woman Executive Secretary	Woman President
National Executive Committee	20 of 94 (21%)	2 of 4 (50%)	2 of 10 (20%)	0 of 2	0 of 1	0 of 1
National Board (Junta Directiva Nacional)	132 of 521 (25%)	–	–	–	–	–
18 Regional party organs	n/a	n/a	n/a	4 of 36 (11%)	3 of 18 (17%)	1 of 18 (6%)
51 Provincial and Island party organs	n/a	n/a	n/a	22 of 102 (22%)	17 of 51 (33%)	5 of 51 (10%)

Source: Created from data for 2001 obtained from Partido Popular headquarters.

Notes

– = not applicable; n/a = not available.

the total. Yet, at National Executive Committee level there appears to be less of a gender hierarchy than in the PSOE, since the gap between the portfolio tier and the whole Committee is only one point (20 vs. 21 per cent). One explanation could be that as the PP has not adopted a gender quota, there has been less pressure for the party to open the doors of its leadership to women. There is also a similarity with the PSOE in the lack of women in the very top posts at the nationwide level, and in contrast, their presence in the two very top party posts at sub-national and provincial levels: 11 per cent AP and 12 per cent PSOE in the regions, rising to 22 per cent for AP and 16 per cent for PSOE in the provinces and islands. One should take into account the PSOE figures are three years older than the PP's and the trend is upward, but nevertheless it is interesting that in the PP it seems easier for a woman to rise to individual prominence in the smallest geographical units, whereas in the PSOE there is greater uniformity. Ultimately, there are only a handful of prominent women in either of Spain's two largest parties.

The gender composition of the leftist IU and PCE displays less clear characteristics due to its complex structure, as witnessed in Table 6.3. The IU's top leadership organ, the Permanent Commission, was gender-balanced at 41 per cent, but the internal composition of its Federal Executive Presidency was unbalanced by the very low representation of women among the Co-ordinators of its regional federations and among its portfolio Secretariats, which were in the main run by men with only seven women (26 per cent). One might have thought the IU's main component party, the PCE, would have a similar structure, but it displayed the historic characteristics of communist parties of having three tiers. There were far fewer women in its Permanent Commission: only three of 15 (20 per cent). In terms of gender balance, only the individually elected members of the Executive Committee met the 40 per cent minimum, while the participation of women was curtailed by the exclusively male presence of the political secretaries of the party federations.

Comparing the leadership structures of Spain's three largest parties, three interesting points can be made. Firstly, that the conservative party lagged markedly behind the PSOE, but not by that much at the upper level given that the PSOE's proportion of women is encouraged by quotas, which the PP does not use. As for the United Left (IU), its results were not much more impressive than the PP's considering that it had adhered to the principle of gender balance. Second, in all parties there was a likelihood of women's greater general presence at the national (federal) executive level rather than at the provincial level. This evidence suggests that *where appointments were made from a nationwide pool of candidates, distinguished female political talent was found more easily than when the choice was restricted to a pool of those who happened to live in a particular location (the province or island).* Equally, local-party elites were on the whole less permeable to arguments about gender equity than regional or

Table 6.3a Gender composition of the IU leadership

IU organs[a]	No. of women	Percentage
Permanent Commission (top tier)	7 of 17	41
Federal Executive Presidency		
Secretariat tier with portfolios	7 of 27	26
Individual members' tier	12 of 37	32
Federation Co-ordinators tier	1 of 19	5
Federal Executive Presidency total	13 of 56	23

Note
a ranked from top to bottom by political status.

Table 6.3b Gender composition of PCE leadership

PCE organs		No. of women	%
Permanent Commission (top tier with portfolios)		3 of 15	20
Executive Committee	Individual elected members	15 of 37	41
	Ex-officio Members (Political Secretaries of Federations)	0 of 17	0
	Total	15 of 54	28
Federal Committee	Individually elected members	35 of 97	36
	Elected members from the 'nationalities' (Autonomous Communities)	7 of 42	17
	Total	42 of 139	30
Regional party federations	Political Secretary (top post)	0 of 17	0

Source: Calculated from lists of names for 2001 provided by Izquierda Unida: http://www.iu.es.

national ones. Third, all parties exhibited the feature that when a party organ was divided into an upper and a lower tier, or into power-ranking of posts, then there were more women in the lower tier and among the lower-ranking posts. Fourth, very few women were the single top leader. In all parties the single top post was nearly always occupied by a man, but at local level it was easier for a woman to reach the top post in the PP than in the other parties. The significance of these features for a general understanding of women's collective trajectory of political participation in Spain will be discussed in the section on tiers of leadership after the analysis of the data on public office below.

Towards gender balance in public office?

While parliaments as institutions are under a certain pressure to increase their proportion of women in the name of equity and balanced gender representation, it is the parties who bear the brunt of delivering the women members to parliament, since the road to becoming a member of parliament is controlled by parties – independent candidates everywhere have a poor chance of winning a seat. In this gate-keeping function of parties, the role of the top party leaders is not a straightforward one. National Executive Committees do not have full control of the process of selecting candidates to stand, and the electorate's final decisions, given the secrecy of the ballot, can be both hard to predict and volatile over time. In the Spanish case the decentralised, federal nature of the PSOE, the province-based party list system and the d'Hondt seat allocation method[10] all intervene in the process, adding to the parties' uncertainty of achieving the desired composition of elected representatives. Therefore Spanish advocates of gender equity have tended to look as closely at the candidate lists in the run-up to elections as at the outcome in parliament.

During Spanish election campaigns, there is a certain amount of competition between the parties over the gender composition of their lists. Equity-watchers distinguish between the proportion of *total* candidates, the proportion of candidates *likely to win* a seat, and the proportion of candidate *lists headed by women*. A woman heading a slate is a good indicator, and probably the strongest available, of women's political power in a party, though it is also the most infrequently found. The composition of the constituency candidate lists, being the nexus between internal party life and public office, reflects the overall gender balance of power throughout a party. They usually contain not just the top provincial party leaders but also the heavyweight national figures needing to find a seat outside of the national or regional capital.[11]

Candidates for seats in parliament

In Spain it is possible to study the gender of candidate lists going back to the first democratic elections in 1977, which allows us to study trends, as in Table 6.4. The first thing to note is the marked contrast between the first ten years of elections, in which progress was slow, and the last decade in which all parties saw substantial increases. Secondly, whereas the right and the left were neck and neck in the first decade, the left was outdoing the right in the 1990s owing to a leap forward that coincided with the introduction of quotas in the PSOE and IU. Thirdly, the proportion of candidates was well over the initial 25 per cent quota, a positive feature, though the figures do not reveal what position on the list the women occupied. In fact, when it came to filling up the electoral slates with run-of-the-mill candidates who had no hope of election (a party tends to field candidates for all possible seats), parties did not hesitate to field women. Women often conducted the less glamorous parts of the campaign in the remoter towns and villages, but thereby gained a political training in the eyes of their parties.

Table 6.4 Women candidates fielded by parties on electoral lists for Congress

Party lists	1977		1979		1982		1986		1989		1996		2000	
	No.	%	No.	%	No.	%	No.	%	No.	%	No.	%	No.	%
AP/CD/CP/PP[a]	45	12	54	11.9	48	8.4	51	14.3	89	17.7	91	25	n/a	n/a
conservative	–	–	56	11.5	44	8.6	–	–	–	–	–	–	–	–
UCD centre-right	30	7	36	7.1	45	8.1	–	–	–	–	–	–	–	–
CDS centre democrats	–	–	–	–	56	10.0	–	–	85	16.8	–	–	–	–
PSOE	48	12	44	8.7	46	8.2	48	13.6	135	26.7	129	35.4	171	49
PCE/IU (left)	59	15	54	10.8	54	9.7	38	10.7	137	27.7	133	36.5	n/a	n/a
Other new left parties	n/a	n/a	454	25.1	–	–	555	31.2	n/a	n/a	n/a	n/a	n/a	n/a
PNV Basque nationalist	2	6	2	5.7	4	12.1	4	15.4	n/a	n/a	9	37.5	n/a	n/a
CiU Catalonian nationalist	4	6	5	8.9	4	6.8	5	10.6	n/a	n/a	11	24.4	n/a	n/a
EE Basque left	7	12	3	10.7	6	18.2	7 (incl. HB)	16.7 (incl.HB)	n/a	n/a	–	–	n/a	n/a
HB Basque separatist	n/a	n/a	3	8.6	3	9.1	(incl. EE)	(incl. EE)	n/a	n/a	–	–	n/a	n/a
PSA Andalucía regional	n/a	n/a	9	10.7	–	–	–	–	–	–	–	–	–	–
Far right + other rightists[b]	10	10	57	12.2	n/a	n/a	88	20	n/a	–	n/a	–	n/a	–
Total + other parties in Spain	653	13.1	1226	16.4	1080	16.4	1092	21.8	2504	30.5	373[c]	33.3[c]	–	–

Sources: 1977: Cases et al. (1978: 94–95) 1979 and 1982: own calculations based on Boletín Oficial del Estado, 3 February 1979 and 2 October 1982. 1982 total from Instituto de la Mujer (1984: 17). 1977–1982: AP second set of figures from López Nieto (1988: 86). 1986–1989: Instituto de la Mujer (1990: 30, 48–49). 1996: Federación de Mujeres Progresistas report (1996). 2000: Secretaría de Participación de la Mujer, CEF-PSOE, unpublished data.

Notes

– = not applicable; n/a means not available.

a In 1977, Alianza Popular; in 1979: Coalición Democrática; in 1982–1989, Alianza Popular or Coalición Popular (including the Partido Demócrata Popular of Oscar Alzaga); from 1986, Partido Popular.

b In 1977, Alianza Nacional 18 de Julio and Fuerza Nueva; in 1979, Unión Nacional, led by Blas Piñar; in 1986, all rightists not mentioned separately.

c Out of five parties.

Candidates likely to win

Given their increased expectations, women's advocates draw a line between candidates 'to win' (*para salir*) as an indicator of women's advancement, in contrast to candidates 'to fill up' the list (*de relleno*). This has the merit of highlighting the candidates' chances, but the method used here was that candidates deemed likely to win were those in a position on the list that had won a seat in the previous election, in other words assuming there would be no swings, rather than applying predicted swings. This method was not designed to help predict the outcome but to reflect the parties' political intentions in constructing its lists.

As seen in Table 6.5, the PSOE fielded 33 (17.5 per cent) likely female deputies in 1989, missing their quota of 25 per cent (at the time); the PP fielded ten (9.5 per cent), CIU one (5.5 per cent), HB one (20 per cent) and EE one (50 per cent), with the rest not fielding any likely women deputies. Regionalist parties were the worst offenders when it came to not putting up any women who were likely to win, whereas the Basque left nationalist parties were the best. By 1996 there was a marked increase in the numbers of women placed in a position with a real chance of election: from 46 to 84, almost double the number, with the PSOE remaining firmly in the lead with 52 of these candidates, and giving women more of a chance of winning than the quota demanded. It remained consistent with its gender parity decision in 2000, by fielding more than the minimum 40 per cent of women in positions likely to gain a seat. But for the PP 15.6 per cent in 1996 actually represented a remarkable turnaround, as the percentage of women in the top *half* of the lists had been steadily diminishing over four elections from a high of 28 per cent[12] in 1977 to the low of 9.5 per cent in 1989. The rise was also notable in the nationalist parties PNV and CiU and in the leftist IU.

Leading candidates

Because occupying the top places of a candidate list is an indicator of being in a leadership position in the constituency party, data on leading candidates more closely reflects women's role in internal party politics than the socio-economic environment in which they are standing.

Table 6.6 shows that in 1989 the PP was the party to field the highest number of woman-headed lists, six out of 52 constituencies. The IU followed with five, the PSOE with three, and the CDS with one. Although the PSOE had adopted a 25 per cent quota the year before, the rule did not straightaway cause women to reach the very top in their constituency parties. The total figure of 15 women electoral list leaders out of a potential 208 (52 constituencies × four nationwide parties) was not impressive – a mere 7 per cent. By 2000, the PSOE and IU had adopted the parity principle, but there was absolutely no gender balance at this key political level,

Table 6.5 Women candidates 'likely' to gain a seat in Congress

	1989		1996		2000	
	No. of women	% of party's candidates	No. of women	% of party's candidates	No. of women	% of party's candidates
PSOE	33	17.9	52	32.7	72	42
PP	10	9.5	22	15.6	–	–
IU	0	0	5	27.7	–	–
CiU	1	5.5	4	23.5	–	–
PNV	0	0	1	20	–	–
HB (Basque separatist)	1	20	0	–	–	–
EE (Basque left)	1	50	0	–	–	–
Total/average	46	–	84	24.7	–	–

Sources: 1989: Barbadillo et al. (1990: 110). 1996: Federación de Mujeres Progresistas (1996). 2000: El País, 30 January 2000, p. 29; Secretaría de Participación de la Mujer, CEF-PSOE, unpublished.

Notes

– = not applicable/not available.

Table 6.6 Women heading constituency candidate lists

Party	1989	1996	2000
Out of a possible 52 lists per party (all constituencies)			
PSOE	3	8	10 (19.2%)
PP	6	7	–
IU	5	5	9 (17.5%)
CDS	1	–	–
Out of a possible four lists per party (four constituencies)			
CiU	0	0	–
PNV (Basque nationalists)	0	0	–
EE (Basque left)	2	–	–
Out of a possible three lists (three constituencies)			
BNG (Nationalist Galician Bloc)	1	–	–

Sources: 1989: Barbadillo *et al.* (1990, Table 5: 130, 132). 1996: Federación de Mujeres Progresistas (1996). 2000: PSOE and IU offices.

Note
– = not available.

reflecting the fact that it was not governed by the imperative of reaching a quota. The results show that top constituency-level leadership was still heavily male-dominated in the nationwide parties at the start of the twenty-first century, although the trend was clearly positive. One reason put forward was that large nationwide parties felt obliged to offer a discourse that was progressive and reflected women's desire to participate in politics, but when it came to top seats, parties held back from giving them to women because they lacked confidence in women's leadership ability (Barbadillo *et al.* 1990: 129). Another is that the figures reflected the internal situation of the parties, as seen earlier, and that women were rarely the party leaders at provincial (constituency) level. Any analysis of the situation in the nationalist parties is hampered by lack of information, as this sort of data was not monitored effectively.

Women elected to Parliament

There was a fundamental change in the participation of women in Parliament from the first decade of democracy to the second, and by the end of the millennium women had achieved a 'critical mass' in the Spanish lower house. The growth in participation was all the more remarkable in view of the starting point: at the beginning of the democratic period very few women's voices were heard either in the newly instituted Congress of Deputies or in the Senate. From 1977 to 1982 only 21 or 22 women (6 per cent of all deputies) shared with nearly 330 men the crucial task of amending and approving the new Constitution and the key phase of law-making that followed it. And, as Table 6.7 reveals, the situation in Congress

Table 6.7 Women in congress of deputies as percentage of party group

Parliamentary group	Constituent assembly 1977–1979		Legislature I 1979–1982		II 1982–1986		III 1986–1989		IV 1989–1993		V 1993–1996		VI 1996–2000		VII 2000–2004	
	No.	%	No.	%	No.	%	No.	%	No.	%	No.	%	No.	%	No.	%
AP/CP/PP conservative	1	6.3	1	11.0	2	1.9	8, 6[a]	7.6, 7.5[a]	10	9.3	21	–	22, 29[a]	14.9	45, 46	24.6, 25.1
UCD/CDS centre–right	7	4.2	10, 11[a]	6.0, 6.6[a]	0	–	–	–	–	–	–	–	–	–	–	–
PSOE socialists	10, 11[a]	8.5, 9.3[a]	5, 6[a]	4.0, 5.0[a]	18	8.9	13	7.1	34	19.4	28	17.6	39, 44[a]	27.6, 31.2[a]	46	36.8
PCE <'82 '86 > United Left IU	3	15.0	2	8.7	–	–	–	–	2	11.8	4	22.2	7, 7[a]	33.3, 31.3[a]	2	25.0
CiU Catalan nationalist	–	–	1	12.5	1	9.1	1	5.6	1	5.6	1	5.9	4	25	2	13.3
PNV Basque nationalist	–	–	0	0	2	25	–	–	–	–	–	–	1	20	1	14.3
EA Basque nationalist	–	–	–	–	–	–	–	–	–	–	–	–	1	100	1	100
HB/EH Basque separatists	–	–	–	–	–	–	1	20	–	–	1	50	1	100	0	0
Mixed group[b]	–	–	–	–	–	–	PDP 2	5	4	28.6	ERC1	100	2; ERC1	100; 100	CC2; CC1	50; 25
Total in Congress %/350	21, 22[a]	6.0, 6.3[a]	20, 21[a]	5.7, 6[a]	18, 22[a]	5.1, 6.3[a]	23–25	6.5	51	14.6	56	16	77, 87[a]	22, 25[a]	99	28.3

Sources: Own compilation using: 1977–1979: Cases et al. (1978). 1979–1982: J. de Esteban and L. López Guerra, eds, (1979). 1982–1986 and 1986–1989: Instituto de la Mujer (1992) p. 58, Instituto de la Mujer (1990), p. 45. 1993–1996 and 1996–2000: Ministry of Social Affairs press release, 7 March 1996, and Servicio de Información del Congreso de los Diputados, personal communications. 2000–2004: personal communications from parties, Congreso and Instituto de la Mujer website.

Notes

a Where two figures are given, the top row is the number arising from the election and the bottom row the count at the end of the legislature. New women deputies came in after the resignation of a male deputy when they were the next eligible candidate on the party's list at the last election.

b Mixed Group has a changing composition, e.g. in 1996–2000 it included one Eusko Alkartasuna, one Partido para la Independencia, one Nueva Izquierda and one Iniciativa per Cataluña, but the latter have been inserted in the IU cell.

remained stagnant until the end of the 1980s. Matters were no better in the Senate: for the first four legislatures the proportion of women senators only crept up from 3 per cent to 5 per cent, a remarkably poor showing.

Matters only began to change when in 1989 the PSOE for the first time obtained its own 'critical mass' of 34 women deputies, two-thirds of the total number of women in Congress, a year after adopting its 25 per cent quota. The conservatives took a leap forward in 1993 and the PSOE did so again in 1996, and all three main parties improved in 2000. Despite losing two elections, the PSOE retained around half all the women deputies in Congress in spite of the PP's new cohort of 45 women. In fact, Spanish women's parliamentary participation had already overtaken the EU average by the mid-1990s, gaining the rank of 6th from the top (19th from the top in the world classification).[13] The growth of Spanish participation rates were among the fastest (Uriarte and Ruiz 1999: 208) and were at a level with those of Germany and Austria, thereby breaking the concept of a north–south divide in this form of political involvement. The VII legislature (2000–) contained 99 women, over 28 per cent of the total, again a healthy achievement in comparative terms, retaining 6th place (excluding Norway and Iceland as they are not in the EU).

As to the Senate, it was harder for women to gain access even though it captured far less of the political limelight than the Congress: their presence in the upper house remained steadily around three percentage points below it:[14] 12.5 per cent in 1993–1996 and 15 per cent in 1996, still well behind Congress's 22 per cent, and then rising to 26 per cent in 2000, almost catching up with the Congress. Success in the Senate elections in 2000 was almost entirely due to the PP, to whom 40 out of the 54 women senators belonged. At 32 per cent this was a higher party proportion of senators than the PSOE's 17 per cent.[15] There is no European trend to compare this with, given that some upper houses or a part of them are indirectly elected and the European average is severely lowered by the British House of Lords' heavy preponderance of men.[16] But in the Spanish context the Senate has been lagging, a subject we will return to later.

Tiers of power

Analysis of women's participation in sub-national party politics, while highly desirable, would require an independent study of the party system in each autonomous community, which is beyond the frame of this chapter. Instead, here follows an analysis of the way women participate in a representative capacity in the geographical hierarchy of institutions of public and party governance. The following two tables survey public posts as well as the internal party positions in the two main parties. Table 6.8 reveals the striking patterns of women's presence as elected representatives in differing tiers of public power. The table is a reminder of just how many new elective positions were created after the return of democracy:

9906 excluding local councillors and 66,439 in all. Evidently, there was a sudden and substantial opening-up of the political opportunity structure: at the start of the transition, the parties only had a fraction of the members they subsequently needed to stand for elections. This phenomenon of a surge in opportunities in fact puts a different gloss on the issue of intra- and inter-party 'competition' – a matter we will return to later.

The distribution of gender representation among institutions, ordered in Table 6.8 by their geographical ambit, revealed that the wider the ambit, the more women were to be found. There was a greater proportion of women in the European than in the national parliaments; a similar proportion was to be found at autonomy level, but this, in turn, was much higher than at local council level. One explanation is that Spanish local councils and the Senate have less prestige and fewer powers – seen from the practitioner's point of view – so that the national and European parliaments are perceived as more rewarding venues by politically active women. In a complementary fashion, it may be that it is a question of the candidates on offer, namely that there are more politically active women to be found among the more highly educated elites from which candidates for the national and European elections are recruited. In addition, it may be that national and European-level politics have acquired a more gender-sensitive political culture. Similarly, the European Parliament may have more women deputies because dealing with the European Union involves a wider, more complex set of concerns and a more international outlook that suits politically active women better than dealing with local affairs. The success of representation in the European Parliament has been noted for other countries (Jenson and Sineau 1995; Kauppi 1999) but remained unexplained. For France, however, Kauppi found that French politicians, men and women alike, perceive the EP as a 'modest' source of political power. It occupies a 'marginal position' in French politics, where 'space has been left for women'. Yet the EP had increased its powers considerably, without an increase in French male politicians (Kauppi 1999:

Table 6.8 Women in elective posts (all parties)

Elected representatives	Year of data	No. women	% women
European Parliament Deputies (64)	1999	22	34.4
Congress Deputies (350)	2000	99	28.3
Senators (208)	2000	54	26.0
Autonomy Parliaments Deputies (1181)	1999	340	28.8
Mayors (8103)	1999	779	9.6
Local Councillors (56,537)[a]	1995	9300	16.5

Sources: Compiled from data collected by Instituto de la Mujer: www.mtas.es.instituto; EP (1999) *Results and Elected Members*, pp. 6, 6a.

Note
a 202 municipalities returned no data.

338–339). Some of this may be true for Spain, though as the EP has flourished in parallel with Spanish democracy, it is probably not seen to be as marginal as in France and – marginal or not – it enjoys considerable prestige as an institution in Spain and among women activists.

There is also evidence in this table of an interesting, intra-institutional tiered pattern, similar to the one found in the internal party organs. It appears that peak, single-person posts, such as a local government mayor (or an Autonomy Assembly's spokesperson as seen in the next table) or the head of a party organ, still tend to be occupied by men. Similarly, the small dip in representation of women found for the Senate can be related to the fact that it is elected on a 'single-member plurality' system that requires individual women candidates to be selected by the voter from a list, instead of the voter picking a whole list that also contains women. This would favour known figures who in turn are more likely to be incumbents, making it harder for newcomer female candidates to be picked. But as Spanish voters can simply select all the candidates from their preferred party, without paying attention to who they are, some of the gender factor can be ironed out – there is insufficient exploratory research on gender in Senate elections.

As for each of the main parties' contribution to this pattern, a similar gendered hierarchy of power-sharing and tiers are found in each of them, as seen in Table 6.9. The first revelation is that this is a dynamic picture. Up until 1996–1998, the PSOE was consistently in the lead, yet the elections held in 1999 and 2000 showed the PP winning many more seats for women as part of its overall gains. By 2000 the PSOE had implemented the parity principle and this brought another cohort of new women in, albeit as part of the party's reduced share of public posts. Both parties displayed a comparable pattern of greater participation of women in the national and European levels – a marked pattern in the case of the PSOE in 1995. The local government level lagged behind, and here the PSOE's quota was not fully implemented. It appears that while the progress in the PSOE can be related to their policy decision, in the case of the PP it was the sudden expansion of opportunities for women, created by winning more seats than previously, that allowed more women to be chosen to participate by party gatekeepers. In other words, the opportunity structure made a favourable impact on PP women from the second half of the 1990s.

Breaking into party politics: some explanations

Amongst the many theories of women and power, it is helpful to differentiate between some of the different types of explanation they offer. Structural explanations pose that women's participation in politics is dependent on 'structural' factors such as the overall development of a country, the proportion of women in employment or in secondary and higher education. This is because these theorists hold that political participation rates

Table 6.9 Women in elected posts held by PSOE and PP, by institution

Elected representatives	Year of election	No. women PSOE	% women PSOE	Year of election	No. women PP	% women PP
European Parliament deputies	1994 1999	8	36	1999	7	29
Congress deputies	1996 (141 PSOE)	44	31	2000	47	26
Senate	1996 (97 PSOE)	22	23	2000	45	30
Autonomous Community legislature spokesperson	–	–	–	1999 (18 PP)	1	6
Autonomous Community deputies[a]	1995 (381 PSOE)	99	26	–	–	–
Mayors of provincial capitals	–	–	–	1999 (28 PP)	2	7
Mayors	1995 (2444 PSOE)	146	6	–	–	–
Local councillors	1995 (20482 PSOE)	3517	17	1999	763	22

Sources: PSOE: own elaboration from data in Secretaría de Participación de la Mujer (1998) – years chosen to be post-25 per cent quota but pre-40 per cent parity. PP: data obtained from Partido Popular headquarters (2001).

Note
a Elections held in different years, though mostly in 1995.

reflect the general process of socio-economic modernisation. In the European context, Greece and Portugal would be examples of this (Uriarte and Ruiz 1999: 210–211). But these authors discard such explanations for the case of Spain, together with the 'cultural' explanation of the prevalence of Catholicism as a deterrent to participation, because neither Spain nor Austria (nor the UK for that matter) fit the theory. A quick glance at the world rankings shows that the top 20 countries with over 25 per cent of women in their lower or single houses of parliament range from the Scandinavian states to Mozambique and Rwanda, Argentina and Cuba, Bulgaria and Turkmenistan, with Britain coming 44th and France 61st (Inter-Parliamentary Union 2002).

Other types of explanation are grounded in political developments, and may focus on the political time-lag in the occurrence of events between one country and another, or highlight features of the electoral system or of institutional behaviour in order to explain differences. In Spain, however, most advocates of women's political participation have not put their faith in the simple passage of time (Martínez Ten 1990: 64). Neither does the evidence illustrate the time-lag proposition, particularly since it is the actual narrowness of the lag and the speed with which it was overcome that is notable. Spanish socialist and conservative women have overtaken their sisters in quite a few of the longer established European parties.

This leads us to more institutional types of explanations, such as the impact of the electoral system. Spanish women's share of legislative power in the lower chamber overtook that of women in Britain and France soon after democracy returned, which suggests that the adoption of an electoral system of 'reinforced' proportional representation with particular features (d'Hondt method of seat allocation in medium to large multi-member constituencies) was more favourable to women than the British single-member plurality or French single-member majority (two-rounds) systems would have been for the Spanish Congress, even in the early years of low awareness of gender balance and long before quotas. It confirms Norris's comparative findings on electoral systems (Norris 1993: 312–314). In this way, Spain serves to illustrate the thesis that the electoral system is a 'crucial enabling condition' (Henig and Henig 2001: 93) for women to increase their participation in institutional politics.

Such reasoning is reinforced by the case of the Spanish Senate, which is elected on a plurality system with a single, mixed list of candidates from all parties for each constituency. Those with the most votes get the seats (two, three or four depending on the constituency). The proportion of women has always lagged in comparison to the lower house, the Congresos, and it has been suggested that where a single individual is chosen, a male is often the first choice. The electorate may be agreeable to voting for a list that contains women, the argument goes, especially if it is headed by a man, as most are, but voters are less agreeable to singling out women candidates from among a male-dominated list, as would be required for the Senate.

Yet, other kinds of evidence point in a different direction. The case of the Senate also shows that, where conservative women are concerned, they manage to obtain more seats in it – despite its plurality system – than they do in the Congress (30 per cent vs. 25 per cent). This suggests that matters also depend on which party it is, independently of the electoral system. Indeed, a strong emphasis on the electoral system as an explanatory factor may be inappropriate in Spain. For in the first two elections under the new electoral system in the late 1970s, heralded as a great period of change in Spanish politics, women voters supported the change while being minor participants in electoral politics. In fact, in European terms, Spanish women's position remained below the European average until the second half of the 1980s. Then suddenly they forged ahead. The surge in their presence coincided with the PSOE's leftist turn on social policy in its last seven years in power roughly from 1989 to 1996. This is one phenomenon that suggests that a better explanation regarding the increased proportion of women in political representation lies with something that happened inside the parties to make them facilitate access to public office for women.

A second phenomenon concerns the placement of the largest proportions of women discussed in previous sections. Evidence pointed to a new trend that belied previous findings that it is easier for women to break into representative politics at the local rather than the national level (reviewed in Randall 1987) and that in terms of participation rates, the closer to the centre of institutional power, the fewer women there are to be found. In the Spanish case, we found the opposite: the Autonomous assemblies and local government do *not* provide a more accessible forum for women politicians – the national and the European parliaments do. While the EP's power remained comparatively weak in the context of the EU decision-making, at least until 1997, it is the only elected European forum and so, as an electoral tier for national level politicians to aspire to, the EP is the most distant centre of power from the local council. The third phenomenon that pushes us to look beyond the electoral system is that this 'room at the top' is also found in internal party politics where more women are to be found in the higher national tier of the parties than at federation or provincial level, though not among the one-person top posts.

Internal party politics and women's representation

The political party was one of a set of three factors established by Norris and Lovenduski (1995) and Norris (1993) for explaining the recruitment of women, though it has often been seen as playing a constraining function, such as in the case of Britain, or a gate-keeping role, rather than overtly facilitating women's participation.[17] Here developments inside the PSOE are considered from the perspective of its role as the first and chief party to increase women's representation, in order to understand how far it was a major facilitator of women's access to leadership and representative positions. Placing a party at the centre of the search for an explanation also fits in with non-feminist approaches emphasising the way social-democratic and leftist parties have taken on board the feminist discourse, even though this perspective appears at first glance to shift the credit to the male-dominated parties. Furthermore, earlier research on the case of the PSOE went beyond conventional analyses of the role of the party to show that it was the strategies of party feminists advocating greater prominence for women that were successful (Threlfall 1998).

The beginning of the shift in the PSOE can be traced back to the internal political debate of the mid-1980s that culminated in the acceptance of minimum quotas of 25 per cent of women for party-controlled internal and public posts in January 1988. The issue of the lack of women in political posts had been criticised by its feminist caucus *Mujer y Socialismo* ever since the late 1970s, with slow and irregular progress being made. But members had lobbied party structures skilfully until they got it approved. It should be pointed out that the timing coincided with a similar discussion taking place in the Socialist International, of which the PSOE has long been an active member, in which the women's section, Socialist International Women, had been pressing for quotas in the 1980s as well (Socialist International Women 1995). They are both examples of successful peak-level pressure by organised party feminists and form part of the phenomenon of female and male 'enlightened elitism'.

So, instead of being the product of a static situation caused by a permanent electoral mechanism and an entrenched political culture, the origins of the rise of women in party politics in Spain can be directly linked to the impact of the feminist lobbies and to party decisions regarding quotas. The Scandinavian example should be borne in mind since their high proportions of women in the lower house arise from the adoption by some parties of a 40 per cent quota in the 1970s and from later legislation on gender balance (Porter 1998: 29). In fact, the effectiveness of the quota mechanism for bringing more women into public life is widely endorsed in Spain (Barbadillo *et al.* 1990; Gallego and Durán 1994; Federación de Mujeres Progresistas 1996; Martínez-Hernández and Elizondo 1997). This should come as no surprise as its concrete effect was immediate. At the very first parliamentary elections held after the quota was agreed by the PSOE, there was an astonishing 89 per cent and 116 per cent rise in the number of PSOE women elected to the national and regional parliaments, respectively – see Table 6.7 above. The Partido Popular did not believe in the quota concept, with high-ranking female politicians calling it 'discrimination' and 'the Wonderbra quota' (Jenson and Valiente 2003: 86), and the leftist Izquierda Unida did, but only later on – and it shows. It is only at the turn of the millennium that the share of political responsibilities given to women in the PP has reached a quarter or a third of posts, mainly attained with the party's unexpectedly large majority in 2000. Their change of tack on this issue has been interpreted as a 'response effect' (Uriarte and Ruiz 1999: 211) and 'mimetic behaviour' (Valiente 2001: 58), and can be compared to Sweden, where the Social Democrats' dominant position 'led the other parties to compete, and even outbid, the Social Democrats as champions of equality', resulting in a convergence of trends across the parties (Norris 1993: 321). Interestingly, during her time as President of the Congress, Luisa Fernanda Rudí claimed that the first four prominent PP women 'arrived' in 1986 because the veteran PP leader and former Francoist minister Manuel Fraga simply said there had to be more women on party lists (Rudí 2001) – an outspoken claim of 'enlightened elitism'.

While not absolutely essential to women's advancement, the effect of the quota mechanism has arguably been sufficiently evident in Spain to be considered the key explanation of the rise of women in party politics. What is not so clear is how and why such a powerful instrument to lever women into power was adopted. A further question is whether it is an unfailingly effective tool or not. And if not, what does its effectiveness depend on? The next section will explore some of these questions.

The introduction of gender balance through the adoption of quota of male and female representatives was a political decision of a party, which once voted on and written into its statutes, can arguably be compared in the way it functions to a law. Like all laws, its impact is dependent on its practical implementation. Therefore, its long-term effectiveness will only be sustained by political willpower backed up by a supportive political culture (whether at the mass or elite level is another matter) with actual law enforcement as the last resort.

The fact that the quota had a positive impact in Spain was not a fore-gone conclusion from the moment of its introduction. A cursory glance at the experience of France and several Latin American countries – relevant contexts given their long-standing channels of communication with Spain – highlights some of the difficulties that can be encountered. The French process has been described a 'sequence of two linked, yet analytically distinct, policy-cycles: the one focused on legislating for minimum quotas; the other on legislating for gender parity' (Lovecy 2000: 445). In France, the first policy-cycle was a response to the extraordinarily limited presence of women in political representation, but was seen as a failure that stimulated the search for an alternative principle – a quest that in turn was by no means an immediate success, enduring for a good ten years (Lovecy 2000: 446–447). Spain also experienced two cycles, the first leading up to the 1988 decision and the second lasting for the next decade, yet the 25 per cent goal was not perceived as a failure in Spain but as a first step that pushed the slow-moving political snowball. In other words, Spanish feminists went in for the incremental approach. Unlike a change in an electoral law, quotas can be increased step by step in small doses and have a ratchet effect.

On the other hand, parties may prove not to be open to persuasion nor permeable. Research in Latin America has shown that parties are quite capable of ignoring exhortations to implement the quota. In Spain there was no legal compunction on parties, yet the socialist party went ahead and implemented its own 'law', albeit not faultlessly, in advance of others. Even in countries where the quota for candidates has been instituted by national legislation such as in ten Latin American nations, it has been found to have made little immediate difference in about half the countries (Jones 2000: 42, Table 2), partly because those parties, in sharp contrast to the PSOE, simply did not respect the law.

In fact, for the Latin American countries, the effectiveness of the quota seems to be dependent on a number of key factors, such as: the use of mandatory 'zipping' (at least one woman in every third position on the list, if not every second); the existence of closed as opposed to open lists for elections (to prevent individualised campaigning by candidates out for themselves); and of larger constituencies in which each party was likely to gain more than one or two seats, ensuring some spread, otherwise the first two seats would invariably go to the leading male candidates (Jones 2000: 42–44). This suggests that, in terms of predictive power, the rise of women in politics is likely to occur in the following political circumstances: a political decision ('it shall be so') adopted either in the form of a party statute, or of national legislation, in a PR electoral system with closed lists in multi-member constituencies, and a two-to-three party, as opposed to a multi-party, system.

All of this existed in Spain – except the zip lists, though these may soon come to be seen as the icing on the cake. Spain has closed lists of candidates (though the merits of open lists are often discussed), has constituencies with an average of seven seats and tends towards a two-party system outside Catalonia and the Basque Country. From this one can conclude that Spain has some objectively favourable electoral features but, crucially, has not legislated nor even adopted zip lists to force women up the ladder of the candidate list. Spain has experienced success with a method that makes the parties ultimately responsible for their own image and reputation.

Once the objective mechanism for increasing women's representation has been identified, we still need to explain the PSOE's openness to persuasion. If one attributes the improvements to the Spanish parties' – at least, the PSOE's – willingness to implement quotas at all levels and to place women in positions where they are likely to be elected, then one has to ask why. Why would a party decide to shoehorn women into its own structures of power via a decision reached centrally or even taken at the top? Again, a number of explanatory arguments can be brought to bear on the question. It is possible to privilege the role of women activists, in this case the socialist-feminists who turned their attention on the PSOE from the 1970s onwards with increasing success in achieving agenda status for gendered public policies. They persuaded the party elites such as the executive commissions at national and regional levels (Threlfall 1997, amongst others).[18] After seeing the effect of the 25 per cent quota in the 1989 elections, PSOE women activists set their sights on 40 per cent and argued for this steep rise – far steeper than what the Socialist International was asking for – as part of general demand for parity democracy. Parity was, in turn, incorporated into a wider claim to gender-sharing of household tasks, work and power made by a range of feminists and submitted by the Federation of Progressive Women (*Federación de Mujeres Progresistas*) to the PSOE's 34th Conference of 1997 (PSOE 1997).

But in so doing, one is also asking why the elites did not put up any strong resistance. It highlights the possibility that the existence of 'persuadable' elites may have been a crucial corollary to success in Spain, even more so than in countries where policy advocates can deploy a law as part of their weaponry for forceful implementation of the quotas. For instance, in Argentina, women activists in parties were also present but they had to resort to threatening to take their party to court for non-compliance. So, the 'willingness to act in good faith' is key, as Jones puts it (2000: 44), at least key to success but perhaps not to sustainability. Precisely because Spanish women's advancement rested on persuasion and the readiness to be persuaded, some observers consider the situation in Spain to be unstable and to lack the guarantees that a law would provide (Balaguer 2000: 53).

Second, there is the influence of the European political environment to consider. The second policy-cycle containing the arguments for the wider, more principled concept of parity democracy in the PSOE was influenced by the parallel European discussion with which it coincided in the 1990s (Navarro 2000: 247), launched by the French feminist Gisele Halimi (see Halimi 1994). It was being strongly defended by women in France on pragmatic as well as principled and philosophical grounds (see Perry and Hart 2000). The claim for parity was endorsed as a general feminist claim at the European Summit of Women in Power held in Athens in 1992, where it was agreed that no more than 60 per cent nor less than 40 per cent of either sex should be represented anywhere in politics. By 1994 the Socialist International's council was asking all its members to increase their women candidates by a minimum of 10 per cent in every election, with the goal of 50/50 gender parity by 2000 (Socialist International Women 1995: 7). Yet, while it is easy to see how this environment was influential, there is nothing binding about the Socialist International's policies, which leads us back to the issue of political will and good faith.

A third possibility for explaining the readiness to be persuaded of PSOE elites is therefore to look at internal party responses to political conjunctures. The demand for increased quota and parity representation coincided with a period of decline in the electoral fortunes of the PSOE. At the 1993 elections, the party lost its overall majority and in 1994, the conservatives won control of a majority of the autonomous communities, leaving the PSOE in overall control of just three (Andalucía, Extremadura and Castilla–La Mancha). Though still in power nationally, its heyday had passed. Over the previous decade it had won four parliamentary elections, dominated the autonomous communities and governed city councils of major population centres, carrying out a programme of democratic consolidation and modernising regional and urban development. By then the PSOE was also facing a complex internal crisis (Heywood 1993). Once a growing party with a young leadership, headed by an unusually popular and persuasive leader who had gained a creditable international standing, the winning formula could not last indefinitely.

Already it had attempted a rethink. In its 'Manifesto 2000' adopted in 1991, it had recognised that profound social changes were taking place, initially beyond its borders, but due to take hold in Spain later. These were bound to create 'a new society' which included 'the women's revolution' (PSOE 2000). But the resurgence of factional conflict (Gillespie 1994) and the split between Felipe González and party vice-president Alfonso Guerra were to plunge the PSOE into internal turmoil. González recognised the need for change in the 1993 campaign, promising to turn over a new leaf (*'el cambio dentro del cambio'* [change from the previous change] as he put it). After a narrow win, he told a wide audience 'I've got the message'. Part of that message concerned the place of women. According to the feminist activists who had thrashed things out with him in a key meeting in the run-up to the election, González recognised that quotas and even parity were an extension of democracy (personal communications). Since then, he has privately been referred to as a late convert to feminism. So the interpretation suggested here is that the pending party renewal process, which was to drag on in fits and starts until 2000, became bound up with new demands for political representation. 'More women' and 'more youth' began to appear as part of the solution in the rhetoric of party renewal.

The need for party renewal is a new way of explaining the upsurge of women as politicians, which is not part of the established literature. The thesis is based on personal observations, interviews and communications over a number of years, as well as the evidence supplied by recent developments. A continuous leitmotiv in the PSOE's process of self-reflection and political discussions since the early-to-mid-1990s has been the need to ensure the party is ready for the twenty-first century (for instance, in its *Manifiesto 2000* programme and party congress documents), to reverse the trend of an ageing membership and to seek new sources of electoral support. There was a tough-minded aspect to this: the search for a way of stemming the electoral decline of a party that perceived its traditional working-class electorate as numerically insufficient. Rather than looking to the middle classes in occupational terms, the PSOE could view women, whether homemakers or employed, young or old, even educated and middle class, as a great new discriminated sector – or at least a less-privileged one – which might be attracted to the PSOE's concerns. González had already seen the need to take on board the concerns of the non-working 'passive classes' in the late 1970s (see his 1979 long interview with the political thinker Fernando Claudín).

By the time of the 34th party conference in 1997, renewal and parity were closely bound up. Negotiations between feminists and party leaders had led to a pre-conference consensus over the statutory change and González had in fact endorsed with his signature a document written by a feminist group calling for gender balance in all spheres of life which had been circulated to all party delegations as part of the outgoing Executive's political discussion document. In other words, the message about parity emanated from the peak leadership of the party, who behaved in this case as an 'enlightened' elite, but the conference, with all its regional leaders and political factions vying for places on the new Federal Executive Commission, first had to approve it. Most of these leaders were men, so they were facing the possibility of having to substitute some of their closest political allies, possibly even themselves, as candidates. Even though González resigned abruptly during the opening session, the decision was not ignored. The relevant change in party statutes was approved and carried forward to the federations' conferences that followed after the federal conference and were approved in all cases, in a further set of 'enlightened' decisions originating at the national centre. There is no research on the political debates about parity inside the party federations, but as conference decisions are binding in a classic social-democrat decision-making structure such as the PSOE's (as per party Constitution – *Estatutos*), proportions of women nearing 40 per cent were achieved everywhere. It appears therefore that national-level leadership, backed by the votes of conference delegates and the 'law' of party statutes, provided enough of a stimulus for all the branches of the PSOE to promote women into representative posts, however reluctant individual members or sections might have been.

Matters did not stop here. To seek legal endorsement of parity was adopted as policy by the PSOE soon after. Two years later in November 1999, the PSOE leader and prime ministerial candidate for the March 2000 elections, Joaquin Almunia, announced his intention to see the electoral law amended to ensure all parties fielded a minimum of 40 per cent from either sex as parliamentary candidates,[19] although a bill was never presented (Jenson and Valiente 2003: 85). The socialist Andalusian leader Manuel Chaves promised that if he won the autonomy elections again, 50 per cent of his new *government* would be composed of women (*El País* 7 November 1999: 24).[20] Despite the PSOE's profound electoral defeat in 2000, parity continued to be associated with renewal in the party's search for a new leader following Almunia's resignation immediately after the March defeat. At the 'Extraordinary' party conference that followed in

July, no less than two of the four candidates for Secretary-General of the PSOE were women, with the odds being on either of two known party figures, one man and one woman, rather than on the two men (personal communications and interviews during the conference). José Luis Rodríguez Zapatero, the surprise winner by nine votes, immediately endorsed parity and the key role of women in society in his two conference speeches and put together a leadership team which gave women seven of the important portfolio posts on the Federal Executive (47 per cent of the top tier, 40 per cent of the total Executive), including the high-profile position of Secretary for International Relations. With Rodríguez Zapatero's victory, the party renewal process came to an end, yet parity was simultaneously endorsed and given a new lease of life, to be implemented throughout the rest of the party and given scholarly endorsement by some of its intellectuals (see the article by Martínez Ten and Paramio 1997). Whether the two concepts and processes will continue to be so closely bound up in the PSOE is a question to watch.

All in all, the achievement of gender parity took over ten years from start to finish as an internal PSOE development (1987 to 1998), excluding the later campaign of institutionalisation through law. It was in fact achieved without coercion, leaving a reform of the electoral law on the agenda in feminist and socialist circles (Caraballo 2000: 31). The reason that gender-based reform was accepted rather than resisted was, as we have suggested, that the PSOE has been undergoing a process of party and leadership renewal that saw women's representation as another mechanism of internal democratisation.[21]

Not all would see the introduction of gender parity as motivated by enlightened intentions. From a different perspective, critics believe parity has been favoured by PSOE leaders because it benefits their interests as it allows them to better control the process of political appointments (Navarro 2000: 25), meaning that the limitation on posts for men and the inclusion of women has enabled leaders to reshape their teams of allies more selectively, and find 'new blood' to their political liking. Navarro, while Director-General of Women in Castilla–La Mancha Autonomous government, believed this generated political conformism. Nor did the system promote greater participation by women as a collective: sometimes it diffused or deactivated the feminist struggle, favouring co-optation and encouraging a party culture in which people are not valued for their abilities or suitability, but for belonging to the right political friendship group (Navarro 2000: 26).

Use of the term 'enlightened elitism' is not meant to suggest that the Federal Executive Committee leaders (in the past the FEC has always included some autonomous community-based politicians) are of themselves more enlightened than others, as people. Anecdotal evidence suggests that far from all Executive members were, as individuals, enthusiastic about bringing more women into leadership positions. But, as a collective, it appears that the party perceived, even if only in a hazy way, that women and parity represented 'the future' (personal communications). There were enough individuals in key positions who were 'enlightened' in so far as they took a broad long-term view of where the party was going and understood that it needed to change organically, not just in its manifesto. Presumably, they thought they themselves would not lose their posts. Promoting women, even if only as fresh faces, but also as possible political innovators, could be an intrinsic part of that renewal and save the PSOE from further decline, and thus women candidates and voters might save the day for them as well. The individual role of González must also be acknowledged to be a persuasive influence on other male leaders since his alleged conversion to feminism on the road to anticipated electoral defeat in 1993.

Furthermore, the existence of a top-down internal dynamic in the PSOE in addition to the formal bottom-up, elective decision-making structures must be taken into account. Regional (federation) conferences follow rather than precede the national conference, giving the Federal Executive the opportunity to influence political, ideological and policy decisions taken in the lower tiers of the party. It also enables charismatic leaders such as González to project his views or set the tone for ensuing debates. The issue this raises is how far it has been the national leadership that has enjoyed sufficient independence of power to adopt a radical new policy and to enforce it throughout the party. Women's representation has benefited from top-down pressure in a party that is, albeit formally a decentralised federal party, nevertheless politically led from the centre.

Women in party politics: the Spanish paradox

As the previous account suggests, the receptiveness of leaders and the permeability of parties such as the PSOE and to a lesser extent the Partido Popular and Izquierda Unida are key to an understanding of the advancement of women in party politics in Spain. The analysis of the case of the PSOE highlights the role of internal party dynamics and the political will of the leadership, coupled with women's advocacy work, above other factors such as the Spanish electoral system, while still regarding the latter as an essential base facilitating women's access. Without feminist networks and presence in organised structures within the PSOE, in other words without women's agency, choices and personal resources of persuasion and effectiveness, the PSOE could simply have remained deaf to gender parity arguments, and, even if forced into a renewal process, could have chosen – or lurched down – a different road. Where party feminists have been active, such as in the United Left, parity has also been implemented, though not quite as evenly.

Many European parties have been concerned with raising the profile of women politicians. What is striking about the Spanish story is that it was unexpected and paradoxical. The party that gained access to the greatest number of public posts in the first two decades of democracy, the PSOE, and effectively offered its members the likelihood of public recognition, an income and a career as politicians, was a very predominantly male party. Its roots in Marxism and the labour movement, and the cumulative impact of the Second Republic, the Civil War and decades of Francoist dictatorship gave it strongly motivated male gatekeepers, the bearers of its historic legacies, the sons of the exiled and the dead. Yet, this very male party led a great opening-up of politics to women.

True, the general expansion of its popularity and consequent access to positions at national regional and local levels, which steeply increased the public posts to be filled by its elected representatives, made it that much easier. But, even more paradoxically, it was not in fact during the PSOE's period of greatest expansion of the early to mid-1980s that entry to women was facilitated nor took place. It would have been understandable if, in the move from clandestinity and no public posts in 1977 to a situation where the PSOE needed to field thousands of candidates for municipal as well as national elections in 1979, adding hundreds more for the autonomy elections from 1983–1984 onwards, hundreds of women had been recruited. But, in reality, the expansion of female recruitment took place well after that original wave, and continued throughout the PSOE's period of national and regional electoral *decline* in the 1990s.[22]

This again suggests that the political opportunity structure and favourable electoral system were not the main factors in the PSOE's case, since these would have predicted massive entry for women in the first phase, not the second. It leads one back to the consideration that in the first phase, when the PSOE had few women members, Spanish feminism had not yet caught on widely and was not demanding quotas. The Socialist International and the EU had not yet turned its attention to the problem of women's under-representation and male leaders were not persuaded. By the later 1980s, matters were different. Equality policies towards women were proving to be popular, membership drives among women had borne fruit and Spain was a member of the EC. By 1988, the leadership was open to persuasion. But even then, good will among a few leaders would not have been enough. The political decision to introduce the 25 per cent quota was what created the watershed separating stagnant from growing representation. Yet, in the period of slow electoral decline from 1989, one might expect competition between candidates to hold on to seats to be highest, with male gatekeepers at their most active. Surprisingly, this was when the PSOE (as well as the already much reduced IU) started to make room for women. To accommodate them, the PSOE must have closed off quite a few opportunities to the men-in-waiting and passed them on to women instead.

For the PP, the figures point to a reverse process. The PP always had more women members than the PSOE, but did not field them. Their political representation grew much later, after the debate about equality had become part of common discourse and the visibility of women candidates was seen as electorally advantageous. It also grew in a period of expansion of party posts due to electoral success, lessening the cost of bringing new women in. Again, the leadership was persuaded, but to a different extent. While not supporting gender parity or intending to introduce a law, the current governing party has nonetheless given women great prominence at elite level, though it remains to be seen whether women will maintain their 25 per cent proportion if the Partido Popular loses seats. The case of the PP also requires further investigation, since too little is known about its party dynamics in this regard.

The pessimistic view of Aurora Navarro is relevant. Raising quotas step by step injects small doses of new blood into parties, but once 40 per cent has been reached in all of them, we do not know whether the process will come to an end or if 40 per cent of women will become the new 'glass ceiling'. The link with party renewal may be broken for the PSOE, and never become an issue for the PP. In time, the new blood may even become the old guard. Another fear, albeit expressed in a Latin American context, is that quotas may lead male politicians to 'enforce a gendered division of political labour' (Jaquette 1994: 232), in which they no longer have to take any responsibility for policy on women. Ultimately, the answer will lie with what happens to the new-blood women politicians who won leadership positions after 1997 in the PSOE and IU and after 2000 in the PP. Will they be able to consolidate their political careers? Will there eventually be a backlash in these parties? It is the next challenge for researchers. In the meantime, the Presidents of both Spain's houses of Parliament were women in 2002 – a first in Europe.

Notes

1 A stereotype that originally arose from a heated debate in the 1931 Republican parliament over the granting of female suffrage. It was reinforced by the fact that the Left parties lost the 1933 elections, the first in which women voted, and forever blamed them, even though leftist candidates had stood against each other and split the progressive vote, as shown in the detailed evidence presented by Clara Campoamor in her book *El voto femenino y yo*, published in 1936.
2 For instance, support from as many Federations as possible is needed by any aspiring leader (whether the incumbent, a challenger or a new consensus candidate) for the formation of the new Federal Executive Committee at conference. The norm in the PSOE is for Federation leaderships to play a key role in negotiating a consensus candidate before the one delegate/one vote election, rather than offer delegates a choice of competing candidates for leader. Federation leaderships can influence the delegates during this election, which is in fact more of an endorsement process (personal observation).
3 Grupo Federal de Estudios Sociológicos (1981): 6.
4 This was the opinion of the PSOE women's caucus, *Mujer y Socialismo* (personal communication).

5 Grupo Federal de Estudios Sociológicos (1981): 15.
6 Information provided by the Organisation Secretariat for 1982.
7 See Joyce Squires (1996) for a fuller discussion of these issues.
8 My own calculations from data in Tables 9, 14 and 15 of Secretaría de Participación de la Mujer (1998): 39, 46–47. The distribution was as follows: six Provincial Presidents (Cordoba, Huesca, Teruel, Ciudad Real, Guadalajara, Toledo); two Provincial Secretary-Generals (Sevilla, Cáceres); three Provincial deputy Secretary-Generals (Almería, Toledo, Soria); and two Secretaries of Organisation (Alava, Cáceres).
9 A study of Basque women in politics found that the Parliamentary Committees with by far the highest proportions of women were Education and Culture, and Employment and Health (Martínez-Hernández and Elizondo 1997: 457).
10 The d'Hondt system (named after the person who devised it) shares out the available seats among the competing parties according to a formula which is not purely proportional but allocates relatively more seats to larger parties. Instead of 'winner-take-all', it is 'winner-takes-most', and often, in practice in Spain, it is 'top two winners-take-all'.
11 Briefing by Isabel Martínez Lozano, PSOE Secretariat for the Participation of Women, 26 January 2000.
12 See López Nieto (1988): 85, 105, 118.
13 Inter-Parliamentary Union figures in European Commission (1999). Spain's world ranking subsequently improved to 12th in 2002.
14 Government of Spain (1994): 50–51.
15 One should remember that the Senate is elected via a plurality system with up to four members for the same 52 constituencies as the Congress.
16 European Parliament data for 1993.
17 Despite the fact that gates may, technically, open up as well as close off access, the image of gatekeeping mostly has constraining connotations.
18 Once the deputy Carmen Romero, Felipe González's wife, adopted the parity argument, the idea that elite men were influenced by their feminist wives became a topic of private and media gossip, as if to belittle the achievement by reducing it to a matter of the boudoir. Undoubtedly there were such cases, and a different spin can be put on the phenomena by asking why were these men of the political elite married to feminist professional women in the first place. This merely confirms that they were both members of an educated, 'enlightened' elite.
19 'Almunia propone cambiar la ley electoral para que las mujeres ocupen el 40% de las candidaturas', *El País*, 7 November 1999, p. 24.
20 A promise he did not keep (only five of 14 of the Junta de Andalucía's portfolios were held by women in 2001, as calculated from the names of the consejeros/as on the Junta de Andalucía's website), but parity in *public* appointments is not mandatory.
21 The other mechanism for renewal was the introduction of one-member-one-vote secret balloting to elect the party's candidate for prime minister in national and autonomous community parliamentary elections.
22 Something similar is claimed for French politics and the socialist party, where the parity debate was taken up at a time when the public was becoming disaffected and the parties needed to 'jump on the bandwagon of equality for women in politics, if they were not to lose massive support'. Also the electoral system is considered a secondary issue (Perry and Hart 2000: 10).

References

Arenal, C. (1974) *La emancipación de la mujer en España*, selected writings edited by Mauro Armiño, Madrid: Ediciones Jucar.

Balaguer, M.L. (2000) 'Una legislación favorable a las cuotas electorales no es inconstitucional en España' in P. Saavedra Ruiz (ed.) *La democracia paritaria en la construcción europea*, Madrid: CELEM, pp. 53–55.

Barbadillo Griñan, P., Juste Ortega, M.G. and Ramírez Mayoral, A. (1990) 'La mujer en el congreso de los diputados: análisis de su participación en as candidaturas electorales de 1989', *REIS Revista Española de Investigaciones Sociológicas*, 52 (90): 101–135.

Brooksbank Jones, A. (1997) *Women in Contemporary Spain*, Manchester: Manchester University Press.

Campoamor, C. (1981, first published 1936), *El voto femenino y yo*, Barcelona: Ediciones laSal.

Caraballo, J.M. (2000) Speech in P. Saavedra Ruiz (ed.) *La democracia paritaria en la construcción europea*, Madrid: CELEM, pp. 29–32.

Cases, J.I., López Nieto, L., Ruiz de Asúa, M.A. and Vanaclocha, F. (1978) *Mujer y 15 de junio*, Madrid: Ministerio de Cultura.

Claudín, F. (1979) 'Entrevista a Felipe González', *Zona Abierta*, 20, May–August.

de Esteban, J. and Lopez Nieto, L. (1979) *Las elecciones legislativas del 1 de marzo de 1979*, Madrid: Centro de Investigaciones Sociológicas.

European Commission (1999) *Women of Europe Newsletter*, No. 87, July/August.

Federación de Mujeres Progresistas (1996) *Políticas sobre igualdad de oportunidades para la mujer*, unpublished press dossier for the 1996 general election.

Federación de Mujeres Progresistas (1997) 'Por un nuevo contrato social mujeres-hombres: documento que aporta al debate la Federación de Mujeres Progresistas', pp. 209–217 of PSOE, *Ponencia Marco del 34 Congreso*, Madrid: PSOE.

Fernández, B. (2000) Speech in P. Saavedra Ruiz (ed) *La democracia paritaria en la construcción europea*, Madrid: CELEM, pp. 23–24.

Gallego Méndez, M.T. (1983) *Mujer, Falange y franquismo*, Madrid: Taurus.

Gallego Méndez, M.T. (1994) 'Women's political engagement in Spain' in B. Nelson and N. Chowdhury (eds) *Women and Politics Worldwide*, New Haven, CT: Yale University Press, pp. 660–673.

García de León, M.A. (1982) *Las élites femeninas españolas*, Madrid: Queimada Ediciones.

García de León, M.A. (1990) *Discriminated Elite: Spanish Women in Politics*, paper to the XII International Congress of Sociology, Madrid.

García Mendez, E. (1979, 2nd edn) *La actuación de la mujer en las Cortes de la IIa República*, Madrid: Ministerio de Cultura.

Gillespie, R. (1989) *The Spanish Socialist Party: A History of Factionalism*, Oxford: Oxford University Press.

Gillespie, R. (1994) 'The resurgence of factionalism in the Spanish Socialist Workers' Party' in D.S. Bell and E. Shaw (eds) *Conflict and Cohesion in Western European Social Democratic parties*, London: Pinter.

Government of Spain (1994) *Report to the IV UN World Conference on Women, Beijing, 1995*, Madrid: Ministry of Social Affairs.

Grupo Federal de Estudios Sociológicos (1981) *Perfil del Militante Socialista*, Boletín PSOE, Madrid: March.

Halimi, G. (1994) *Femmes, moitié de la terre, moitié du pouvoir: plaidoyer pour une démocratie paritaire*, Paris: Gallimard.

Henig, R. and Henig, S. (2001) *Women and Political Power: Europe since 1945*, London: Routledge.

Heywood, P. (1993) 'Rethinking socialism in Spain: Programa 2000 and the social state', *Coexistence*, 30: 3.

IDES (1988) *Las Españolas ante la política*, Madrid: Instituto de la Mujer.

Instituto de la Mujer (1984) *Situación social de la Mujer en España 1983*, Madrid: Ministerio de Cultura.

Instituto de la Mujer (1990) *La Mujer en España: Política*, Madrid: Ministerio de Asuntos Sociales.

Instituto de la Mujer (1992) *La mujer en cifras 1992*, Madrid: Ministerio de Asuntos Sociales.

Inter-Parliamentary Union (2002) 'Women in national parliaments', compilation at 3 October: http://www.ipu.org.

Izquierda Unida (undated) *Estatutos*, Madrid: Izquierda Unida.

Jaquette, J. (ed.) (1994, 2nd edn) *The Women's Movement in Latin America*, Boulder, CO: Westview Press.

Jenson, J. and Sineau, M. (1995) *Mitterand et les Françaises: un rendez-vous manqué*, Paris: Presse de Sciences Po.

Jenson, J. and Valiente, C. (2003) 'The feminist movement and the reconfigured state in Spain' in L. Banaszak, K. Beckwith and D. Rucht (eds) *Women's Movements Facing the Reconfigured State*, Cambridge: Cambridge University Press.

Jones, M. (2000) 'El sistema de cuotas y la elección de las mujeres en América Latina' in P. Saavedra Ruiz (ed.) *La democracia paritaria en la construcción europea*, Madrid: CELEM, pp. 35–47.

Kauppi, N. (1999) 'Power or subjection? French women politicians in the European parliament', *European Journal of Women's Studies*, 6 (3): 329–340.

López Nieto, L. (1988) *Alianza Popular: estructura y evolución electoral*, Madrid: C.I.S.

Lovecy, J. (2000) 'Citoyennes à part entière? The Constitutionalization of gendered citizenship in France and the parity reforms of 1999–2000', *Government and Opposition*, 33 (4): 439–462.

Lovenduski, J. and Hills, H.J. (eds) (1981) *The Politics of the Second Electorate*, London: Routledge and Kegan Paul.

Marín, K. (1999) 'Ellas se las juegan', *El País Semanal*, 6 June 1999, pp. 44–58.

Martínez-Hernández, E. and Elizondo, A. (1997) 'Women in politics: are they really concerned about equality? An essay on the Basque political system', *European Journal of Women's Studies*, 4 (4): 451–472.

Martínez Ten, C. (1990) 'La participación política de la mujer en España' in J. Astelarra (ed.) *Participación política de las mujeres*, Madrid: C.I.S.

Martínez Ten, C. and Paramio, L. (1997) 'Un nuevo contrato social entre hombres y mujeres', *Leviatán: Revista de Hechos e Ideas*, 69, Madrid: Funación Pablo Iglesias, pp. 85–103.

Mossuz-Lavau, J. and Sineau, M. (1981) 'France' in J. Lovenduski and H.J. Hills (eds) *The Politics of the Second Electorate*, London: Routledge and Kegan Paul.

Navarro, M. (2000) 'Proposed modification of the Spanish electoral law to introduce parity democracy' in P. Saavedra (ed.) *Towards a Parity Democracy: Analysis and Review of Current Electoral Legislation*, Madrid: CELEM Seminar Report.

Navarro Zárate, A. (2000) Speech in P. Saavedra Ruiz (ed.) *La democracia paritaria en la construcción europea*, Madrid: CELEM, pp. 25–27.

Norris, P. (1993) 'Conclusions: comparing legislative recruitment' in J. Lovenduski and P. Norris (eds) *Gender and Party Politics*, London: Sage.

Norris, P. and Lovenduski, J. (1995) *Political Recruitment: Gender, Race and Class in the British Parliament*, Cambridge: Cambridge University Press.

Partido Popular (1999) Documentos Políticos, Madrid: Partido Popular.

PSOE (Partido Socialista Obrero Español) (1997) Comisión Ejecutiva Federal, *Ponencia Marco*, 34 Congreso, 20–23 de junio, Madrid: PSOE document.

PSOE (Partido Socialista Obrero Español) (2000) 'Manifesto 2000', Madrid: PSOE.

Perry, S. and Hart, S. (2000) 'Parity in French politics' in L. Twomey (ed.) *Women in Contemporary Europe: Roles and Identities in France and Spain*, Bristol and Oregon: Intellect Books, pp. 9–28.

Porter, E. (1998) 'The political representation of women in Northern Ireland', *Politics*, 18 (1): 25–32.

Randall, V. (1987, 2nd edn) *Women and Politics*, London: Macmillan.

Rudí, L.F. (2001) Interviewed by A. Espada, *El País Semanal*, No. 1310, 4 November, p. 16.

Ruiz Franco, M.R. (1995) 'Nuevos horizontes para las mujeres de los años 60: la ley de 22 de julio de 1961', *Arenal*, 2 (2): 247–268.

Secretaría de Participación de la Mujer (1998) *La participación de las mujeres en el PSOE y en las instituciones públicas*, Madrid: PSOE.

Socialist International Women (1995) *A Quota for Women: Promoting Gender Equality*, leaflet (14 pp).

Squires, J. (1996) 'Quotas for women: fair representation?' in J. Lovenduski and P. Norris (eds) *Women in Politics*, Oxford: Oxford University Press.

Threlfall, M. (1998) 'State feminism or party feminism?, *European Journal of Women's Studies*, 5 (1): 69–93.

Threlfall, M. (1979) 'Presencia de la mujer en las elecciones legislativas', *Zona Abierta*, 19: 56–70.

Uriarte, E. and Ruiz, C. (1999) 'Mujeres y hombres en las élites políticas españolas: diferencias o similitudes?', *REIS*, 88: 207–232.

Valiente, C. (2001) 'Movimientos sociales y Estados: la movilización feminista en España desde los años sesenta', *Sistema*, 161 (March): 31–58.

Part III
Changing gender relations?

7 Securing a foothold in the labour market

Christine Cousins

Introduction

Employment growth in Spain since the end of recession in 1995 has been one of the highest in Europe. The increase in women's employment rate has been twice the rate of the European Union average and that for men has been nearly four times the European average. Unemployment, too, has fallen from its very high level of 20 per cent in 1994 to 11 per cent in 2002. However, Spanish labour markets retain their distinctive features with, for example, the highest unemployment rate in the OECD and the EU, one of the lowest employment rates in Europe, the highest proportion of temporary fixed-term contract workers and a large informal economy. The aim of this chapter is to generate insights into the implications of these employment trends and conditions for gender relations, household structures and coping strategies in Spain. As discussed below, the perspective adopted is one which makes gender central to the analysis and also takes into account the interaction between household and family circumstances, employers' strategies, labour-market policies and the welfare state.

One initial limitation, however, is that statistical data on labour-market participation can tell us little about changes in gender relations either in the home or in the workplace. As Perrons and Gonas (1998) have noted, changes in gender roles, for example women's increased involvement in paid work, can occur alongside little or no change in gender relations. It may be, as these authors argue, that more ethnographic data for any particular country is required. It is recognised also that the structuring of gender relations and household formations are neither independent of, nor determined by, wider economic and employment pressures but are relatively autonomous of these (Rubery and Fagan 1994). This, therefore, means that the nature of the gender 'contract' in a specific country must also be examined, together with tax and social-security systems, labour-supply characteristics and policies and provisions for combining paid work and family life.

Fagan and O'Reilly (1998) have argued that a 'gender systems'

Figure 7.1 'Multi-tasking' – poster created by a Catalan women's group, the Vocalía de Dones de l'Associació de Veins de l'Esquerra de l'Eixample, 1977. Border contains a list of demands: 'Down with exploitation of women – Out with macho society - No discrimination in education – No to job discriminatin – For a secure job – Socialization of domestic work – For freely-decided motherhood – No to unemployment – Anullment of repressive and anti-feminist laws.

approach is the most appropriate for analysing cross-national differences in employment patterns. This approach, which draws predominantly on the work of Hirdmann (1998), Pfau-Effinger (1993) and Duncan (1995), focuses on 'how particular institutional arrangements and "gender contracts" give rise to particular forms of gender relations and how the inherent tensions can be identified within a given society' (Fagan and O'Reilly 1998: 22). As Duncan explains, the idea of the gender contract arose in Scandinavian countries when substantial change in women's roles was occurring yet gender divisions were being maintained nonetheless. In each society and over time there develops a social contract between the genders, a notion of appropriate behaviour and roles of each gender. This contract is founded, though, on an asymmetry of power in which the male domains are systematically and structurally assigned a higher value. It would also seem that the gender contract in any one society differs by region, education or class level, by generation and by ethnicity, although space in this chapter permits only a brief examination of these differences (see the work of Duncan 1995, Solsana 1996 and González López 1997 for regional differences in the UK and Spain respectively). One criticism that may be made of the term 'gender contract', however, is that it implies consent or consensus between men and women, whereas in reality there may be little choice in accepting prevailing norms and assumptions about gender roles.

The 'gender systems' approach suggests that if national institutional structures change, for example during periods of rapid economic and social transformation, then gender relations in a particular country may be at variance with the different societal institutions. This may increase tensions and contradictions in the existing 'power-balance' between men and women leading to a process of re-negotiation of gender relations by individuals or collective actors (Pfau-Effinger 1998). This re-negotiation may be at the level of individuals coping with employment changes and opportunities in everyday life (see, for example, the work of Tobío 2001) or by collective actors in political or public spheres. As Pfau-Effinger notes, factors which make the process of change stronger and more dynamic include both the extent to which the traditional gender culture was entrenched before a period of change, and the scope actors have to find consensus on new gender arrangements in relation to existing social integration and political practices (1998: 179). In the case of Spain, which has experienced profound economic, social and political changes in the past 30 years, this framework would appear to be particularly fruitful.

Hirdmann's work (1998) focuses on gender conflict and the negotiation of different gender contracts in Sweden. For Hirdmann gender conflict arises as the unintended result of women's integration into both the labour market and the political sphere since it challenges the previous gender order built on gender segregation and the male norm. At a theoretical level, solutions to this conflict in Sweden involved negotiations between men and women for new gender contracts. The first of these she calls the 'housewife' contract evident between 1930 and 1960, with women's 'dual role' a further variant in the 1940s and 1950s. This gave way in the 1960s and 1970s to an 'equality contract' 'stating the individuality of men and women in the family as well as society' (Hirdmann 1998: 41). This new contract was based on a discourse of men and women as similar and equal as the full-employment concept was extended to women and a range of policies was introduced which enabled women to combine work and family life.[1] The entry during the 1970s and 1980s of women into paid work in the public sector, especially in part-time jobs, was, Hirdmann says, a way of opening up a new and special 'space' for women to occupy without threatening men's position: 'There seems to be an almost structural way of avoiding the gender conflict exploding, by opening up new areas' (1998: 43). In view of the fact that the labour market in Sweden is highly segmented, with men and women doing different jobs, this appears to be a particularly apt description of what happened there in the 1970s and 1980s.

Other writers have noted that in Germany and the UK the 'space' for women's integration has obviously been through part-time work and, for many women, low-paid part-time work (Fagan and O'Reilly 1998). In this view part-time work 'is essentially a gender compromise across national boundaries: women are able to enter the labour market and meet the requirements of service sector employers without disrupting men's traditional breadwinner status at the workplace or in the home' (Fagan and O'Reilly 1998: 23).

Whichever perspectives or concepts are used it would appear that an examination of women's integration into the labour market must take place within a framework which makes gender central to the analysis. A similar plea for inclusion of a gender perspective into all social and labour market analysis has been put forward by Rubery *et al.* (1998) and Fagan and O'Reilly (1998). Both sets of authors consider that analysis (or cross-national comparison) of labour markets should incorporate a framework which takes account of the interaction between household and family circumstances, employers' strategies, labour-market policies and the welfare state. This chapter reflects these theoretical positions and seeks to extend our understanding of the impact of the changing nature and forms of employment in the context of a specific welfare regime, on household structures and strategies and changing gender relations in Spain. The following discussion also focuses on the nature of women's integration into the labour market and the extent to which this has been accompanied by an intensification of differentiation between men and women and different groups of women in participation and terms and conditions of employment.

The segmentation of Spanish labour markets

The Spanish labour market is now highly segmented into at least four different labour markets (see Pérez-Díaz and Rodríguez 1995 and Cousins 1994, 1999a for reasons why this has occurred). The first segment derives from the historical legacy of the Franco regime which privileged core workers with regard to labour-market status and income maintenance. During the Franco regime, in the context of a ban on trade unions, political parties, strikes, and free collective bargaining, employment security was granted to workers by Franco to provide a modicum of political legitimacy for the regime. This protected core of the labour market still exists and the rigid rules for exit and entry to the labour market have been applied for about five decades without interruption though with regular readjustments. The persistence of the core has also been a determining factor in the creation of other quite different labour markets, each with its own rules (Pérez-Díaz and Rodríguez 1995).

A second labour market contains those on temporary-fixed-term contracts, nearly one third of the employed workforce (see Table 7.1). In the context of high unemployment and under employers' pressure for liberalisation, legislation of 1984 introduced fixed-term contracts as a way of circumventing the employment protection rules attached to permanent workers and as a means to promote the creation of new employment. Since then virtually all new entrants to the job market, and mainly young workers and women, have been employed on fixed-term contracts, with lower pay and little training prospects (Jimeno and Toharia 1994; see also below). New employees may be contracted for a few months and then work informally or enter unemployment, before returning to legally contracted temporary work. Employers, especially in the small firms (firms with less than 50 workers constitute 98 per cent of all businesses) are reluctant to transform temporary contacts into permanent ones. With respect to part-time employment, it is less important as a form of flexible

Table 7.1 Trends in non-standard employment in Spain 1991–2002 (% employment)

	Part-time		Fixed-term contracts		Self-employment	
	1991	*2002*	*1991*	*2002*	*1991*	*2002*
Spain						
Female	11.5	16.7	38.9	34.1	18.7	12.5
Male	1.6	2.5	30.1	29.0	18.8	17.8
EU average						
Female	28.8	33.5	12.5	14.2	12.7	10.7
Male	4.2	6.5	10.2	12.0	18.5	17.6

Source: Employment in Europe (2003).

work although since labour-market reform in December 1993 this has increased, especially for female workers (see Table 7.1 and the discussion below).[2]

A third labour market consists of those workers in even more precarious work in the underground economy. Estimates of the submerged economy ranged from 22 to 30 per cent of total employment in 1986 (Pérez-Díaz and Rodríguez 1995 and Cousins 1994). In this sector there is low pay, no social-security contributions and no protection from dismissal. The fourth sector is that of the officially ex-employed or unemployed population. Although the informal economy is extensive it does not appear to substantially modify the figures for unemployment. Unemployment has declined in the past few years, but women's unemployment is still twice as high as that of men, 16 per cent and 8 per cent respectively in 2002 (Employment in Europe 2003; see also Table 7.2). Women also form the major part of the worst forms of unemployment, those out of work for long periods and first-time job seekers. Further, over one quarter of young women under 24 years are unemployed (this is almost twice the European average) compared with 18 per cent of young men (see Table 7.3).

Trends in women's activity rates – late 1980s and 1990s

Women's employment rate is one of the lowest in the European Union (see Table 7.4), although, as we discuss below, it has been increasing since the mid-1980s and especially in the 1990s. However, initially, women's

Table 7.2 Unemployment rates 1993–2003 for men and women in Spain and EU15

	1993 Female %	2002 Female %	1993 Male %	2002 Male %	1993–2002 Female % change	1993–2002 Male % change
Spain	24.1	16.4	15.5	8.0	7.7	7.5
EU15	11.4	8.7	9.1	6.9	2.7	2.2

Source: Employment in Europe (2003).

Table 7.3 Youth unemployment rates[a] 1993–2002 for men and women in Spain and EU15

	1993 Female %	2002 Female %	1993 Male %	2002 Male %	1993–2002 Female % change	1993–2002 Male % change
Spain	42.8	27.3	35.1	18.4	15.5	16.7
EU15	20.8	15.5	19.8	14.8	5.3	5.0

Source: Employment in Europe (2003).

Note
a Youth unemployment is % of labour force aged 15–24.

Table 7.4 Female employment rates[a] and activity rates[b] in EU member states 2002

	Female employment rates as a % of working-age population	Female activity rates as a % of working-age population
Sweden	72.2	75.8
Denmark	71.7	75.5
Finland	66.2	72.8
Netherlands	66.2	68.3
UK	65.3	68.3
Austria	63.1	66.0
Portugal	60.8	65.0
Germany	58.8	64.2
France	56.7	62.7
Ireland	55.4	57.8
Luxembourg	51.6	53.7
Belgium	51.4	56.2
Spain	**44.1**	**52.8**
Greece	42.5	50.1
Italy	42.0	47.9
EU15	**55.6**	**60.9**

Source: Employment in Europe (2003).

Note
a Employment rate refers to females aged 15 to 64 years who are in employment, divided by the working-age population.
b Activity rate refers to females aged 15 to 64 years who are in labour force (employed and unemployed), divided by the working-age population.

increased economic activity from the second half of the 1980s contributed to the growth of the labour force, but with the persistence of high unemployment and an increase in frustrated job seekers. All in all, an increase of 1.8 million jobs between 1985 and 1991 was accompanied by a decrease of only 500,000 unemployed (Toharia 1997). The recession of 1992–1994 (which was so steep that it has been described as a second industrial restructuring process) resulted in a high loss of manufacturing and permanent jobs, a process more intense but shorter than the similar process in the early 1980s.

Since the end of recession there has been a strong growth in female employment rates, as a proportion of the female population, during the 1990s. The percentage change has been more than double the European average (see Table 7.5). There has been significant growth in the employment rates of prime-age women (as a proportion of women aged 25–54), increasing from 40 per cent in 1995 to 54 per cent in 2002 (Employment in Europe 2003). Young women in particular are now entering the labour market before marriage and remaining in work after the birth of their children. This reverses the traditional pattern established during the Franco regime when women withdrew from the labour market on marriage.

Table 7.5 Employment rates 1993–2002 for men and women in Spain and EU15

	1993 Female %	2002 Female %	1993 Male %	2002 Male %	1993–2002 Female % change	1993–2002 Male % change
Spain	30.7	44.1	63.0	72.6	13.4	9.6
EU15	49.2	55.6	71.0	72.8	6.4	1.8

Source: Employment in Europe (2003).

Other writers have noted, however, that the extremely rigid structure of the Spanish labour market means that once women leave their jobs they find it very difficult to re-enter employment. Therefore only a small proportion of women in full-time jobs leave their jobs if they marry or have children (González López 1997). The choice of part-time work as a means to combine work and family that women make in many north European states is not an option for most Spanish women (see below). González López (1997) found that the proportion of women aged between 26 and 45 years living in full-time dual-earner households was the same as in Britain (about a quarter of households in both countries) despite the fact that women's labour-market participation is considerably higher in the UK. Threlfall (2000: 37) calculated that there were almost as many Spanish prime-age (25–49) women in full-time work as in the UK, as a proportion of the female population: 38 per cent and 41 per cent respectively – despite their lesser participation and higher unemployment rates. There were, however, significant regional differences in Spain with full-time dual earner families more likely to come from the industrial and urbanised regions.

There is, therefore, a polarisation between younger women who now follow continuous full-time careers and the entirely disrupted careers of older full-time homemakers (see also Chapter 8), although, as discussed below, the situation is more complex than this as there is also polarisation between those in secure and insecure work. Nevertheless, one important polarisation is between generations as it is now possible to distinguish a profound break in the experiences of different generations of women. Garrido (1992), for example, speaks of the 'two biographies' of women in which the life experiences of younger and older women have progressively diverged. Women's employment rates are also very dependent on their levels of education. In the 1980s and 1990s women's increased entry into higher education coincided with an expansion of professional jobs so that women have substantially increased their share of such jobs. For women with university or professional qualifications, employment rates are some 14 percentage points below men with the same qualifications at 67 per cent and 82 per cent respectively (Employment in Europe 2001). However, employment rates of women with low levels of education are less than half the rate for comparable men, at 32 per cent and 70 per cent respectively.

Uneven economic development in Spain has also resulted in strong regional differences between the more advanced urban areas and less developed agricultural regions. Female participation rates therefore vary significantly from region to region. In the Girona province in Catalonia, for example, the female participation rate was 47 per cent compared with 28 per cent in both the provinces of Ciudad Real and Cuenca in 1998 (EPA 1998).

Women as 'outsiders' in the labour market

As Moltó (1996) has argued, as latecomers to the labour market, women tend to be 'outsiders' as they have entered the labour market at a time when unemployment was high and increasing, the use of fixed-term contracts spreading rapidly and the economy undergoing rapid restructuring, particularly in traditional industries, leading to an increase in the informal economy. Women, therefore, have been disproportionately integrated into the labour market in the temporary/informal and unemployed segments. Only just over one third of women had a 'typical' or standard employment relationship of permanent full-time work in 2002 (see Table 7.1).

Virtually all young workers have taken fixed-term contract work as they have entered the labour market since the 1980s. However, such contracts are not exclusively a feature of work for young people but are a working reality for a significant proportion of the adult workforce. In 2002 temporary contracts affected 30 per cent of all male wage earners and 34 per cent of female wage earners (Table 7.1). Furthermore, Spain shows one of the highest levels of involuntary temporary working, with 70 per cent of all temporary workers involuntarily employed, that is one in four of all those employed (Employment in Europe 2001). Unfortunately, women's share of temporary work has been increasing, rising from 38 per cent in 1994 to 42 per cent in 2000 (Carrasquer 2001).

Fixed-term contracts were more prevalent in the private sector, although as we discuss below, more recently they have been used increasingly in the public sector because of budgetary restraints. The growth of temporary fixed-term contracts for young people and for women has created a new world of precarious work with workers moving from short-term contracts to unemployment and back to a further short-term contract (OECD 2000).[3] In the retail sector, for example, there is a 'contractual rotation' through which workers rotate from temporary work to unemployment and then back to temporary employment once again to fill vacancies left by other temporary workers who have left. Firms thereby have a pool of temporary workers who continuously fill a number of jobs (García-Ramón and Ortíz 2000).

A major labour reform in May 1997 (following an agreement between employers and trade unions) introduced legislation which aimed to promote permanent contracts and to transform fixed-term contracts into permanent jobs.[4] This reform encouraged the creation of more permanent contracts but the number of these has never exceeded more than 9–10 per cent of the total (EIRO Feb. 2002). Ferreiro and Serrana (2001) argued that while the 1997 reform created jobs for skilled workers (in that they have benefited most from the new permanent contracts and conversion of temporary into permanent jobs) at the same time a new form of segmentation was generated. That is, the proportion of workers with very short fixed-term contacts increased, leading, in turn, to increased rotation in jobs.[5]

Part-time work in Spain has been low in comparison to levels in northern Europe (for reasons see Note 2). However, in 1994 legislation was introduced to remove the legal impediments to part-time employment and such employment has increased, especially for female employees (see Table 7.2).[6] Commentators suggest that the increase in part-time work is led by employers wishing to increase staffing levels during peak periods and is not a form of work which helps women to combine paid work and family (Moltó 1996; EIRO June 2001). 'Part-timers are forced to accept highly deregulated hours of work that make it difficult to reconcile work with family and social life' (EIRO June 2001: 1).

There is a low level of voluntary part-time work; in fact Spain shows one of the lowest levels in Europe, with around only 5 per cent saying they did not want a full-time job. This compares with 70 per cent of part-timers in the UK and Germany (Employment in Europe 2001). Female part-timers are, therefore, not in these jobs by choice but because of the characteristics of the occupation or because they were unable to find a full-time job (EIRO June 2001).[7] A high proportion (58 per cent in 1999) of part-time jobs are also temporary fixed-term contracts. Part-time work is therefore associated with high job instability.

Official statistics provide only a partial account of women's paid work. The informal and unrecorded economy is also an important source of jobs for women. Many of the features of the labour market in Spain create favourable conditions for the increase in irregular forms of working, namely the decline in regular, stable jobs, the persistence of high unemployment, the presence of foreign immigrants from Third World countries and the subordinate position of many women in the family providing a subordinate workforce in the labour market. Whilst work in the informal economy is not new, rather it is a long-standing and integral aspect of the economy, the rounds of industrial restructuring during the economic recessions of 1975–1985 and the early 1990s have extended the importance of this type of work. Firms have relocated elsewhere, decentralised production and increased networks of subcontracting in an effort to cope with international competition. Informal working includes unpaid family work, homeworking, domestic work, unregistered casual or seasonal work, and work in unregistered subcontracted workshops in a range of innovative and traditional sectors. Estimates of the size of the informal economy vary but all show higher proportions of women working in this sector. Since many of the workers in the informal sectors are women they, therefore, do not fit into the 'normal' EU definitions of workers associated with trade unions as social partners, or with regulated conditions of work or protected by social security (Vaiou and Stratigaki 1997).

Frequently there is a hierarchy of firms from the formal to the informal sectors, especially in the labour-intensive industries such as clothing, textiles, footwear and food. As the aim is to lower costs of production, firms seek female workers who are willing to accept low wages and precarious conditions, especially those who live in rural areas where there is a lack of alternative work opportunities (Baylina and García-Ramón 1998).

Baylina and García-Ramón's research on industrial homeworking in four rural areas of Spain found family income to be derived from a model of pluriactivity at the household level. However, there were regional disparities in the contribution that women's earning made to family income which reflected the social structure of the regions. In Andalusia women's industrial homeworking was necessary to complement an unstable family income based on agriculture. In Galicia, this work offered an income to women 'trapped' in isolated rural areas and contributed to other diverse forms of family income. In Catalonia, women's earnings raised the stable income of a husband. In Valencia, footwear homeworking was the best way for unemployed women to maintain their family budget.

Pay

The average pay of women in 2000 was 25 percentage points lower than men, although this varied considerably between the autonomous communities, sectors and occupations (EIRO Jan. 2002).[8] However, it should be noted that statistical sources on earnings leave out workers in agriculture, the public sector and in the domestic sphere, as well as in small firms with less than 10 employees. Thus, some 43 per cent of female wage earners are excluded from the statistics as they form the majority in these sectors (ibid.). And as some of these sectors (agriculture, domestic and small firms) are low-paying sectors, the gender pay gap is likely to be underestimated. Further, in general women are overrepresented in the sectors of low-paid work, as well as in temporary and part-time work which are both associated with low pay. One recent study reported that the pay of temporary workers in the private sector was 65 per cent of the average wage for men and 54 per cent of that of women (EIRO Sept. 2002a). As the period of recruitment is short, annual income is also low.

Nevertheless, surprisingly low pay is not a main cause of poverty in Spain.[9] Rather, as we discuss below, the structure of the family and its relationship to the labour market explains the lack of association between low pay and the working poor. That is, most low-paid jobs are taken by young people and women who, in the main, live in households where the males are earning higher wages. There are two exceptions to this pattern: single-parent households, where the mother's low pay is the cause of poverty, and immigrants, where the men also tend to be concentrated in the low-paid sectors (EIRO Sept. 2002a).

The Spanish national minimum wage is one of the lowest in Europe with only Greece and Portugal set at a lower level. In 2002 the minimum wage represented 40 per cent of the average wage, at 516 euros per month (about £325), and its level has been falling over the past 20 years (EIRO Sept. 2002b). Whilst only a small proportion of the regular workforce receive a wage at the level of the national minimum, some 5–6 per cent, it is nevertheless important for macroeconomic and budgetary objectives. That is, many non-contributory benefits are established as a proportion of the national minimum wage, especially unemployment benefits and pensions. As we discussed in Chapter 3, the low level of non-contributory benefits (disproportionately taken by women) is one reason for poverty amongst those who are not in paid work.

Private and public sector employment

It should come as no surprise that the public sector was one of the main sectors for employment expansion for women, as they increased their educational qualifications and entered professional occupations.[10] The public sector, in which about 25 per cent of female employees work, favours greater gender equality through recruitment, promotion and training programmes, and greater use of permanent and full-time contracts. The expansion of the public sector in the 1980s and early 1990s was associated with the modest growth of the welfare state (as Spain sought to catch up with other European countries) and with the staffing of the newly established autonomous communities and other public institutions. By the late 1990s, however, preparations to comply with the criteria to join the single currency led to a lack of growth in public expenditure and jobs[11] and there was also a substantial rise in recourse to temporary fixed-term contracts. According to Ferreiro and Serrana (2001), 77 per cent of new jobs created in the public sector between 1995 and 1999 were in the form of temporary fixed-term contracts. This contributed to making even the public sector an insecure workplace for women: women's temporary recruitment went up from one out of five in 1994 to almost one in four by 2000 (Carrasquer 2001).

On the other hand, the private sector does not offer the same working conditions as the public sector, and traditionally has made much greater use of fixed-term and part-time contracts; for example, in 2000, 37 per cent of women's jobs in the private sector were temporary fixed-term contracts compared with 24 per cent in the public sector (Carrasquer 2001). The private sector employs 64 per cent of all Spanish workers, and consists predominantly of small and medium-sized firms, 99.8 per cent of which have less than 250 employees and 93 per cent less than ten. Small firms offer lower wages, less stable employment contracts, more irregular working hours, less safety and fewer opportunities for training (EIRO Jul. 1999). Small firms also have high start-up and closure rates and more frequent job turnover than large plants, so although SMEs created more new jobs than larger firms in recent years they also caused more job losses. Furthermore, employees had far fewer opportunities to defend themselves from compulsory redundancies and lower pay: the 1999 EIRO study found small firms in Spain to have lower unionisation rates and a lack of collective bargaining. The relationship between the small employers and their workforce is more paternalistic, based to a greater extent on individual treatment, and can also be more authoritarian.

The reconciliation of work and family life

Women's integration into the labour market is influenced not only by the system of labour-market organisation but also by the nature of the welfare state, the family and differences in gender roles and gender relations. The differing patterns of women's labour-market participation are shaped by the configurations of social policies adopted in each country, especially those which encourage or discourage the reconciliation of employment and family life. While the incorporation of policies to reconcile paid work and family at the European Union level (for example, the employment guidelines) signals an important development for gender-equality policy, such policies have to be implemented in terms of the pre-existing policy and cultural frames in each country and the particular 'gender order' underlying the welfare state (Ostner and Lewis 1995; Cousins 1999b; Hantrais 2000).

Esping-Andersen's (1996, 1997, 1999) perspective, which identifies a nexus of labour market–welfare state–family in different regimes, is a useful way in which to analyse women's employment opportunities. There are very large differences in employment opportunities for women in the so-called 'insider–outsider' labour markets of countries such as Germany and the southern European countries in comparison with those of the Scandinavian countries which provide 'women-friendly' policies and an 'employment-maximising' approach. With respect to the continental European welfare states (in which he includes Spain), Esping-Andersen argues that where entire families are locked into welfare dependency on one male earner there is a tendency to preserve and even strengthen job protection and social rights for those in the core workforce (the 'insiders') 'even if it is clear that this is exactly what causes exclusion of the "outsiders"' (1997: 142).

Employment in Spain is concentrated on key breadwinners who financially support others in the family who are not in work or work intermittently. Data from both the OECD (1998) study and the Gregg and Wadsworth (1996) show Spain to have the highest incidence of households in which one adult only is employed. The family therefore takes much of the strain of high unemployment and temporary fixed-term contract work, which in practice means a woman running the household on one full wage with occasional smaller contributions. The family is the key to the stability of Spanish society, with a variety of sources of incomes from different labour markets, pensions or unemployment benefits being pooled (see Pérez-Díaz and Rodríguez 1995 and Esping-Andersen 1999). The ideal is to have one key worker located within the core labour market.[12] This is especially important for those without previous work experience who are not entitled to receive any benefit (see Chapter 3). Families are then dependent on the main wage earner not only for earnings but also social-security benefits. More recently this has changed as the growth in employment in the past five years has meant that more young people and women have been able to take up low-paid jobs (EIRO Sept. 2002a). Whilst this increases the family income, for women such a dispersion of jobs perpetuates the traditional family structure and the division of labour within it. For young people too it perpetuates their dependence on the parental home, as the level of pay does not allow them to have the same standard of living if they leave home (ibid.).

As discussed in Chapter 3 cash transfers predominate in the Spanish welfare state and there is a lack of welfare services for the care of sick, disabled, or elderly people or for children under 3 years. Further, family obligations in Spain involve legal obligations to care and this extends beyond nuclear-family members. There is therefore an obligation to care which in practice falls mainly on women (see, for example, Chapter 9). As González López (1997) argues families play a decisive role in women's intergenerational solidarity networks in the absence of extended child or elderly care provision. Reliance on family help, especially grandmothers for child care, is a well-established practice, especially given the lack of part-time work and the full-time working hours of women (Moltó and Domingo 1998; Ruivo *et al.* 1998). Tobío (2001), in her interviews with working mothers, found that one third are helped daily by grandmothers and this rises to two-thirds in unusual circumstances such as when a child falls ill or during school vacations. Geographical closeness of different generations in the family contributes to these intergenerational networks. Nevertheless, the use of family help in childcare may hinder geographical mobility and also with increased female employment this form of help may become less available in the future.

Other strategies for working mothers include paying other women, often immigrants, who may help on an irregular basis with childcare and domestic responsibilities, especially for more highly paid couples. In fact the large and increasing demand for these services may encourage an inflow of female immigrants to southern European countries (Moltó and Domingo 1998; Gregson *et al.* 1999). An additional strategy is that of self-employment in a family business or homeworking, as this enables women to have flexible hours and to combine work with the care of young children. Tobío (2001) also mentions a range of other strategies. These include: organisation, planning and control, time strategies, using fathers as a resource (but see Chapter 8), spatial strategies, and simplifying and reducing domestic work. However, as Tobío argues, working mothers are dealing individually with the problems that being both a mother and a worker pose. New practices in employment have not been matched by public policies or practices within families.

More recently, as a response to the European Union directive on family leave, a new law to promote the reconciliation of work and family life was implemented in November 1999. This law extends the mother's maternity- and parental-leave rights and promotes the father's use of family-leave arrangements and working-time reductions. However, the issue of lack of childcare provision for children under three years is not addressed (see also Chapter 8) and unpaid parental-leave schemes are of little use to those on short fixed-term contracts.

Young people and women are also the most likely to take temporary fixed-term contracts but this type of work is not sufficiently stable or continuous to support an autonomous family. Some writers have suggested, therefore, that the same process of segmentation which occurs in the labour market is also to be found in opportunities to marry and form a family (for example, De Ussel 1995). Those young people who do not have access to the labour market, have intermittent or occasional work and are without prospects of continuity of employment generally tend to have a prolonged dependency on their families, often until their late twenties or even later (see Chapter 3). Not only has the rate of marriage in Spain declined but the age of marriage has risen and the rate of fertility at 1.2 is now one of the lowest in the world. The dramatic fall in the birth rate appears to be one response to the difficulties of obtaining stable work and combining paid work and family life. For example, one study of perceptions of the family found that the majority of respondents gave 'economic reasons' as to why couples do not want children or have fewer children (Cruz Cantero 1995).

Conclusion

The 'space' for women's labour-market activity in Spain has been disproportionately in the more precarious sections of employment, namely temporary fixed-term work, the informal economy and unemployment. We have also examined the implications of precarious employment at the level of households. Low and intermittent wages can only be supplemented by other stable incomes or social-security benefits. As previously argued such a dispersion of jobs will do little to modify traditional gender relations. Nevertheless, as we have also seen, about a quarter of young women are living in full-time dual-earner households.

Moltó (1996: 92) has remarked that there is a segmentation among Spanish women which is shaped by the currently high unemployment and temporality of employment:

> Highly educated women in professional and public administration jobs show a permanent attachment to the labour market, along the life-cycle, while poorly educated women, working in ancillary services and living in households out of employment networks are likely to cluster in the secondary segment of the labour market, with many interruptions in their labour market participation along the life-cycle.

The integration of women into the labour market, therefore, shows a 'double movement' (Carrasco *et al.* 1997): an increase in inequalities between male and female workers in different labour-market segments and increasing differentiation between women themselves.

An increasing polarisation between women workers has also been found in other European countries and especially the UK (see, for example, Bruegel and Perrons 1996 and Bulletin No. 5 and 6 1995). With respect to gender relations in Spain, however, the transition from private patriarchy to one of an 'equality' contract is likely to be highly varied by generation, by region, by education and by employment conditions. Barriers to equality include the nature of the segmented labour market in which, as we have seen, women are concentrated in the most vulnerable and non-core segments as well as the nature of the welfare state (see Chapter 3). Indeed, Guillén (1997) has remarked that the combination of the welfare state with low family benefits and services and the segmented labour market generate a vicious circle from which it is difficult to escape and makes it difficult to modify traditional family roles.

At the same, however, issues of gender equality are on the political agenda in Spain as well as at the European Union level. At an individual and household level we can also expect continued re-definition and re-negotiation of gender relations as women's aspirations move away from traditionally assigned roles. Inés Alberdi, lead author of the major government report commissioned on the occasion of the United Nations International Year of the Family, points out with considerable insight that the socialising function of the modern family is strategically aimed at achieving personal success for each and every one of its members (Alberdi 1995: 462–463). Alberdi argues that in the modern age, the traditional sacrifice of one member's well-being (that of the mother) for the sake of the others cannot be expected, and simply leads to conflict and family breakdown – the fall of one leading to the fall of all, so to speak. Therefore if the family is to have any future it must be a co-operative enterprise (Alberdi 1995: 463). In this context, the ability of young women to earn enough of an independent living and that of mothers to maintain enough financial autonomy for a modern family to be sustainable, together with a gendered understanding of the dynamics of the labour market, become the key to the whole society's future.

Figure 7.2 Street sweeper in Valencia, 2002.

Notes

1 Although many commentators would argue that there is still not an 'equality contract', women's options have been extended and they have become more economically independent.

2 The low level of part-time working in Spain appears to be due to the lack of tradition for such work. This can be traced back to restrictions placed on such contracts prior to the Workers' Charter 1976 in which the worker and employer were required to pay social-security contributions as if the job were full-time. The labour laws of 1980 and 1984 called for the principle of equality and proportionality between full-time and part-time work in rights conferred by the social-security system and the existence of a written '*contrato de trabajo a tiempo parcial*' (Kravaritou-Manitakis 1988). In 1994 legislation was introduced to remove the legal impediments to part-time. The rights of some part-timers were reduced by the legislation: if the working time was less than 12 hours per week, the worker had no right to unemployment benefit or transitory illness payments. This has now been amended by the April 1997 agreement with the introduction of equal social-security treatment between full-time and part-time workers who work fewer than 12 hours per week.

3 Adam and Canziani (1998) found that between 1987 and 1996 on average 76 per cent of fixed-term contract workers find themselves in a precarious situation from one year to the next, with only 14 per cent on average gaining a permanent contact one year later.

4 New permanent contracts were introduced with reduced severance payments and social-security contributions and support was also provided for converting certain types of temporary jobs into permanent ones, for example through apprenticeship and practical training contracts.

5 However, the turnover of fixed-term contracts is striking. In 1998, new contracts with a duration of one month represented 58 per cent of the total number of contracts and those with a duration of less than three months represented 82 per cent (ibid.). In 1995 the proportion of temporary workers with contracts below 3 months was 37 per cent, by 1999 the proportion was 46 per cent (Ferreiro and Serrana 2001: 48).

6 The increase in part-time employment has been in the service sector, in retail, teleworking, fast food, care services as well as more traditional services such as cleaning and domestic work, hotels and catering (EIRO June 2001).

7 Evidence from the European Labour Force Survey 1996 showed that only 3.7 per cent of female part-timers in Spain gave as their reason 'did not want a full-time job', compared with an average of 65.9 per cent of part-time women in the EU15 countries who gave this reason (Eurostat 1997).

8 This compares with a gap of 19 percentage points and 18 percentage points in the UK and Sweden respectively (EIRO Jan. 2002).

9 As explained in Chapter 3 poverty is associated with inactivity, retirement and unemployment (mainly because of the low levels of benefits).

10 For example, in 1964 there were 17 women for every 100 male public employees. By 1991 this figure had increased to 70/100 and for the age group 25–29 years there were 105 female public employees to every 100 male employees (Moreno 1998). Between 1980 to 1991 women also increased their share of medical professional jobs from 23 to 37 per cent, accountancy jobs from 11 to 21 per cent, legal professional jobs from 7 to 22 per cent and university professional jobs from 21 to 28 per cent (Rubery and Fagan 1995).

11 While there was an increase of more than 300,000 jobs in the public sector as a whole (excluding public enterprises) between 1990 and 1997 there has been no further growth in central government since 1997. In order to restrain

current outlays and achieve Maastricht convergence criteria, central government only replaced one out of every four permanent positions lost by retirement or quits (OECD 2000). As a consequence there has been a decline of more than 10 per cent in central government and social-security administration since 1997.

12 Toharia (1997), analysing data from the Spanish Labour Force Survey (EPA) since 1977, found that, despite the very high increase in unemployment since then, 60 per cent of the unemployed lived in households where at least one person worked. There was a small proportion who lived in households where no one was in receipt of pensions or unemployment benefits (since 1987 less than 10 per cent of the unemployed). However, this proportion has increased since 1992 due to cutbacks in unemployment compensation although it was still less than 10 per cent in 1996. As Toharia suggests, the households provides an important safety net for the unemployed (and one could add for those on fixed-term contracts and in informal work) and provides an explanation for the lack of significant social tensions.

References

Adam, P. and Canziani (1998) 'Partial de-regulation: fixed-term contracts in Italy and Spain', Centre for Economic Performance, London: London School of Economics, Discussion Paper 386.

Alberdi, I. (ed.) (1995) *Informe sobre la situación de la familia en España*, Madrid: Ministerio de Asuntos Sociales.

Baylina, M. and García-Ramon, M.D. (1998) 'Homeworking in rural Spain: a gender approach', *European Urban and Regional Studies*, 5 (1): 55–64.

Bruegel, I. and Perrons, D. (1996) *Deregulation and Women's Employment: The Diverse Experience of Women in Britain*, London: Gender Institute, London School of Economics.

Bulletin No. 5 and No. 6 (1995) *Bulletin on Women and Employment in the EU*, European Commission Director-General for Employment, Industrial Relations and Social Affairs, Brussels.

Carrasco, C., Alabart, A., Mayordomo, M. and Montagut, T. (1997) *Mujeres, Trabajo y Políticas Sociales: Una aproximación al Caso Español*, Ministerio de Trabajo y Asuntos Sociales, Instituto de la Mujer 51.

Carrasquer, P. (2001) 'Precarious employment and gender inequality': http://www.eiro.eurofound.ie./2001/09/Features/ES109201F.html.

Cousins, C. (1994) 'A comparison of the labour market position of women in Spain and the UK with reference to the "flexible" labour debate', *Work, Employment and Society*, 8 (1): 45–67.

Cousins, C. (1999a) 'Changing regulatory frameworks and "non-standard employment" in Europe' in A. Felstead and N. Jewman (eds) *Global Trends in Flexible Labour*, London: Macmillan.

Cousins, C. (1999b) *Society, Work and Welfare in Europe*, London: Macmillan.

Cruz Cantero, P. (1995) *Percepción social de la familia española*, Madrid: Centro de Investigaciones Sociológicas.

De Ussel, J.I. (1995) 'Trabajo y Familia en España', *Revista Internacional de Sociología*, 11 (May–August): 171–198.

Duncan, S. (1995) 'Theorising European gender systems', *Journal of European Social Policy*, 5 (4): 263–284.

EIRO (April 2000) 'Wage discrimination against women and temporary workers': http://www.eiro.eurofound.ie./2000/04/InBrief/ES000428ln.html.

EIRO (June 2001) 'Spain: part-time employment examined': http://www.eiro.eurofound.ie/2001/06/feature/es0106245f.html.

EIRO (Jan. 2002) 'Comparative study of gender pay equity: the case of Spain': http://www.eiro.eurofound.ie./2002/01/word/ES0110201s.doc.

EIRO (Feb. 2002) 'Spain: unemployment rises again': http://www.eiro.eurofound.ie./2002/01/Features/ES0201209F.html.

EIRO (Sept. 2002a) 'Comparative study on low wage workers and the working poor: the case of Spain', http://www.eiro.eurofound.ie./2002/08/word/ES0205109s.doc.

EIRO (Sept. 2002b) 'National minimum wage is among lowest in EU': http://www.eiro.eurofound.ie/2002/09InBrief/ES0209202Nhtml.

Employment in Europe (2001, 2003) DG for Employment, Industrial Relations and Social Affairs, Office for Official Publications of the European Communities, Luxembourg.

EPA (1998) *Encuesta de Población Activa*, Madrid: Instituto Nacional de Estadística.

Esping-Andersen, G. (ed.) (1996) *Welfare States in Transition: National Adaptations in Global Economies*, London: Sage.

Esping-Andersen, G. (ed.) (1997) 'Do the spending and finance structures matter?' in W. Beck *et al.* (eds) *The Social Quality of Europe*, Bristol: Policy Press.

Esping-Andersen, G. (1999) *Social Foundations of Post-industrial Economies*, Oxford: Oxford University Press.

Eurostat (1997) *Labour Force Survey 1996*, Luxembourg: Office for Official Publications of the European Communities.

Fagan, C. and O'Reilly, J. (1998) 'Conceptualising part-time work: the value of an integrated comparative perspective' in J. O'Reilly and C. Fagan (eds) *Part-time Prospects: An International Comparison of Part-time Work in Europe, North America and the Pacific Rim*, London: Routledge.

Ferreiro, J. and Serrana, F. (2001) 'The Spanish labour market: reforms and consequences', *International Review of Applied Economics*, 15 (1): 31–53.

García-Ramón, A.M.D. and Ortíz, A. (2000) 'The fixed-term contract, the Spanish route to flexibility? Women in the retail sector in the Barcelona region', *Economic and Industrial Democracy*, 21 (3): 311–333.

Garrido, J.G. (1992) *Las Dos Biografias de la Mujer en España*, Instituto de la Mujer, 33, Madrid: Ministerio de Asuntos Sociales.

González López, M.J. (1997) *Do Modern Welfare States Foster Democratic Family Arrangements? Comparative Case Studies of Britain and Spain*, London School of Economics, Gender Institute, Working Paper Series, Issue 2.

Gregg, P. and Wadsworth, J. (1996) *It Takes Two: Employment Polarisation in the OECD*, Discussion Paper No. 304 Centre for Economic Performance, London: London School of Economics.

Gregson, N., Simonsen, K. and Vaiou, D. (1999) 'The meaning of work: some arguments for the importance of culture within formulations of work in Europe', *European Urban and Regional Studies*, 6 (3): 197–214.

Guillén, A.M. (1997) 'Regímenes de Bienestar y Roles Familiares: un Análisis del Caso Español', *Papers: Revista de Sociología*, 53: 45–63.

Hantrais, L. (2000) 'From equal pay to reconciliation of employment and family life' in L. Hantrais (ed.) *Gendered Policies in Europe: Reconciling Employment and Family Life*, London: Macmillan.

Hirdmann, Y. (1990) 'Genussystemet' in Statens Offentliga Utredningar, *Demokrati och Makt i Sverige*, Stockholm: SOU.

Hirdmann, Y. (1998) 'State policy and gender contracts: the Swedish experience' in E. Drew, R. Emerek and E. Mahan (eds) *Women, Work and the Family in Europe*, London: Routledge.

Jimeno, J. and Toharia, L. (1994) *Unemployment and Labour Market Flexibility: Spain*, Geneva: ILO.

Kravaritou-Manitakis, Y. (1988) *New Forms of Work: Labour Law and Social Security Aspects in the European Community*, Luxembourg: European Foundation for the Improvement of Living and Working Conditions.

Moltó, M.L (1996) *Trends and Prospects for Women's Employment in the 1990s in Spain*, Spanish Report for the EC Network Women and Employment Equal Opportunities Unit DGV Commission of the European Union.

Moltó, M.L. and Domingo, T. (1998) *Women and the Labour Market in the Southern Countries*, València: Institut Universitari d'Estudis de la Dona, Universitat de València.

Moreno, L. (1998) 'Safety net in southern Europe', paper presented to the 2nd International Research Conference on Social Security, Jerusalem, January.

OECD (1998) *Employment Outlook*, June, Paris: OECD.

OECD (2000) *Economic Survey: Spain*, Paris: OECD.

Ostner, I. and Lewis, J. (1995) 'Gender and the evolution of European social policies' in S. Leibfried and P. Pierson (eds) *European Social Policy: Between Fragmentation and Integration*, Washington, DC: The Brookings Institution.

Perez-Diaz, V. and Rodriguez, J.C. (1995) 'Inertial choices: an overview of Spanish human resources, practices and policies' in R. Locke *et al.* (eds) *Employment Relations in a Changing World Economy*, Cambridge, MA: The MIT Press.

Perrons, D. and Gonas, L. (1998) 'Introduction: perspectives on gender inequality in European Employment', *European Urban and Regional Studies*, 5 (1): 1–12.

Pfau-Effinger, B. (1993) 'Modernisation, culture and part-time employment: the example of Finland and West Germany', *Work, Employment and Society*, 7 (3): 383–410.

Pfau-Effinger, B. (1998) 'Culture or structure as explanations of differences in part-time work in Germany, Finland and the Netherlands?' in J. O'Reilly and C. Fagan (eds) *Part-time Prospects: An International Comparison of Part-time Work in Europe, North America and the Pacific Rim*, London: Routledge.

Rubery, J. and Fagan, C. (1995) 'Gender segregation in societal context', *Work, Employment and Society*, 9 (2): 213–240.

Rubery, J. and Fagan, C. (1994) 'Does feminisation mean a flexible labour force?' in R. Hyman and A. Ferner (eds) *New Frontiers in European Industrial Relations*, Oxford: Blackwell.

Rubery, J., Smith, M., Fagan, C. and Grimshaw, D. (1998) *Women and European Employment*, London: Routledge.

Ruivo, M., Do Pilar González, M. and Varejão, J.M. (1998) 'Why is part-time work so low in Portugal and Spain?' in J. O'Reilly and C. Fagan (eds) *Part-time Prospects: An International Comparison of Part-time Work in Europe, North America and the Pacific Rim*, London: Routledge.

Solsana, M. (1996) 'La segunda transición demográfica desde la perspectiva de género' in M. Solsana (ed.) *Desigualidades de Género en los Viejos y los Nuevos Hogares*, Instituto de la Mujer, Madrid: Ministerio de Asuntos Sociales.

Threlfall, M. (2000) 'European employment: a new approach to analysing trends', *European Journal of Social Quality*, 2 (2): 13–50.

Tobío, C. (2001) 'Working and mothering: women's strategies in Spain', *European Societies*, 3 (3): 339–372.

Toharia, L. (1997) *Labour Market Studies: Spain*, report prepared for European Commission Directorate General for Employment, Industrial Relations and Social Affairs.

Vaiou, D. and Stratigaki, M. (1997) 'Women in the south: diverse experiences of work in a unifying Europe' in A.G. Dijkstra and J. Plantenga (eds) *Gender and Economics: A European Perspective*, London: Routledge.

8   The changing roles of men in families in Spain

Celia Valiente

Introduction

Dramatic changes in gender relations, particularly the position occupied by men within families, have taken place over the last few decades in most western societies, with developments along two main dimensions. Firstly, 'the general movement away from paternal authority as a major organising principle in family life' (O'Brien 1995: 48), which has had consequences both for family law and for relations among family members. Parental authority is now attributed to both parents and not just the father as was previously the case, and family life is currently based much less on wives' and children's obedience to husbands/fathers and more on dialogue and negotiation between family members. Secondly, some men's role in the family is no longer restricted to that of breadwinner, which has led to changes in public policy and family relations. Some policies now recognise fathers' caring functions and allow or encourage them to take paternal leave, such as in Sweden (Bergqvist and Jungar 2000), and what is more, men's vision of fathering has begun to change. A significant number of fathers have come to see their function as entailing more than simply being the material provider. These men wish to be nurturers, companions, playmates and role models for their children (Cohen 1993: 12; O'Brien and Jones 1996: 135). The bonds between some fathers and their children have become closer than in the past, and the time fathers spend in caring work (and domestic tasks) has increased somewhat in recent decades in countries such as the United States (Ishii-Kuntz 1993: 48; Pleck 1993: 219–220) and the United Kingdom (O'Brien 1992: 178).

Although these changes in the position of men within families consti-tute a broad, cross-national tendency, significant variations exist among western countries at least in terms of the extent of such a transformation. In this chapter we look at the Spanish case, analysing how far it illustrates prevailing trends between 1975 and 2000. We conclude that the first dimension of this transformation – the shift away from exclusively paternal authority – has clearly already taken place in Spain. In contrast, it is far from obvious that the second dimension of change – the move towards a model of fatherhood in which the man's role is not restricted to breadwinning – has advanced as far as in other countries. The first part of the chapter describes the diminishing importance of the principle of paternal authority in the organisation of family life in Spain. The second examines the persistence of the idea that breadwinning is men's sole family obligation. Finally, the third discusses the reasons why only very timid changes have actually taken place in the position of men as breadwinners. Secondary sources and results of surveys constitute the main data used.

The fading of men's authority within the family

Paternal authority is no longer one of the fundamental principles of family law in Spain. Generally speaking, men and women are now treated equally in family law. Firstly, both now have equal obligations and rights within marriage, unlike in the past when the principle of inequality between spouses was embedded in family law.[1] For instance, until 1975, article 57 of the Civil Code (CC), which is the main legal source for the study of family obligations and rights, established that husbands had to protect their wives, whilst wives had to obey their husbands. Moreover, many married women's civil rights were not recognised; for example, until 1975 married women needed their husbands' permission to sign a job contract or engage in trade. Secondly, men and women now also have the same obligations and rights with respect to their children, since parental authority is held by both parents and not just by the father, as was previously the case.[2]

If paternal authority over family life were still legitimate both in principle and in practice, many citizens would agree with the following propositions: important family decisions should mainly be taken by the father rather than by other family members; children must obey and respect their fathers rather than trust them; fathers should treat their offspring strictly; fathers ought to issue orders to their children rather than reason with them; and fathers have the right to punish their sons and daughters in order to discipline them. But as will be seen below, this is not the case. Studies have shown that paternal authority is no longer the ideal nor the *de facto* major organising principle of family life for much of the Spanish population.

In terms of ideals, a survey of males aged 18–65 years carried out in 1987 is very revealing: 52 per cent of respondents disagreed with the statement that 'men have exclusive responsibility for exercising authority within the family', though a large minority of 40 per cent still supported the idea (INNER 1988: 55). Other studies have shown that younger people are more likely to reject such traditional conceptions of family life. For example a 1992 survey of young people of both sexes aged 15–29 found that as many as 77 per cent of respondents disagreed with a similar statement (Navarro and Mateo 1993: 123).

Many people think that family decisions should not be taken by the father alone, but by both parents acting together with their children. A 1990 poll of adults of both sexes asked the question: 'from what age should children's opinions be taken into account regarding important family decisions, such as a change of residence or choosing a holiday?' 20 per cent of respondents answered 'always', meaning at any age; 49 per cent replied that they should be taken into account between the age of 10 to 16; while only 19 per cent felt that their opinions should only count from age 18 onwards. A tiny minority of 2 per cent thought that children's opinions should never be considered (Juste *et al.* 1991: 123).

Furthermore, obedience ceased to be the quality most appreciated in children quite some time ago. Already by 1975, 67 per cent of adult respondents of both sexes thought that 'it was more important for children to trust rather than respect their parents' (De Pablo 1976: 386). So it was not surprising to find that by 1990 only 5 per cent of adults of either sex considered obedience to be one of the three most important virtues that children ought to be taught at home. The majority of respondents preferred other very different qualities: good manners, a sense of responsibility and tolerance, in that order (Alberdi *et al.* 1994: 143–144).

In terms of the realities of family life (as reported by survey respondents), other family members other than the father – namely wives and children – participate extensively in family decision-making (Alberdi *et al.* 1994: 90–91; Alvira *et al.* 1994: 32–33, 104; Meil 1999: 75–80). In an important 1989 survey of Spanish parents and the population in general (henceforth '1989 survey'), parents were asked to reveal who took decisions in their family. In 81 per cent of cases, decisions affecting the whole family were either taken by both parents, either alone or with their children, whereas decisions affecting were taken by an even larger proportion of the sample: 84 per cent (Aguinaga and Comas 1991: 191).

In fact, a large part of the population believes that there are a number of areas in which a father should not decide for his children. The 1989 survey showed many people believed that children and teenagers should take certain decisions on their own, such as choosing their clothes, holidays, studies, managing pocket money, smoking and drinking alcohol, starting from an age range of between 11 and 15 (Aguinaga and Comas 1991: 139). Such opinions made a stark contrast with those expressed in 1975. At that time there was widespread support for parental control over a number of important aspects of children's lives. For example, 56 per cent of those interviewed thought that 'parents should administer the money earned by their children' [emphasis added], though the question did not ask until what age; whilst 68 per cent even believed that 'parents should control their children's friendships' (De Pablo 1976).

Attitudes changed so rapidly that already by the 1989 survey Spanish parents were reporting that they were much less strict with their daughters and sons than their own parents had been: as many as 74 per cent of parents thought that they were 'not strict' or 'not very strict' with their offspring, with only 23 per cent of parents believing that they were 'very' or 'rather' strict (Aguinaga and Comas 1991: 185). Interestingly, in the more informal context of discussion groups organised prior to the 1989 survey, parents also expressed the view that raising children was more complicated nowadays than in the past, since they were now obliged to justify their orders and explain their decisions to their kids (Aguinaga and Comas 1991: 44–45).

Many Spaniards think that dialogue and reasoning as opposed to imposition and coercion constitute the best way to bring up children. In a 1990 survey of adults of both sexes, 85 per cent of respondents agreed with the sentence 'dialogue is the best means of ensuring that children understand'. But these declarations of support for dialogue and communication should be taken with a pinch of salt, since a large number of adults also supported the use of punishment (of the 'light' corporal type) when necessary. Half of all respondents (51 per cent) still agreed with the statement 'children should be taught to obey from a young age, even if this is done through punishment' and as many as 65 per cent agreed that 'a smack in time prevents more serious problems'. Similarly, while most parents no longer believed in the effectiveness of punishment (only 45 per cent disagreed with the assertion that 'punishment achieves nothing with children'), 55 per cent still thought that teachers should have the right to punish their pupils (Juste *et al.* 1991: 110, 118). Finally, anecdotal evidence that parents in Spain continue to resort to punishment comes from that fact that it is still possible (although increasingly rare) to see parents spanking or otherwise physically punishing their children in public, such as in the street or in the park.

Nonetheless, children themselves confirm that patterns of authority in family life are now largely based on communication. A 1992 survey of children aged 8–14 living in seven major cities reported that 61 per cent of children believed that, by and large, 'parents do not punish their children very much'. Referring to their own families, 71 per cent said that their parents were not very strict with them and that 'my parents normally punish me when I deserve it'. Equally, a large majority (68 per cent) reported that their parents respected their opinions when they differed from their own (Pérez *et al.* 1993: 59–64). Despite this trend towards better communication between parents and their children, a minority of kids lived in families in which arbitrary and recurrent punishment was the norm, and where children do not trust their parents enough to talk to them about a range of important subjects. Twenty-one per cent of children declared that, as a rule, parents punished children a lot; 14 per cent of children that their parents punished them without good reason; and 12 per cent that their parents were too strict with them. Thirteen per cent did not even dare to talk with their parents (Pérez *et al.* 1993: 59–64). Another source, from 1991, found that only 5 per cent of children (one in every 20 who lived in a family with two parents or a widowed parent and at least one child under 16) agreed with the statement 'I think that my parents smack and punish me too much' (Alvira *et al.* 1994: 66). The picture is, on the whole, encouraging, and shows that male authority has waned and that most fathers have found less punitive ways of expressing themselves.

More than just the breadwinner?

Men's legal family obligations

The Spanish legal system establishes women and men's equal obligation to support and care for family members. Both spouses have equal responsibility for helping each other financially, physically and psychologically, as well as for contributing to support the household to the best of their abilities. Both parents, whether biological or adoptive, have the same legal duty to support and care for their children, as well as the right to 'correct' their children (a softer word than 'punish') reasonably and in moderation.

Both parents retain the same duties after separation or divorce. If such a separation or divorce leaves one partner financially much worse off than the other, the more affluent parent must pay alimony to the poorer one. Responsibility for maintaining and caring for children falls to both biological and adoptive parenthood independently of their civil status, and consequently the duty of care is not extinguished after separation or divorce either.

Men's attitudes towards domestic and caring tasks

So much for the law. Attitudes may of course be a wholly different matter. In fact, men's (and women's) attitudes towards domestic and caring tasks have substantially changed in western countries in recent years, with many men and women now thinking that household duties should be shared (Haas 1993: 238). The same can be said for Spain. Back in 1975 the majority of Spaniards thought these tasks were entirely women's responsibility of women, yet by the late 1980s this was no longer the case. Thus in 1975, we find 81 per cent of men and an even larger proportion of women (83 per cent) agreeing with the statement 'household chores are for the woman; only in the case of the wife's illness should the husband do them' (De Pablo 1976: 378). Similarly a 1977 survey of young people aged 15–20 found that only 25 per cent of boys and 19 per cent of girls agreed with the idea that 'men and women should share domestic tasks equally' (Linz 1978: 113), meaning that the whole lot could safely be left to women. In contrast, only a decade later a 1987 survey of Spanish men aged 18–65 found that fewer than half (46 per cent) of respondents went along with the statement 'household chores are women's tasks', while even more (49 per cent) actively disagreed, especially the younger and more educated respondents, and, revealingly, men married to working women also disagreed that their wives should do all the chores (INNER 1988: 23–25). By 1995, a majority of Spanish adults of both sexes (60 per cent) disagreed with the proposition 'man's duty is to earn money; woman's duty is to take care of home and family' (CIS 1995),[3] showing that the notion of clearly separate spheres, so energetically revived and exalted in the Franco era, has today lost credence to a more complex view of household arrangements.

In fact such changes in people's view of the desirable division of household labour can be related, at least in the case of the younger generation, to their understanding of what makes marriage successful, or at least prevents it disintegrating. By the 1990s large majorities of 15–29-year-olds of both sexes (79 per cent of men and 89 per cent of women) considered that the sharing of household duties was one of the key factors for the success of a couple, coming third place after fidelity and a satisfactory sexual relationship in the hierarchy of recipes for success (Navarro and Mateo 1993: 118–120).

Men's time, women's time

Of course, what is crucial in addition to attitudes towards family life, domestic chores and caring is the actual amount of time that men are willing to spend on all this in practice. Much evidence from other countries suggests that there is quite a gap between what men think and what they do (Haas 1993: 238, 249), with time-use studies being the tool whereby such discrepancies have been revealed. As these are a relatively recent development in Spain, it is impossible to know the real extent of change in this respect, though on the whole it is thought that the trend is positive: men really are more involved in caring and domestic tasks than they were (INNER 1988: 34; Menéndez 1994: 89).

But if the exact time spent on family life is measured, all the time-use studies point to a persistently large gender difference. Time spent each day on chores traditionally performed by women (cooking, cleaning the house, washing and cleaning, grocery shopping, sewing and childcare) was 1 hour and 6 minutes by employed men, 4 hours and 48 minutes by employed women, and 6 hours and 12 minutes by housewives, showing that when women went out to work, they incurred a double burden of tasks. But the overall burden was to some extent counter-balanced by the activities traditionally performed by men (repairs to the house and to cars, driving family and work vehicles, paperwork and accounts), on which men spent 1 hour and 42 minutes, employed women 30 minutes, and housewives only 6 minutes (OTR/IS 1988: 16, 24). All in all, though, women, whether they were working at home or outside, ended up contributing considerably more time to the household than men – almost five hours a day on average (Durán 1987; INNER 1988: 23–38; Izquierdo *et al.* 1988: 29–48; Ramos 1990, 1994; Carrasco 1991: 111–150; Menéndez 1994: 89; Alberdi 1995;

Tobío 1995: 57–60; Álvaro 1996). Therefore the gender division in the use of time is particularly intense.

One of the issues in this regard is that part-time work is uncommon, so that most women who work outside the home do so on a full-time basis.[4] That is part of the explanation of why they end up with a double shift. But let us also take into account that men do not spend that much time at work: the same 1987 time-use study found that the average time spent in waged work by working men, working women and housewives was, respectively, 4 hours and 48 minutes, 4 hours, and 12 minutes; while the additional time spent in 'matters related to work performed outside working hours' was, respectively, 1 hour and 6 minutes, 42 minutes, and 0 minutes (OTR/IS 1988: 49). This reminds us that not all men fit the image of the hard-working male provider; many are studying, retired or unemployed but still do not do much housework.

The picture did not alter much over the coming decade. When all working hours, whether professional or domestic, were added up, women's overall burden in 1996 was considerably more onerous than men's: 8 hours and 58 minutes per day in contrast to men's 6 hours and 15, despite the latter devoting more time to paid work. Izquierdo *et al.* (1988: 97) make the insightful point that this gender difference makes men as a whole dependent on women's work, while women as a whole are *not dependent on men's work but men's income* because men's working hours are mostly paid. Rather than a simple paradox, this situation is a manifestation of women's exploitation by men in our society. It has also been suggested that the gender difference in the use of time is detrimental to women's health (Izquierdo and Martí 1992), though one has to acknowledge their greater longevity.

In short, despite men's increasingly favourable attitude towards sharing domestic chores and care with women, a clear-cut division of labour along gender lines still exists within most Spanish families. Wages from work outside the home represent the main (or almost only) way in which a large number of men contribute to family life, whilst women devote much more time than men to household and caring tasks whether they are bringing in a wage or not. The next part will consider possible explanations for the persistence of this gendered division of labour.

Spanish men's breadwinner role: an interpretation

Several explanations can be offered to explain the persistence of bread-winning as the main or exclusive family function of Spanish men, based on the different position of men and women in the labour market; men's lack of domestic and caring skills as a result of their upbringing and training; the negative image of domestic work; the widespread assumptions regarding the lesser importance of female employment; the centrality of mother-care for small children; and the absence of public policies to encourage, not just enable, men to become more involved in caring work.

Beginning with the labour market, the gender gap in activity and employment rates is greater in Spain than in other western countries. The proportion of employed women in Spain remains low. To illustrate this, I will focus on the situation of women of either under 45 or over 50, since there are great variations to be found by age groups (see also Chapter 8).

The great majority of women over the age of 45/50 in Spain remain full-time housewives. Their husbands mostly spend a significant part of their time working outside the home. The women specialised many years ago in care work and housework, performed with little or no help from other members of the household, whether husbands, children or relatives. If they were ever in it, they abandoned the labour market a decade or two ago. Given high unemployment rates, their chances of returning to employment are slim. Thus they are in a weak position from which to negotiate any alteration to the traditional division of labour in the household.

The picture is of course rather different for later generations of women where a majority are active, whether employed or still seeking work. Many will not stop working after marriage and childbirth, and the consensus is increasingly that household chores should be shared by the couple. At the same time, a not-so-hidden revolution has taken place in parental attitudes towards girls' education with parents investing similar amounts of expectations and resources into their sons' and daughters' education (Escario *et al.* 1987: 49; Aguinaga and Comas 1991: 181–183) and no longer believing in the traditional idea that boys needed be educated for a career whilst girls could just be trained for marriage (De Pablo 1976: 378). Even more importantly, parents have behaved in a manner consistent with their egalitarian beliefs, so that most young women are now as qualified as the men of their generation and social class.

So why is it then that most young men still play only a very small role in housework and care compared to their partners? In part, it reflects their continued lack of domestic skills arising from a privileged upbringing. For in spite of receiving a similar education, daughters and sons are still treated differently at home: daughters are required to help with household and caring tasks to a greater degree than sons (De Zárraga 1985: 60–61; Escario *et al.* 1987: 104–106; INNER 1988: 37; Navarro and Mateo 1993: 125–126; Pérez *et al.* 1993: 67–69; Finkel 1997: 72–80). Sons are still not taught the skills required to run a household.

Paradoxically, such gender inequality in the practice of domestic skills and chores has lasted longer in Spain than in other western countries, not least because a larger proportion of young adults live with their parents until their mid- or late-twenties. In 1996, as many as 77 per cent of young people aged 15–29 lived at home – even 53 per cent of those aged 25–29 did so (Ministerio de Trabajo 2000). Even daughters did more housework than fathers (Finkel 1997: 72–80). And where the participation of fathers in household tasks was limited, that of their adult sons was even more reduced (INNER 1988: 37).

Furthermore, most young people in Spain only leave their parents' home to marry and form a new household, and when they do, only the women have any domestic skills – though not as many as in the past. Therefore it is entirely up to the young woman to 'teach' her partner, who is often reluctant and needs a great deal of persuasion to contribute to domestic work. This often leads to rows between the couple and later with the children. Time-use studies suggest that young women are to some extent successful in persuading their partners to help them with (rather than share) household duties, since a larger proportion of young men (mainly those aged 25–35) do actually participate in these activities (INNER 1988: 36).

But the point is that pressure from female partners is the main factor encouraging Spanish men to learn domestic skills and perform household tasks. A study of individual parents who were members of the parents' association at their children's primary and secondary state schools found that 30 per cent of fathers and 54 per cent of mothers said that 'men performed household and caring duties only when women demanded them to do so' in their own cases (Finkel 1997: 92).

In fact, young Spanish men have never had it so good. On the one hand, they live with their parents where they are relieved of the obligation to do housework and deprived of the opportunity to acquire domestic skills since their mothers do it all for them until they get married. On the other, while in other western countries, high rates of divorce put many men under 'structural pressures to do housework' either as a threat or because they no longer have a partner to do it for them (Fassinger 1993: 195), Spain's low divorce rates reflect the fact that few men find themselves forced to learn.[5]

Additionally, in trying to 'teach' or encourage their partners, young women are up against widespread negative images of domestic work, common societal assumptions about the lesser importance of female employment and the belief that maternal care for small children is crucial. Spaniards consider domestic tasks to be tedious, repetitive and uninteresting (Escario *et al.* 1987: 68; Institut d'Estudis Metropolitans de Barcelona 1995: 127; Finkel 1997), so it is not surprising that anyone who has not been brought up to do this work tries to resist becoming involved in it. In fact, there is even a trend among those who have (namely daughters) to try to give up housework as well (Escario *et al.* 1987: 104–105).

As to women's employment, many Spaniards still see it as a voluntary activity that provides women with a supplementary income ('pin-money'), social relations or even entertainment. A study of attitudes towards family change based on discussion groups of middle-class men aged 18–50 living in four large cities concluded that listening to men talking about their wives' jobs one would think that they were talking about some privileged group who spent their time in the most pleasant and amusing jobs surrounded by a great work atmosphere. The hours were short, and far from being tired after work their wives came home happy and ready to do all the housework waiting for them (Escario *et al.* 1987: 53). In contrast, men's employment was seen as essential rather than an option. They were under an obligation to provide the family's main income (Alberdi *et al.* 1984: 49; INNER 1988: 51–52). Indeed, a significant proportion of Spaniards still thought that married women should not chose to work if it was not strictly necessary: 46 per cent of respondents to a 1990 survey disagreed with the statement 'a married woman has to work even if her salary is not completely necessary for the support of her family' (Alberdi *et al.* 1994: 117). As in other respects, the younger the people are, the higher their level of education, and if they are married to working women, the less frequently they express such views, but nonetheless, because women's employment is still seen as an option and sometimes even as a bad choice, women find it difficult to persuade their partners to do a greater share of domestic chores by arguing that they also have jobs (Escario *et al.* 1987: 46–64).

As to child-rearing, it is commonly assumed that a mother's care is essential during the first years of the child's life at least, that women have natural instincts for caring that men lack and therefore that fathers may help but should not share the task on an equal basis (De Pablo 1976: 377–382; Iglesias 1984: 8–10; Escario *et al.* 1987: 84–88; INNER 1988: 54; Aguinaga and Comas 1991: 33). Evidently, all these beliefs are obstacles to the involvement of fathers in child care. Such ideas explain why many Spaniards believe that mothers' full-time employment jeopardises the upbringing of small children (De Pablo 1976: 375–376; Escario *et al.* 1987: 55; INNER 1987: 54; Juste *et al.* 1991: 38–39). A 1990 survey showed 55 per cent of adults of both sexes agreeing with the statement 'it is probable that a child under six suffers if her/his mother works'. But when the question referred to children of any age, there was greater acceptance of working mothers: in fact 61 per cent agreed with the statement 'a working mother can have as warm and safe a relationship with her children as a housewife' (Alberdi *et al.* 1994: 98–101). Nevertheless, the idea that female employment is detrimental for small children discourages women, for a number of years at least, from committing to waged work in order to play a pivotal role in child care, which, in turn, also distances fathers from care work.

It is in this context that the profound Spanish mistrust of any 'institutionalisation' of children should be understood. Many parents view childcare centres as one of the least preferable options for their children, especially if they are under three, if not afterwards as well. Mother care is the preferred option. When the mother cannot stay home night and day to take care of her youngster, the second preference is for another woman to replace the working mother at home, mimicking the full-time housewife–mother role. But of course only a minority of couples can afford to pay for a full-time child minder and so many other children are looked after by their grandmothers (Escario *et al.* 1987: 89–94; Aguinaga and Comas 1991: 33–35, 170–172; Juste *et al.* 1991: 43–44; De Miguel 1994: 820). As these are frequently ready and able to look after grandchildren, since most older women are full-time housewives, young couples chose to live close to one of their parents. It can be argued, therefore, that mistrust in the 'institutionalisation' of small children creates incentives for women to remain at home with babies and toddlers while encouraging men to concentrate on breadwinning, especially when a family cannot afford the cost of a childminder or a grandmother is not available.

Is Spain getting its policies right?

Sweden provides the best example of public policies designed to enable people to combine their professional and family duties in a way that successfully promotes men's involvement in family tasks (Bergqvist and Jungar 2000). Some public policies of this type do exist in Spain and, together with other equal opportunities measures, have been characterised as progressive and advanced. In some quarters, it is thought that such policies are well ahead of social practice, and that if the population behaved in accordance with the ideas embedded in policy, Spanish society would be much more egalitarian in gender terms (Instituto de la Mujer 1990: 108; 1993: 27). But there is another set of arguments, such as those made here that, broadly speaking, Spanish policies have allowed but not encouraged men to play a greater role in domestic and caring tasks; that many policies are useless in practice both because they do not provide women with sufficient resources to negotiate the distribution of these tasks with their partners; and because they stigmatise men who want to perform the role of nurturing fathers.

A common element of most Spanish programmes intended to help citizens to make their work and family responsibilities compatible is that they may be taken advantage of either by the mother or the father. Very few programmes provide benefits that are lost if fathers do not take them up, being specifically designed for them. Consequently, the overwhelming majority of people 'benefiting' from these measures are women. This is the case of two of the most important of these measures, maternity leave and child-feeding breaks. Working mothers who have made social-security contributions through employment for at least 180 days within the five years preceding childbirth are entitled to 16 uninterrupted weeks of paid maternity leave. Working mothers decide when to take this leave (before and/or after childbirth), with the only condition that 6 weeks have to be taken after delivery. The level (which is proportional to the salary) and period of social-security contributions are used to calculate the so-called regulatory base. The amount of money received during paid maternity leave is 100 per cent of the regulatory base. The mother is also guaranteed the right to return to her job. Since 1989 (Law 3 of 3 March), if both parents work the father may take as many as four of the final weeks of paid parental leave. If the father takes this opportunity, the mother must return to work. If the man does not do so, the mother can remain on paid leave. In 1999 (Act 39 of 5 November), the number of weeks of father's leave was increased from four to ten; in other words he could in theory start to look after the baby only six weeks after the start of the mother's leave. This again suggests that the law is rather in advance of social practice.

There is also provision for unpaid parental leave to care for small children in Spain. It lasts a maximum of three years, beginning from the moment of childbirth. Only one of the parents may take this leave. The beneficiary is guaranteed a return to his/her exact job anytime during the first year and a post 'in the same professional category' (but not necessarily the same job) is guaranteed for the remaining two years. In addition, the period of leave is counted as effectively worked with respect to professional seniority and promotion. As such parental leave can only be taken by one parent, it is not hard to guess which one usually benefits from it.

As for child-feeding breaks, since 1900 working women have had the right to take these during the working day. Since 1989, the father may also take these nursing breaks in the place of the mother if both are working, but the two parents cannot both take them. Nursing breaks consist of either a one-hour break (or two breaks of 30 minutes each), or a reduction of 30 minutes from the working day. These breaks are always considered as time effectively worked.

Do fathers make the most of such opportunities to care? The number of fathers who take maternity/paternity leave is small but not irrelevant. The Spanish quarterly Labour Force Survey provides data broken down by sex of employees who did not work in the 'week of reference' (the week the questionnaire was administered) and the reasons for not working that week are asked. Unsurprisingly, 97 per cent of employees who did not work due to maternity leave (1998, 4th quarter) were women, and the remaining 3 per cent were men (Instituto Nacional de Estadística 1999: 204). No data is available on the number of fathers taking advantage of unpaid parental leave and child-feeding breaks, but it seems likely that the number would be insignificant. Since these measures can be taken either by the mother or the father, employers and most workers of both sexes consider it 'natural' that they should be taken by the mother. As has been shown to be the case in other countries (Pleck 1993: 233), men who take these measures are not only seen as uncommitted to work but also as unmasculine.

The same attitude does not arise in Spain in the case of benefits which are unique to fathers and are lost if not taken by them, the best example being the right to two days off work (at full-pay) in the case of childbirth, serious illness or death of a close relative. (The number of days off rises to four if the worker has to travel to another locality.) These days off do not generally stigmatise the father, since they are considered to be 'his' by right and if he were not to take them the main beneficiary would be seen to be his employer, since the employee is entitled to full pay. In contrast, when time off from work can be taken either by the father or the mother, this possibility is conceived by many employers and workers as 'her' right.

A final point is that the argument that benefits available only to fathers have a greater impact on their involvement in care is only applicable in the case of measures which guarantee full or almost full pay. On average, working men earn higher salaries than women. When father-only benefits are unpaid or paid at a rate well below the full salary, some couples may think that they are losing an important part of the man's salary. They may also decide that this is too high a price to pay for the man's involvement in care work.

Conclusion and future research

This chapter has shown that recent decades have seen profound changes to the average Spanish family. There has been considerable reform to ensure equal rights in marriage and family law. Paternal authority no longer provides the backbone to family life and children have a greater say in their lives. But an overall assessment of the degree of equity in the Spanish family must take into account that there has been little rebalancing of the gender division in household labour. The main or sole household responsibility of many men is to serve as the breadwinner, while women take responsibility for most domestic and care work whether they go out to work or not. The factors which explain why wage-earning constitutes almost the only way in which many men contribute to their families are: the different position of women and men in the labour market; men's lack of domestic skills arising from the different upbringing given to boys and girls; shared societal assumptions regarding the lesser importance of female employment; the priority given to maternal care of small children; and the lack of policies which not only permit but also encourage men to participate in domestic tasks and caring.

In fact – and this has come as something of a surprise – some men, especially the middle-aged and elderly, have seen a reduction in their family responsibilities over the last decades. Traditionally, they were not only supposed to be breadwinners but also the source of authority within the family. By and large, the exercise of this authority required the father's presence and energy, since decisions had to be made for the rest of the members of the household, and men were also responsible for their children's (and wife's) discipline, and were often the only ones who could drive the car. Now some men no longer exercise these forms of authority, without their participation in domestic tasks and care increasing substantially. Thus we come to the stark conclusion that some men are doing less for their families than they used to and are less involved with than in the past. It is not clear whether this is occurring in other countries in the same way.

Spain is even more of an odd case since overall male activity rates are lower than in other countries. For example, the activity rate of 55–59-year-olds was 75 per cent and that of 60–64-year-olds was only 40 per cent (4th quarter 1998; see Table 1). A topic for future research will be the role that inactive men play in their family. Some still maintain the status of providers since they make a financial contribution to the family budget in the form of unemployment or disability benefit, early retirement or redundancy lump sums, or pensions. By contrast, a group of inactive men can be identified who are neither wage-earners nor contribute in any way to the family income. It would be reasonable to assume that one response would be for them to compensate for their loss of status as providers by playing a more active role in domestic and caring tasks. However, our knowledge of both Spain and other countries shows that this is rarely the case.

Another somewhat pessimistic conclusion is that, in some respects, the changes in families described in this chapter have taken place at women's expense. Women have secured a greater role in the exercise of authority in families while keeping their responsibility for housework and care, and some have also gained the opportunity to earn their own income from employment. They have acquired many rights but also an increasing number of responsibilities, while their male partner's family responsibilities have generally been reduced to financial support alone. Together with the rest of the family men have gained a higher family income as a result of women's employment, yet they have not been burdened with new duties. To note this is not to lament a past when women held a subordinate status in families organised around the principle of paternal authority. Rather, it seeks to suggest that men are much more willing to share some rights or duties (to exercise authority within families and earn wages in the labour market) than others (to care for others and perform household tasks). Future research will have to consider how women are managing to cope with so many new and old functions at the same time.

Recent changes in families have also put pressure on other types of men, especially those younger ones who do not want to imitate their fathers or male relatives, but who lack alternative role models. Other studies will have to explain how these 'new' men are inventing 'new' family roles for themselves. Finally, another aspect which requires further research is the question of the way in which paternal authority actually functioned in the past. This chapter started from the assumption that during the last few decades there has been a move away from paternal authority as the formal, institutionalised, organising principle of family life in all western countries. However, in Spain at least, we still do not know how paternal authority was actually exercised. Laws established that husbands/fathers had formal authority within families, but more research is needed in order to gain an understanding of which prerogatives men actually exercised, and which they left to the people in charge of the daily management of the household: women. It is therefore premature to conclude whether gender relations have actually become significantly more equitable than they were before.

Notes

1 An earlier version of this chapter is Valiente (1996). In this chapter, the terms 'spouse', 'husband' and 'wife' are used to refer to married people, not cohabiting partners. Spanish family law does not encompass the latter – with recent, minor exceptions. Cohabitation is much less common in Spain than in other western countries. In 1994, only 3 per cent of people aged 16 and over living as a couple were cohabitees (similar to Ireland and Portugal). This was the second lowest in the European Union (after Italy and Greece, with 2 per cent), significantly lower than the EU average (8 per cent) and that of other member states, such as the United Kingdom (11 per cent) (European Commission 1998: 60).
2 Parental authority encompasses the obligations and rights in respect of children under 18 that the law ascribes to parents because they are deemed responsible for maintaining and caring their children.
3 Other studies corroborated this and similar views (Escario *et al.* 1987: 68; Cruz and Cobo 1991: 142; Juste *et al.* 1991: 27; Navarro and Mateo 1993: 124; Pérez *et al.* 1993: 66–69).
4 In the fourth quarter of 1998, 83 per cent of working women (and 97 per cent of working men) had full-time jobs (calculated by the author from Instituto Nacional de Estadística 1999: 241).
5 In 1995, Spain had the second lowest crude divorce rate in the EU per 1000 population (0.8) after Italy (0.5). The EU average was 1.8 and the UK rate was 2.9 (provisional and estimated figures, European Commission 1998: 63). The crude divorce rate is the ratio of the number of divorces over the mean population in a given year.

References

Aguinaga, J. and Comas, D. (1991) *Infancia y adolescencia: la mirada de los adultos*, Madrid: Ministerio de Asuntos Sociales.
Alberdi, I. (ed.) (1995) *Informe sobre la situación de la familia en España*, Madrid: Ministerio de Asuntos Sociales.
Alberdi, I., Escario, P. and Haimovich, P. (1984) 'Actitudes de las mujeres hacia el cambio familiar', *Revista Española de Investigaciones Sociológicas*, 27: 41–59.
Alberdi, I., Flaquer, L. and Iglesias, J. (1994) *Parejas y matrimonios: actitudes, comportamientos y experiencias*, Madrid: Ministerio de Asuntos Sociales.
Álvaro, M. (1996) *Los usos del tiempo como indicadores de la discriminación entre géneros*, Madrid: Instituto de la Mujer.
Alvira, F., Blanco, F., Sandi, M. and Torres, M. (1994) *Relaciones padres/hijos*, Madrid: Ministerio de Asuntos Sociales.
Bergqvist, C. and Jungar, A. (2000) 'Adaptation or diffusion of the Swedish gender model?' in L. Hantrais (ed.) *Gendered Policies in Europe: Reconciling Employment and Family Life*, 160–179, London: Macmillan.

Carrasco, C. (1991) *El trabajo doméstico y la reproducción social*, Madrid: Instituto de la Mujer.

Centro de Investigaciones Sociológicas (1995) Study Number 2, 194, October, available on 30 November 1999 at: http://www.cis.es/cgi-bin/contenidobin? nest=2194).

Cohen, T.F. (1993) 'What do fathers provide?: Reconsidering the economic and nurturant dimensions of men as parents' in J.C. Hood (ed.) *Men, Work, and the Family*, 1–22, Newbury Park, CA: Sage.

Cruz, P. and Cobo, R. (1991) *Las mujeres españolas: lo privado y lo público*, Madrid: Centro de Estudios Sociológicos.

De Miguel, A. (ed.) (1994) *La sociedad española, 1994–1995*, Madrid: Complutense.

De Pablo, A. (1976) 'La familia española en cambio' in Fundación Foessa (ed.) *Estudios sociológicos sobre la situación social de España*, 345–405, Madrid: Euramérica.

De Zárraga, J.L. (1985) *Informe juventud en España: la inserción de los jóvenes en la sociedad*, Madrid: Instituto de la Juventud.

Durán, M.Á. (ed.) (1987). *De puertas adentro*, Madrid: Instituto de la Mujer.

Escario, P., Alberdi, I. and Berlín, B. (1987) 'Actitudes de los varones ante el cambio familiar: informe de investigación' (unpublished).

European Commission (1998) *Social Portrait of Europe*, Luxembourg: Office for Official Publications of the European Communities.

Fassinger, P.A. (1993) 'Meanings of housework for single fathers and mothers: insights into gender inequality' in J.C. Hood (ed.) *Men, Work, and the Family*, 195–216, Newbury Park, CA: Sage.

Finkel, L. (1997) *El reparto del trabajo doméstico en la familia: la socialización en las diferencias de género*, Madrid: Confederación Española de Asociaciones de Padres y Madres de Alumnos.

Haas, L. (1993) 'Nurturing fathers and working mothers: changing roles in Sweden' in J.C. Hood (ed.) *Men, Work, and the Family*, 238–261, Newbury Park, CA: Sage.

INNER (1988) *Los hombres españoles*, Madrid: Instituto de la Mujer.

Institut d'Estudis Metropolitans de Barcelona (1995) *Las mujeres y el uso del tiempo*, Madrid: Instituto de la Mujer.

Instituto de la Mujer (1990) *I Plan para la Igualdad de Oportunidades de las Mujeres 1988–1990: evaluación*, Madrid: Instituto de la Mujer.

Instituto de la Mujer (1993) *II Plan para la Igualdad de Oportunidades de las Mujeres 1993–1995*, Madrid: Instituto de la Mujer.

Instituto de la Mujer (2000) Survey on the use of time, data available on 16 April 2000 at: http://www.mtas.es/mujer/mcifras/202.htm.

Instituto Nacional de Estadística (1999) *Encuesta de Población Activa: Resultados Detallados, Cuarto Trimestre de 1998*, Madrid: Instituto Nacional de Estadística.

Ishii-Kuntz, M. (1993) 'Japanese fathers: work demands and family roles' in J.C. Hood (ed.) *Men, Work, and the Family*, 46–67, Newbury Park, CA: Sage.

Izquierdo, J., Del Río, O. and Rodríguez, A. (1988) *La desigualdad de las mujeres en el uso del tiempo*, Madrid: Instituto de la Mujer.

Izquierdo, M.J. and Martí, O. (1992) 'Factores socioculturales condicionantes de la salud' in M. De Onís and J. Villar (eds) *La mujer y la salud en España: informe básico*, 3, 153–228, Madrid: Instituto de la Mujer.

Juste, M.G., Ramírez, A. and Barbadillo, P. (1991) *Actitudes y opiniones de los españoles ante la infancia*, Madrid: Centro de Investigaciones Sociológicas.

Linz, J.J. (1978) *Informe de la encuesta sobre la juventud 1977*, Madrid: Instituto de la Juventud.

Meil, G. (1999) *La postmodernización de la familia española*, Madrid: Acento.

Menéndez, S. (1994) 'La implicación del padre en la crianza y la educación de sus hijos: análisis exploratorio con una muestra andaluza' (unpublished).

Ministerio de Trabajo (2000) 16 April: http://www.mtas.es/injuve/estudios/juven-cifras/tablas2.html.

Navarro, M. and Mateo, M.J. (1993) *Informe juventud en España*, Madrid: Instituto de la Juventud.

O'Brien, M. (1992) 'Changing conceptions of fatherhood' in U. Björnberg (ed.) *European Parents in the 1990s: Contradictions and Comparisons*, 171–180, New Brunswick, NJ: Transaction.

O'Brien, M. (1995) 'Fatherhood and family policies in Europe', *Cross-National Research Papers*, 4: 48–56.

O'Brien, M. and Jones, D. (1996) 'The absence and presence of fathers: accounts from children's diaries' in Ulla Björnberg and Anna-Karin Kollind (eds) *Men's Family Relations: Report from an International Seminar*, 135–152, Stockholm and Gothenburg: Almqvist & Wiksell and Gothenburg University.

OTR/IS (1988) 'Síntesis del estudio sobre uso del tiempo desde la doble perspectiva de la conducta masculina y femenina' (unpublished).

Pérez, P.M., Marín, R. and Vázquez, G. (1993) *Los valores de los niños españoles 1992*, Madrid: SM.

Pleck, J.H. (1993) 'Are "family-supportive" employer policies relevant to men?' in J.C. Hood (ed.) *Men, Work, and the Family*, 217–237, Newbury Park, CA: Sage.

Ramos, R. (1990) *Cronos dividido: uso del tiempo y desigualdad entre mujeres y hombres en España*, Madrid: Instituto de la Mujer.

Ramos, R. (1994) 'El trabajo de la mujer desde la perspectiva del uso del tiempo' in Dirección General de la Mujer de la Comunidad Autónoma de Madrid (ed.) *El trabajo desde una perspectiva de género*, 49–67, Madrid: Dirección General de la Mujer de la Comunidad Autónoma de Madrid.

Tobío, C. (1995) 'Formas de supervivencia de las familias: la posición de las familias en la estructura social' in Instituto de Demografía (ed.) *II Jornadas sobre demografía urbana y regional: ponencias y comunicaciones presentadas*, 163–176, Valencia: Instituto de Demografía.

Valiente, C. (1996) 'Men's family roles in post-authoritarian Spain (1975–1995)' in U. Björnberg and A.-K. Kollind (eds) *Men's Family Relations: Report from an International Seminar*, 11–32, Stockholm and Gothenburg: Almquist & Wiksell and Gothenburg University.

9 Conclusion

From progress to resistance?

Monica Threlfall and Christine Cousins

Any book on Spain is tempted to challenge or concur with the famous defensive quip '¡Spain is different!' made by a Francoist Minister during the dictatorship as he vainly struggled to justify the country's lag with respect to accepted European norms of good governance. Subsequent writers played with the idea that Spaniards thankfully no longer had to be so defensive, Spain could now boast of having a 'democracy without adjectives' (to qualify or excuse it). The historian Juan Pablo Fusi suggested Spaniards could enjoy living in a merely normal country.

In this book the comparison with other European states has in fact been deliberately eschewed. Yet the desire to be different need not refer to other countries; it can reflect a people's dream of metamorphosis into a new *civitas* unlike the one incarnated before, a dream of national rebirth and regeneration. Indeed, to escape the past and become like others was the longing of the generation who accomplished the transition to democracy. Therefore the chance of accelerated and profound change away from the past was a constant, even dominant, theme of the Spanish political discourse after the dictator's death. The slogan 'For Change' was so evocative that the PSOE was able to ride to a triumphant victory on the back of it in 1982.

Yet, evocative as it was to many, the change heralded by the politicians in their various guises never carried explicit promises to bring liberation to women. Few political leaders realised at the time how much and how many women longed for another life, and if not for themselves at least for their daughters. So, given this unpromising start of the post-Franco era, it is a credit to the many feminist activists that they persisted in putting injustices to rights, offered tangible progress to women and articulated a new discourse on gender equality so resonant that half the population of Spain heard and the other half began to listen.

What is certain is that Spain *is* now different – undeniably different from before. Much of that difference – as yet unknown and insufficiently acknowledged – has to do with gender, making it necessary to re-read gender into the story of that metamorphosis. After all, Spain has reached 14th from the top on the UN's Gender Empowerment Index that measures the participation of women in political and economic spheres, only a few places behind the US, which is ranked 10th (United Nations 2003). Although this task of gendering the Spanish polity may never be satisfactorily accomplished, we have attempted to make a start. We have traced both the impact of gender struggle on the political life of the transition and the democratic life of parties and parliament, and the gender fault-lines embedded in policy-making and policy implementation, as well as the shifts in gender relations in the labour market and the institutions of social citizenship and social security. The focus has been on the development of, and constraints to, the installation of practices that are more equitable to women and men, and on the problems that have not been tackled or have proved intractable.

A point to note before reaching any overarching conclusions is that the changes have not affected all Spanish women substantially in the same way. The deep cleavages within Spanish society in the mid-1970s meant that the social transformations achieved since then have impacted differently on women and men in the different autonomous communities, in urban and rural areas, and by generation, education and social class. In fact the differences between the generations of women may now be greater than before. Some have gone as far as to use the term 'polarisation' of the experiences of different generations of women and Garrido (1992) spoke of the 'two biographies' of women in which the life experiences of younger and older women had progressively differed. There is, therefore, a new divergence between younger women who now aspire to a continuous full-time employment career path and the full-time homemaking careers of older women. And there is also another fundamental generational gap: that between women of pre- and post-fertile age, between those who are well past the experience of coupledom and motherhood and those who are planning to embark on them, because the latter have gained the key freedom of exercising control over their fertility through birth control, while the former bear a history of fraught pregnancy avoidance or multiple motherhood.

Yet this is not to say that older women have been entirely left behind by the train of modernisation, but rather that they are perhaps travelling in one of the back carriages. As Chapter 3 showed, a basic pension for all was introduced which gives all women a modest entitlement irrespective of their employment history and frees them from the worst indignities of skivvying on into old age. Further, the overall liberalisation of attitudes towards women has granted them much more freedom to go out and about on their own, join social clubs or engage in voluntary work. Even Spain's legion of elderly widows and never-married women have benefited from the re-appraisal of women's skills as enterprising non-governmental organisations search them out for volunteering with needy groups such as released offenders in rehabilitation programmes (Pérez-Lanzac 2002: 106).

There is no doubt that Spanish women made a bid to play a part in the democratisation process and were successful in gaining a foothold in political parties and in national, regional and local government that was sufficient to transform politics from within and to engender the policy-making process, as shown in our reassessment of feminist activism in the 1975–1982 period and in the chapters on harassment and violence. In so doing, feminism galvanised women voters into supporting the parties that stood for change, and avoided the emergence of a reactionary female block – while winning opinion-poll approval in the process. The agenda of the transition and subsequent governments was altered – engendered – by the need to address women's concerns in policy-making, and the new policies served to regenerate local councils' functions as service-providers and to increase the legitimacy of the new autonomous regions such as Andalucía.

Feminist activists, by not turning their backs on the possibility of exercising power, addressed the political parties with the demand for representation in leadership positions, on the principled grounds that women constitute half the population. Chapter 6 on political participation and parity democracy showed the development of this struggle which ended by placing Spain in the advanced half of European nations. It also showed that male-dominated parties could be persuaded both by principle and by pressure to open the gates of party power. A further persuasive factor was, in the case of the left parties, their own internal crisis and desire for renewal, and in the case of the right, the conviction that to give women visibility in political representation – or at least not to lag too far behind their rivals in this – played well with the electorate.[1] In other words, the gendering of Spanish political life was aided by openings in the political opportunity structure. The first was provided by a constitutional break in which the elite wished to make a great leap forward (1977–1978). The second opening was provided by the 1979 re-launch of elected local councils with strengthened powers, followed by the creation of a whole new institutional tier of elected regional administrations with a service-providing role. Thirdly, an opening was provided by the PSOE's loss of power both at autonomy level from 1994 and nationally in 1996, after which it made a bid to revive its fortunes by taking the bold modernising step of acknowledging the concept of gender parity and instituting it in elective posts.

The presence of women changed the content and styles of political decision-making. The assumption of gender-blindness in policy-making was debunked. Understandings of what constitutes an appropriate area for state intervention were altered and redefined. Institutions were restructured to accommodate women's demands firstly for specialist departments dealing with gender discrimination and equal opportunities, and later for the whole of public administration to take responsibility for instituting equality policies via the process known as gender mainstreaming. As Rowbotham aptly put it, successful liberal feminist movements in the 1990s have been 'adept at negotiating the disintegratory modernising impulse in capitalism and securing a piece of the cake' (1996: 15). In this regard, Spain is no exception.

The discussions in Chapter 2 on gendering the transition and in Chapter 6 on towards parity democracy also contribute to the growing literature on women and gender in political transition processes. This literature emerged in relation to Latin American women's movements and gendered developments in post-Communist states of Eastern Europe and therefore mainly *after* the Spanish case had taken place. But a reappraisal of the prominence of gender in the making of Spanish democracy, such as we offer here and which is also taking place in Spain, shows that the Spanish case provides useful lessons and pointers for future transitions. Apart from providing an example of successful institutionalisation of a women's movement, it also highlights how institutionalisation can have a knock-on effect in facilitating the new parity democracy project, still incipient in Europe and globally. For it is difficult to conceive that the PSOE and IU would have accepted the degree of feminisation of their parties imposed by the parity demand without the socialist feminists' previous history of collaboration. This provides a pointer for the project's future success worldwide.

Let us turn now to the other major question of how far there has been a shift of power in the gendered division of labour. In many respects changes in women's lives reflect the profound changes occurring across all advanced nations. These include women's increased participation in the labour market, increased educational attainments and changes in household and family formation. But in Spain such changes were compressed into a much shorter period than most other European countries, and followed straight on from nearly four decades of institutionalised gender discrimination that was probably more extreme than elsewhere in Europe. It is both the suddenness of the legal break with the past and the speed at which social and ideological change has occurred which makes the Spanish case so interesting. Nevertheless, accelerated change did not take place at all levels, as the economy did not produce sufficient jobs to absorb the new demand by the women entering the labour market. Nor did the state step in to facilitate this aspect of women's emancipation, so, as Tobío (2001) holds, there is a contradiction between their desire to work and the traditional social organisation based on the mother as carer and manager of the home. In this sense it was a disjunctive process.

There are many ways in which Spanish women suffer far greater constraints than their counterparts in north European countries with respect to their employment opportunities and welfare state support. As we have seen, women's integration into the labour market has been distinctive, as they predominate in its more precarious segments. Yet as was discussed in Chapter 7 on the labour market, young women give priority to entering it before getting married and then try to remain in it even after the birth of their children, because gaining work stability and an income is tantamount, from the young women's perspective, to gaining an important preliminary asset for marriage, as it was for men in the past (Flaquer 1999). Having a job is both a guarantee of independence in case of divorce but also of co-resourcing within the family, particularly for purchasing a home. However, whilst young women are refusing to behave like their mothers, motherhood is proving something of an insuperable obstacle, as there is no well-trodden path for them to follow in reconciling the responsibilities that come with parenthood and paid employment, and few institutional practices facilitate it. As Tobío (2001: 366) has remarked: 'The new reality of women as workers is not yet fully acknowledged, thus delaying changes in the family, in the social organisation and in social policy coherent with women's role in paid work.'

Another way in which we show the Spanish case to be significant is with regard to the debate around individualisation, 'late modernity' and the family. The current phase of western development is characterised in sociological terms as one of 'late modernity' in which social relations have become individualised, with a loosening of traditional family roles. For instance, women's ascribed status within the home has changed as they have been drawn into paid employment. For Beck and Beck-Gernsheim, individualisation means the disintegration of existing social forms, for example, the increasing fragility of such categories as class and social status, gender roles, family and neighbourhood (2001). The family in particular tends to become 'marketised', meaning that market processes infiltrate it, with an accompanying dissolution of its social bonds. The case of Spain, however, demonstrates that these developments can vary widely between different European societies.

By contrast, the emergence of a welfare state in Spain (as part of the modernising process) and its late and more limited development has gone hand in hand with the reinforcement, not the decline, of the family as an agency of material and emotional support. For Flaquer (1999) the Spanish family system is, in contrast to the general theory, characterised by a low degree of individualisation and by heavy 'institutional density'. This means that a dense network of family ties persist throughout people's lives to the extent that moral obligations derived from kinship are institutionalised by being made binding in civil and even criminal legislation. The key function of the family in fulfilling caring, financial and material services that elsewhere may be provided by the welfare state have also been discussed in the various chapters in this book.

Several contradictory processes, however, are changing the role of the family. Firstly, we highlighted how younger women's roles, expectations and aspirations with respect to education and employment have been transformed. There has been a reconfiguration of gender roles among young men and women, with the latter staying in paid work after the birth of their children and seeing themselves as essential income-generators responsible for co-resourcing the household (even though this may be in temporary or part-time work). This behaviour clearly sets young women apart from their mothers, on whom they are nonetheless dependent for daily child care or when children are ill, leading observers to ask what will happen when the working mothers of today become unavailable as 'substitute mothers' for their grandchildren in the future (Tobío 2001).

Furthermore, the lack of external supports for the family such as housing, state transfers and welfare services, as well as the difficulties young people experience in obtaining a stable or permanent job, act to restrict their opportunities for family formation. While other factors such as prolonged education also play a role, the result, as we have seen, has been a delay in the age of marriage, a delay in the age of mother's first birth and a decline in the fertility rate until immigrant women reversed it from 1999.[2] On the one hand, this reinforces the role of family in that young people continue to be reliant on their family of origin until their late twenties or early thirties, and intergenerational transfers (for example, housing) become especially important for new families to form. On the other, the family itself is under threat in the long term, given the lack of external support and the difficulties of family formation. As Ferrera argued with respect to the welfare state in southern Europe, 'an institutional configuration originally built to serve the family is now working to erode its own foundation by discouraging, precisely, family reproduction' (Ferrera 2000: 172).

In fact, in the last ten to 15 years the traditional nexus between welfare state, labour market and family – described as one 'in which entire families are locked into welfare dependency on one male earner' (Esping-Andersen 1997: 142) – started to unravel. Thus women's increasing participation in work and the recent difficulties for both young men and women in establishing new households and raising children opens up the question of the extent to which the family and its relationship to the welfare state and labour market can continue to operate in its traditional form. Indeed Esping-Andersen (1999) sees 'the family' as the driver of change in European welfare states and argues that the 'familialism' of the old welfare settlement based on assumptions of traditional duties of men and women is now the 'Achilles heel' of welfare states.

However, others have argued that the concept of unpaid caring work, or social care, needs to be placed at the centre of any analysis of the welfare state (Daly and Lewis 2000). Such a focus helps to account for the gendered nature of social relations in the context of welfare state provision. Daly and Lewis believe that 'Especially important is the distribution of care (giving and receiving) between men and women and among families, the conditions in which this is carried out, and the state's role in affecting such conditions' (2000: 287). They point to the crisis of care affecting all European societies. On the one hand, demographic changes (especially the aging of the population and financial pressures) are increasing the demand for care, whilst on the other, women's greater participation in paid work and changing norms of family responsibilities have decreased the supply of caring work. In Spain, policy-makers do not take on board women's unpaid caring work, although they did respond to the UN call at Beijing to carry out time-budget surveys to determine who does what, and for how long, in the household. This revealed, according to María Angeles Durán, an expert from the National Research Council (CSIC), that two-thirds of all work performed in 1998, in terms of time spent, was unpaid (personal communication 2002). In the future, given the looming shortage of unpaid carers, it may be essential to develop policies that address the issue of the distribution of care and the state's role in this. Particularly important, as we discuss below, is the recognition of women's unpaid care work for entitlements to social citizenship and for policies that support the reconciliation of paid work with family life. As Carole Pateman said a long time ago, 'The impact of the domestic burden upon women and the cultural attitudes which support her continuing responsibility for servicing the family, *although by now a truism* cannot be overestimated' (Pateman 1979, cited in Lovenduski and Hills 1981: 323; emphasis added). Truism or not, its consequences are taking a long time to sink in.

Women in Spain: 'on cats paws but always with claws'?

In this last part some general considerations along the themes of the book will be made. Let us start with the extraordinarily positive endorsement of Spanish feminism by Manuel Castells in his celebrated three-volume work of political economy (1997). Castells holds that the last decades of the twentieth century in Spain had a 'major impact on improving women's legal, social and economic condition, as well as in facilitating the entry of women to prominent positions in politics, business, and society at large' (1997: 190). Furthermore he believes that 'Spanish feminism exemplifies the potential of using politics and institutions to improve women's status' and is a case of 'successful institutionalisation [...] though at the cost of the loss of the autonomous social movement' (1997: 191). Lastly, Castells also concludes that 'attitudes of machismo were dramatically eroded in the new generations' (1997: 190).

There is little to disagree with in these statements regarding Spain which are themselves inspired by examination of similar sources to ours and to some extent echo conclusions reached in Threlfall (1996), Valiente's numerous publications and Cousins (1999). But such an endorsement, based on women doing more and better, still does not tell us enough about shifts in the Spanish gender system, nor whether women are any closer to achieving their ambitioned goals. The system Castells identifies when discussing feminism on a global scale is an undefined 'patriachalism' of which a part, the patriarchal family, was already crumbling slowly (Castells 1997: 136). The point is that to conclude in terms of 'more' and 'better' with regard to women does not tell us enough about the dynamics of gender change.

Let us therefore turn to two useful ways of approaching an appraisal of women's situation in nation-states, which have been deployed by feminist scholars. One is via a discussion of the concept of 'welfare state patriarchy' and the other the concept of 'citizenship'. Neither of these by any means exhaust the terms of the debate but they are well established in feminist thought. And in the absence of major paradigms for assessing gender transformation from a political development perspective, these terms can well be applied to the case of Spain.

It is accepted that there are forms of public as well as private patriarchy (following Walby 1990 and others), and both are the subject of numerous feminist critiques. But there is some ambiguity with respect to whether public patriarchy is entirely a form of domination. The Scandinavian welfare states, though characterised as a form of *public* patriarchy, are considered by some to have liberated women from dependency on *private* patriarchy. This implies that there is an advantage to be gained by women when the shift is made towards a public patriarchy with generous benefits for mothers and children. At its best, a 'woman-friendly' state may emerge (to use Hernes's 1988 original term and subsequent usage). In its turn, the British public patriarchy (the patriarchal welfare state) has for several decades provided entitlements that enable mothers to forgo dependence on a male provider and live on state benefits for accommodation and maintenance for at least 16 years (to the end of their youngest child's compulsory school age). In Germany an allowance (*Erziehungsgeld*) is paid to any new mother to look after a child irrespective of their personal relationships until it reaches school age. The point is that despite feminist critiques of the welfare state as another form of patriarchy, writers such as Bock and Thane (1991) point out that welfare states in Europe and particularly in Sweden have been moulded into being supportive ('friendly') by women's demands. It is clearly arguable that such a redefined gender system resulting from the pro-active and supportive intervention of well-developed welfare states can be seen as an advance over private patriarchy. Setting aside much more recent counter-arguments regarding the poverty trap of mothers who bring up children exclusively on state support and the British Labour government's efforts to modify this system, welfare state patriarchy and the woman-friendly state are useful reference points to use in assessing the case of nations lacking a well-developed welfare state such as Spain's in the 1970s.

However, our conclusion must be that the Spanish state has limited its involvement in supporting social change or gender equity through welfare programmes. There continues to be, for example, no universal national support for lone parents, no housing benefits and little if any social housing for rent. Among other things this impacts negatively on women's abilities to flee from domestic violence to new rented accommodation that may provide a place of safety. Further, as discussed in Chapter 3 on social policy, social-welfare services for the disabled and elderly are at a low level and leave female relatives to cope. We have also seen that there is no national safety-net of social assistance, only that provided by the autonomous communities consisting almost exclusively of a minimum-income scheme which is only a minimum-level means-tested benefit for selective categories of persons in need, and in exchange the recipient has to undergo reinsertion training. In other words, there is no entitlement as of right to a public minimum income as there is in well-developed welfare states. There are also few services to support women experiencing pressing needs because of their traditional role as carers of the young or the elderly.

The concepts surrounding social citizenship, and citizenship for women, also provide useful criteria. While it is accepted that women have gained political citizenship in equal measures to men in most European states, the feminist argument is that they do not hold social citizenship. As Lister explained (1998: 176–179), at its simplest this means that women's care-giving activities are insufficiently recognised even today by the social-security and pensions system. Therefore women as actual or potential mothers will remain 'exiled as a group from full citizenship' (Lister 1998: 199) until the present incompatibility between earning and caring becomes fully taken on board by the state, and resolved.

In this context, the question of whether women in Spain are any closer to achieving a recognised social citizenship does not lead to a positive answer. The manifest difficulties that Spanish women experience, when trying to maintain a place in the labour market of sufficient stability to be able to accumulate social security entitlements, heavily constrains their freedom to achieve the goal of autonomy. As we noted in Chapter 3, Orloff (1993) argued that we need to take into account the extent to which welfare states enable those who do most of the domestic and caring work to form and maintain autonomous households without having to marry to gain access to a breadwinner's level of income and benefits, or be engaged in full-time employment themselves. In Spain, far too many women are faced with the impossibility of maintaining an autonomous household and are forced into shared dependency with parents or a life partner. Only to a small extent has access to social entitlements been 'decommodified', as health and old-age pensions are now a universal provision independent of a citizen's contribution to social insurance through paid employment. Instead, there is a stratified or dual system of social protection in which women disproportionately receive a much less generous and means-tested social assistance.

It it necessary to emphasise, therefore, that until the work that most women actually do – care work – is recognised, they will not have social citizenship and will remain in a fundamentally inequitable position. Women, as the child-bearing gender, are structurally unable to resolve, by themselves, the intrinsically conflictive juxtaposition between, on the one hand, society's requirement that individuals engage in income-generating work *before* their activity is socially recognised and rewarded with full social insurance, and on the other, the inescapable need of all individuals to receive care. The fact that everyone, young, middle-aged and old, requires material and emotional servicing, including of course the care-givers themselves, stubbornly remains a gender-blind spot unrecognised by public policy. The many changes that have taken place in Spanish society constitute only initial steps in this general direction.

Both these debates point towards a more general goal of *autonomy* as desirable for women – at its simplest, the capacity for a woman to enjoy a degree of independence and exercise control over her life. The concept of autonomy has also been linked to political citizenship by Luce Irigaray (1989) who argues that women's citizenship – political and social – must be formalised at state and constitutional level. Developing Irigaray's points, Velu (2000) discusses why women need to be able to be 'autonomous and responsible individuals', not just *de facto* (reflecting the Anglo-Saxon approach) but also *de jure* as a formal status. They argue that their existing formal equality in law is limited because they have neither the 'power to name' nor the 'legitimate citizen's status to impose new forms of inter-action with both male and female subjects acting as equal partners' (Velu 2000: 90–91). In agreement with Irigaray, she holds that if men formally had to recognise women's role as fully-fledged citizens, then mechanisms aiming to limit or exclude women could not function so easily (Velu 2000: 91). This is the essence of the long-term parity democracy project.

In other words, for women's citizenship to be formalised, the existing social system under which citizens earn their living (that at present is not organised to allow women to bear children and earn a full living *as of right)* would have to be comprehensively overhauled in law as well as in practice. If one compares this concept of citizenship with the insights from a parallel debate in another context that discusses the differences in the achievements for women in terms of *procedural* as opposed to substantive equality (Hervey and Shaw 1998), the notion of female citizenship is enriched. It is not just that equality of the sexes must be achieved substan-tively, in the practice of everyday living, but also that women should not be fobbed off with the supposedly Anglo-Saxon practice of muddling-through on a bit of give-and-take, a few concessions and the odd compro-mise, even when they make some sort of 'reconciliation between employment and family life' just about practicable for some. The parity democracy argument is that substantive equality – a gender system that is designed so that women are free from the constant struggle with the inher-ent contradictions of the current set-up – should not only be buttressed by the state, but also be embodied in the realm of the symbolic, in law and in the polity's constitutional structures. Even if women in practice gain the ability to act as autonomous agents in ordinary life, they should addition-ally have that positon, and the reconciliation between employment and parenthood it would bring, legitimised officially.

In our view, then, Spain has not moved beyond procedural equality of legal reform towards an attempt to bring about substantive equality by attacking the root causes and the structures that underpin the preservation of the gender order. This is not to deny that there is a well-developed corpus of laws on formal equality nor that aspects of substantive equality are targeted by laws against sexual harassment (to make everyday working life for women as free from persecutory behaviours as it is for men) and against violence against women (to allow women the same freedom from physical aggression as men enjoy in practice and under the law). But the difficulties of implementation highlighted in the relevant chapters in this book show that the law has been unable to make that promise of equal freedom substantive. More effective practices would require sensitive policy development and finer instruments for the implementation of legal precepts as well as equal opportunities training among the professions, civil servants, law-enforcement agents, employers, trade-union representatives and members of parliament.

The success of feminist advocacy bodies in attaining formal equality policies have, therefore, been constrained in a number of ways. First, and at the most general level, we find a resilience of the pre-existing policy frameworks in addition to institutional constraints. Ostner and Lewis (1995), for example, have argued that gender-equality policies are bound to be implemented in terms of the pre-existing policy and cultural frames, in other words distorted in order to fit the particular gender order underlying public and social policies. 'National social policies rest on underlying assumptions about who is the primary and who is the secondary breadwinner or care giver. These assumptions are crystallised in the various institutions that constitute (a country's) welfare regime' (Ostner and Lewis 1995: 183). Several chapters in this book have demonstrated the strength of the male-breadwinner family model during the Franco regime. Whilst we might now describe the Spanish gender order as one in transition from private patriarchy (Duncan 1995), the ideal of breadwinning as the main or exclusive family function of Spanish men is remarkably persistent. It is sustained in a number of ways: by the different position of men and women in the labour market; by men's lack of domestic and caring skills as a result of their upbringing; the negative image of domestic work; the widespread assumptions regarding the lesser importance of female employment; the centrality of mother-care for small children; and the absence of public policies to encourage men, not just feebly enable them, to become more involved in caring work.

Second, there is a lack of representation at the decision-making level for bodies such as the Institute of Women. As Valiente observed, the Institute of Women 'has neither the power nor the budget to implement most gender equality policies. Instead it has to convince other state offices to develop women's equality policies' (1998: 469). While policy implementation remains in the hands of state units (mainly ministries), gender equality is rarely a priority.

Third, whilst equality is in principle quite well regulated in the labour market, the policy toolkit is small, lacking in what is called the machinery of equal opportunities implementation that ranges from workplace committees and agreements, to targets for employers and trade unions, clauses in collective bargaining agreements and general discussion of the meaning of equal pay in practice at the grass-roots level. As noted, although there are departments in the major trade unions devoted to women's issues, the position of these departments within the unions has always been weak. Research has also shown that collective bargaining plays little or no role in achieving equal opportunities and that little or no attention is paid to 'women's issues' in agreements (EIRO 1997). Where equality issues such as maternity leave and pay or child care are covered by collective agreements, they rarely go beyond the legislative provisions.

Given what we have found, one could say that the absence of an ongoing public project for a full welfare state, for dismantling patriarchy, let alone for a 'social and cultural mutation' (to use Irigaray's 1989 term referring to a profound change of culture through widespread innovative methods and patterns of behaviour), women remain in a fragile position in Spain. They have not gained that real social visibility that would result from the legitimation of the status and rights that define female citizenship. Nor have they gained what is termed *equivalent* rights *that respect Difference* (with a capital D) rather than just equality of rights (Velu 2000: 89). We would conclude that any traditional form of respect for Difference that might continue to exist in Spain is anchored in a patriarchal tradition and therefore represents continuity with the past rather than innovation. Nevertheless, even the traditional Difference of women may still provide a useful heritage to build on in the future.

Where does that leave gender change in Spain? If the explicit criteria for gender equity have not been achieved, what has happened? One way of summing up the process could be Ulrich Beck's image that gender change has been a sub-revolution creeping forward like a cat, softly but effectively – 'on cats paws but always with claws' (Beck 1994: 26) – scratching at the underbelly of society. Though the notion of a 'quiet revolution' is in fact a familiar one, here it suggests gradual and incremental progress that may not be noticeable or even fully visible, but nonetheless has an impact at a deeper level. Yet, on balance, this is not a satisfying or convincing portrayal of the Spanish case except in very general terms. For gender questions *have* in fact had a high profile, *have* moved forward rather quickly, *and* have *not* maintained an even rhythm. The possibility of stagnation and erosion of gains is an open question despite the absence of a backlash (Threlfall 1996: 298–300). We conclude therefore that in Spain, politics, ideology and women's aspirations were transformed more readily than the economy was able to respond to the challenge of women's inclusion, and more profoundly than men were able to adapt to the shift in gender relations.

Given such disjunctive movement, it is fitting to avoid binary or teleological formulations. Scholars of the east European transitions have argued that 'democracy after communism represents not the removal but the reconfiguration of asymmetries of power' (Watson 2000: 103; see also Watson 1996). The same could be said for transitions from an authoritarian regime such as Franco's, respecting the differences. Arguably, democracy provides more freedoms, but Watson's formulation avoids the binary and linear approaches loosely summed up as 'worse before/better after' the political break with the past. For the Spanish case one could insist that some changes have indeed been for the better, yet the overall power relationship between the sexes has remained asymmetrical – and in a different way from before. The particular originality is that *elective power structures proved more permeable to women than productive ones*. This approach is also more akin to certain ideas regarding modernisation processes in general. In Beck's (2000) formulations, linear models of modernisation are avoided in favour of a notion of a multi-level process with contrary tendencies and structures marked by an unfinished dialectic of modernisation and counter-modernisation. And Therborn (1995) warns against seeing modernisation as a unified process or single set of processes, and allows for various *trajectories* through a *terrain* of modernity to be identified.

Should the asymmetry that characterises change in Spain lead to the suggestion that there may be a specific Spanish road to gender equity? Possibly there is a 'family way' towards an eventual formal recognition and social approval of 'what women do' that would absorb and transform the traditional gender order into something different and satisfying without going down the typically European road of almost full incorporation into paid employment. Indeed, the question of satisfaction should not be dismissed. When all is said and done, rewarding family relationships and satisfaction with life must be included amongst the ultimate benchmarks to indicate quality of life. The reconfigured centrality of the family that has been a theme in this book may yet be considered 'the Spanish way' that does have something to offer women, bearing in mind that six million Spanish women are still full-time housewives and 85 per cent of them felt 'satisfied', according to a 2002 survey. Over half even felt that what they did *was* valued by society though 42 per cent complained that it was not (Grande 2002). This corroborates evidence from earlier decades showing Spaniards of both sexes and all ages feel surprisingly positive about their family life and emotional relationships (e.g. Durán 1993: 257–259).

So can it be concluded that an intangible 'bargain with patriarchy' (Kandiyoti 1988) has been struck to keep the Spanish gender order stable as a particularly 'familial' one? Tempting as it is, probably not. A fundamental critique of this kind of survey results on satisfaction is that they do not factor in choice. Whether people have options is a test of the effectiveness of any theoretical freedom to choose. Women may see the avenues of public participation opening up for them, yet not be able to take up the opportunities because of constraints in their everyday lives regarding employment, living arrangements or motherhood. This does not constitute a desirable model. In the same survey referred to above, a large majority of homemakers also complained that they were not paid for their care work, amounting to over 40 hours a week (Grande 2002), which suggests the presence of a rumbling volcano of long-term instability in the gender order. Satisfaction or happiness levels among Spanish women in their present condition are insufficiently well grounded for them not be shifted by new reverberations.

The fact is that no winds of feminist change blow gustily at the moment. Rather than a new fixed bargain, Spanish women have settled into a temporary accommodation with patriarchy to preserve themselves and their family life until they see new openings in the political or economic opportunity structure and the way ahead becomes clearer. Women's interventions so far, whether in the fields of work and the division of labour, or public policy and representation, have altered trends, behaviour and the course of events in a way that is still not yet fully recognised nor theorised. For the road to women's full emancipation and autonomy in the current socio-political environment in Spain is not distinctly laid out. In time a pathway will be forged and it may well diverge and run along separate courses in different parts of the country.

Notes

1 In a survey of future Spanish trends, the statement 'there will be more women in posts of public responsibility than now' was the statement that obtained the broadest range of agreement among respondents (79 per cent), interpreted as a sign of approval (Tezanos 1997: 61).
2 The birth rate rose slightly through 1999, 2000 and 2001 (latest figure available) to 1.24 children per women of fertile age, although this still remains the lowest in Europe, according to the Spanish National Institute of Statistics (INE), who attribute most of the growth to immigrant women (Oficina de Información Diplomática 2002: 13), responsible for over 20,000 births p.a. by 2001 on present trends (estimated by authors on basis of INE data for previous years in above).

References

Beck, U. (1994) 'Self-dissolution and self-endangerment of industrial society: what does this mean?' in U. Beck, A. Giddens and S. Lash (eds) *Reflexive Modernisation*, 174–183, Cambridge: Polity Press.
Beck, U. (2000) *The Brave New World of Work*, Oxford: Polity Press.
Beck, U. and Beck-Gernsheim, E. (2001) *Individualization: Individualized Individualism and its Social and Political Consequences*, London: Sage.
Bock, G. and Thane, P. (eds) (1991) *Maternity and Gender Policies: Women and the Rise of the European Welfare States 1880s–1950s*, London: Routledge.
Castells, M. (1997) *The Power of Identity*, second book of the trilogy *The Information Age: Economy, Society, Culture*, Oxford: Blackwell.

Cousins, C. (1999) 'Gender relations and changing forms of employment in Spain', *Journal of Southern Europe and the Balkans*, 1 (2): 199–215.

Daly, M. and Lewis, J. (2000) 'The concept of social care and the analysis of contemporary welfare states', *British Journal of Sociology*, 51 (2): 281–298.

Duncan, S. (1995) 'Theorising European gender systems', *Journal of European Social Policy*, 5 (4): 263–284.

Durán, M.A. (1993) 'Necesidades sociales y satisfacción en la década de los noventa' in P. Folguera (ed.) *Otras visiones de España*, 213–277, Madrid: Editorial Pablo Iglesias.

EIRO (1997) 'Equal opportunities and collective bargaining in the EU': http://www.eiro.eurofound.ie/1997/04/study/N9704201S.html.

Esping-Andersen, G. (1997) 'Do the spending and finance structures matter?' in W. Beck, L. Van der Maesen and A. Walker (eds) *The Social Quality of Europe*, Bristol: The Policy Press.

Esping-Andersen, G (1999) *Social Foundations of Postindustrial Economies*, Oxford: Oxford University Press.

Ferrera, M. (1996) 'The "southern model" of welfare in social Europe', *Journal of European Social Policy*, 6 (1) 17–37.

Ferrera, M. (2000) 'Reconstructing the welfare state in southern Europe' in S. Kuhnle (ed.) *Survival of the European Welfare State*, London: Routledge.

Flaquer, L. (1999) 'Changes in Spanish families and the implications for employment', ESRC Seminar Series on Parenting, Motherhood and Paid Work: Rationalities and Ambivalences, Bradford: University of Bradford, Dept. of Applied Social Sciences.

Garrido, L. (1992) *Las Dos Biografias de la Mujer en España*, Instituto de la Mujer, 33, Madrid: Ministerio de Asuntos Sociales.

Giddens, A. (1994) 'Living in a post-traditional society' in U. Beck, A. Giddens and S. Lash (eds) *Reflexive Modernisation*, 57–109, Cambridge: Polity Press.

Grande, M.J. (2002) 'Sus labores', *El País*, EPS No. 1332, 7 April, p. 102.

Hernes, H. (1988) *Welfare State and Woman Power*, Oslo: Norwegian University Press.

Hervey, T. and Shaw, J. (1998) 'Women, work and care: women's dual role and double burden in EC sex equality law', *Journal of European Social Policy*, 8 (1): 43–63.

Irigaray, L. (1989) *Le temps de la différence: pour une révolution pacifique*, Paris: Le Livre de Poche.

Kandiyoti, D. (1988) 'Bargaining with patriarchy', *Gender and Society*, 3: 274–290.

Lister, R. (1998) *Citizenship: Feminist Perspectives*, Basingstoke: Macmillan/ Palgrave.

Lovenduski, J. and Hills, J. (eds) (1981) *The Politics of the Second Electorate: Women and Political Participation*, London: Routledge and Kegan Paul.

Molyneux, M. (2001) *Women's Movements in International Perspective*, Basingstoke: Palgrave.

Oficina de Información Diplomática (2002) 'La natalidad aumenta por tercer año consecutivo', *España 2002*, June.

Orloff, A.S. (1993) 'Gender and the social rights of citizenship: the comparative analysis of gender relations and welfare states', *American Sociological Review*, 58 (June): 303–328.

Ostner, I. and Lewis, J. (1995) 'Gender and the evolution of European social policies' in S. Leibfried and P. Pierson (eds) *European Social Policy: Between Fragmentation and Integration*, Washington DC: The Brookings Institution.

Pérez-Lanzac, C. (2002) 'Volver a empezar', *El País Semanal*, No. 1332, 7 April.

Rowbotham, S. (1996) 'Introduction' in M. Threlfall (ed.) *Mapping the Women's Movement: Feminist Politics and Social Transformation in the North*, London: Verso.

Tezanos, J.L. (1997) 'Las imágenes y expectativas del futuro en la sociedad española' in J.F. Tezanos, J.M. Montero and J.A. Díaz (eds) *Tendencias de futuro en la sociedad española*, 41–73, Madrid: Editorial Sistema.

Therborn, G. (1995) *European Modernity and Beyond*, London: Sage.

Threlfall, M. (1996) 'Conclusion' in M. Threlfall (ed.) *Mapping the Women's Movement: Feminist Politics and Social Transformation in the North*, London: Verso.

Tobío, C. (2001) 'Working and mothering: women's strategies in Spain', *European Societies*, 3 (3): 339–372.

United Nations Development Programme (UNDP) (2003) *Human Development Report 2003*, New York: UNDP, also available at http://hdr.undp.org/reports/global/2003/.

Valiente, C. (1998) 'An overview of the state of research on women and politics in Spain', *European Journal of Political Research*, 33: 459–474.

Velu, C. (2000) 'Luce Irigaray and citizenship' in A. Bull, H. Diamond and R. Marsh (eds) *Feminisms and Women's Movements in Contemporary Europe*, Basingstoke: Macmillan.

Walby, S. (1990) *Theorising Patriarchy*, Oxford: Blackwell.

Watson, P. (1996) 'The rise of masculinism in Eastern Europe' in M. Threlfall (ed.) *Mapping the Women's Movement: Feminist Politics and Social Transformation in the North*, London: Verso.

Watson, P. (2000) 'Theorising feminism in postcommunism' in A. Bull, H. Diamond and R. Marsh (eds) *Feminisms and Women's Movements in Contemporary Europe*, Basingstoke: Macmillan, pp. 110–117.

Bibliographical commentary and bibliography of research on gender in Spanish history, politics, public policy, sociology, anthropology and ethnography since the 1920s, published in English (1971–2002)

Monica Threlfall

Bibliographical commentary

It may come as a surprise to the reader that only a handful of monographs on any aspect of Spanish women's lives have been published in English since 1970. Three of these were commissioned papers for international bodies such as the EU and the UN or government reports (Alcobendas 1984 and Moltó 1996 on employment, Instituto de la Mujer 1995), rather than sparked by individuals' interest. Two of them remaining unpublished. This was the fate of the first full monograph that we have identified, Fredericks's (1972) *The Social and Political Thought of Federica Montseny, Spanish Anarchist 1923–1937*, which remains a PhD dissertation. The second monograph, a comprehensive study of feminism in twentieth-century Spain written by British historian Geraldine Scanlon (with financial support from the University of London), never came out in English yet ran to two editions in a Spanish translation (published in 1976 and 1986).

It was not till the first half of the 1990s that scholarly interest led to further monographs. Three of the five new books confirmed what had by then become a constant theme of interest among historians, namely the extraordinary role Spanish women had played in the anarchist movement, in Republican politics and in the Civil War of the 1930s. They are Ackelsburg's (1991) *Free Women of Spain: Anarchism and the Struggle for the Emancipation of Women*, Mangini's (1995) *Memories of Resistance: Women's Voices from the Spanish Civil War* and Nash's (1995) *Defying Male Civilization: Women in the Spanish Civil War*. Then came Brooksbank Jones's broad treatment of the democratic era, already mentioned in our Introduction. The latest monograph in our bibliography is by Morcillo Gómez (2000) on gender ideology and Franco's Spain, the only publication in English to deal exclusively with the long years of 1939–1975.

Luckily scholars, enthusiasts and the merely curious have not had to rely entirely on monographs for their information, as there has long been a growing list of journal articles and book chapters to satisfy their interest. It is instructive to briefly review the list compiled here, which is limited to the post-1970 period and to a range of topics that includes history, politics, sociology, anthropology and ethnography. Historians were the first off the mark, focusing on anarchism, the Republic and the Civil War, with Temma Kaplan's work on women and Spanish anarchism (1971, 1977). But the early interest on the part of anthropologists, kicking off on the theme of machismo, should be noted (Gilmore and Gilmore 1979). At the same time, we note an early focus on individual women, namely those prominent in Republican politics: Margarita Nelken, Federica Monseny and Dolores Ibárruri, and, in the case of the latter, also in the opposition to the Franco regime.

The 1980s saw a new departure with the first attempt to express the new democratic women's movement's demands to an English readership (Ragué 1981) and the first overview of the changing Spanish policy environment for women (Matsell 1981). We also find the phenomenon of authors applying knowledge gained as activists and participants in the process to interpret the new Spanish feminism (Astelarra 1985; Threlfall 1985; Durán and Gallego 1986). At the same time a volume put the Spanish case on the map of comparative studies of women's movements (Dahlerup 1986). In another development, we also see mainly male academic and professional writers acknowledge aspects of the role of gender in the transformation of Spain by including chapters on gender questions in their books (Threlfall's in Torrents and Abel 1984; Hooper 1995; Moxon-Brown 1989; Gibson 1995). The 1980s also see further anthropological or ethnographic studies of gender relations and household practices in Spanish villages, mainly in Andalusia and Galicia.

In the 1990s several new fields became available to English-language readers. Firstly, the labour market began to be covered with the special issue of the now defunct *Iberian Studies* (1991) bidding to be the first to address women's employment in Spain, followed by the work of Cousins (1994). The contributions of Spanish experts to European Union research networks served to present English-language readers with a particularly strong picture of women's disadvantage in the labour market, by studying the informal economy and temporary fixed-term contract work (Miguélez Lobo 1988; Moltó 1996; Moltó and Domingo 1998; Ruivo *et al.* 1998; García-Ramón and Ortiz 2000).

Secondly, the family–employment–social policy nexus was to become a productive field for English-language publications, starting with Tobío (1994) and Frotiée (1994). Thirdly, public-policy analysis emerges, a field that is to be extensively investigated through Valiente's multiple contributions on a wide range of gender policies (Valiente 1995, 2000, 2001). The interest in wider achievements of the women's movement was also consolidated (Kaplan 1992; Threlfall 1996, 1997; Valiente 1995).

Meanwhile in the most recent years we have seen an increase in the number of publications overall and an increase of interest in cultural studies with three edited volumes, two on Spanish culture containing several contributions on gendered themes (Graham in Graham and Labanyi 1995; Jordan and Morgan-Tamosunas 2000) as well as a whole volume on female identity in historical perspective with contributions of relevance to the post-1970 period (Enders and Radcliff 1999). Most recently of all, we are witnessing the arrival of studies of sexuality and sexual identity (Mira in Jordan and Morgan-Tamosunas 2000; Beadman 2000), and the consolidation of studies of social policy (Mangen 2001) and on a range of public policies by Valiente, which also consolidate the available publications on the family-employment nexus.

Nonetheless it is worth noting that straightforwardly political studies of voting and political participation in English remained limited across the whole period covered to Gallego and Mendez (1994), Alexander (1999), Hamilton (2000) and Threlfall (1984, 2001), reflecting the lesser interest of political scientists in gender in the Spanish context. And we should not fail to point out the extreme paucity of publications on women in the Franco era before the 1990s, which make the contributions by Nash (1991) on motherhood, Morcillo Gómez (2000) on womanhood and Preston (2002) on prominent individuals a key starting point for English-language readers interested in this remarkable period.

The picture that arises from our bibliography shows that the coverage for English-reading students of the Spanish gender order is still not comprehensive, revealing the vagaries of scholarly interest in certain topics – for example, the anthropological studies appearing mainly in the US, and the historians manifesting a predilection for research on the Second Republic and Civil War period. We hasten to acknowledge that this state of affairs does thankfully not mirror the situation in Spanish-language publishing where women's history has become a burgeoning field of inquiry (Enders and Radcliff 1999: xi) leading to a wave of new historical research, as well as to reappraisals of the place, role and influence of women in the contemporary Spanish polity, amounting to a rich catalogue of political and sociological enquiry as well as theorisation.

Bibliography (in order of publication)

1971

Kaplan, T. (1971) 'Spanish anarchism and women's liberation', *Journal of Contemporary History*, 6 (2): 101–110.

1972

Fredericks, S.F. (1972) *The Social and Political Thought of Federica Montseny, Spanish Anarchist 1923–1937*, PhD dissertation, University of New Mexico.

1977

Kaplan, T. (1977) 'Other scenarios: women and Spanish anarchism' in R. Bridenthal and C. Koonz (eds) *Becoming Visible: Women in European History*, New York: Houghton Mifflin.

1979

Gilmore, M. and Gilmore, D.D. (1979) 'Machismo: a psychodynamic approach (Spain)', *Journal of Psychological Anthropology*, 2 (3): 281–299.

1981

Kern, R. (1981) 'Margarita Nelken: women and the crisis of Spanish politics' in J. Slaughter and R. Kern (eds) *European Women on the Left: Socialism, Feminism and the Problems Faced by Political Women 1880 to the Present*, 147–162, Westport, CT: Greenwood Press.

Matsell, C. (1981) 'Spain' in J. Lovenduski and J. Hills (eds) *The Politics of the Second Electorate*, London: Routledge & Kegan Paul.

Ragué, M.J. (1981) 'Spain: feminism in our time' in J. Bradshaw (ed.) 'Special issue: the womens's liberation movement: Europe and North America', *Women's Studies International Quarterly*, 4 (4).

1982

Kaplan, T. (1982) 'Female consciousness and collective action: the case of Barcelona', *Signs*, 7: 545–566.

1983

Mullaney, M.M. (1983) 'Dolores Ibarruri, *La Pasionaria*: the female revolutionary as symbol' in M.M.Mullaney (ed.) *Revolutionary Women, Gender and the Socialist Revolutionary Party*, 191–242, New York: Praeger.

Porter, D. (1983) 'The role of women in the Spanish revolution' in D. Porter (ed.) *Vision on Fire: Emma Golman on the Spanish Revolution*, 248–260, New York: Commonground Press.

1984

Ackelsburg, M. (1984) 'Mujeres Libres: individuality and community, organising women during the Spanish civil war', *Radical America*, 18 (4): 7–19.

Alcobendas, M.P. (1984) *The Employment of Women in Spain*, Luxembourg: Office for Official Publications of the European Communities.

Mazur, J. (1984) 'Women's work in rural Andalucía', *Ethnology*, 23.

Threlfall, M. (1984) 'The political participation of women' in C. Abel and N. Torrents (eds) *Spain: Conditional Democracy*, London: Croom Helm.

224   *Monica Threlfall*

1985

Ackelsburg, M. (1985) 'Separate and equal? Mujeres Libres and anarchist strategy for women's emancipation', *Feminist Studies*, 11 (1): 63–83.
Astelarra, J. (1985) 'Feminism and democratic transition in Spain', *Canadian Woman Studies*, 70–73.
Threlfall, M. (1985) 'The women's movement in Spain', *New Left Review*, 151 (June–July): 45–73.
Uhl, S. (1985) 'Special friends: the organisation of intersex friendship in Escalona, Andalusia', *Anthropology*, 9.

1986

Durán, M.A. and Gallego, M.T. (1986) 'The feminist movement in Spain' in D. Dahlerup (ed.) *The New Women's Movement: Feminism and Political Power in Europe and the USA*, London: Sage.
Lever, A. (1986) 'Honour as a red herring', *Critique of Anthropology*, 6 (3): 83–105.

1987

Kaplan, T. (1987) 'Women and communal strikes in the crisis of 1917–22' in R. Bridenthal, C. Koonz and C. Sturd (eds) *Becoming Visible: Women in European History*, 2nd edn, Boston: Houghton Mifflin.

1988

Miguélez Lobo, F.M. (1988) 'Irregular work in Spain' in EEC Survey, *Underground Economy and Irregular Forms of Employment*, Final Report, Brussels.

1989

Moxon-Browne, E. (1989) 'Women and politics: reflections on change', *Political Change in Spain*, London: Routledge.
Nash, M. (1989) 'Milicianas and homefront heroines: images of war and revolution 1936–39', *History of European Ideas*, 11.
Threlfall, M. (1989) 'Social policy towards women in Spain, Greece and Portugal' in T. Gallagher and A. Williams (eds) *Southern European Socialism: The Challenge of Government*, Manchester: Manchester University Press.
Uhl, S. (1989) 'Making the bed: creating the home in Escalonia, Andalucía', *Ethnology*, 28.

1990

Gilmore, D.D. (1990) 'Men and women in southern Spain: domestic power revisited', *American Anthropologist*, 92 (4): 953–970.
Vincent, M. (1990) 'The politicization of Catholic women in Salamanca' in F. Lannon and P. Preston (eds) *Elites and Power in Twentieth Century Spain: Essays in Honour of Raymond Carr*, 107–126, Oxford: Clarendon Press.

1991

Ackelsburg, M. (1991) *Free Women of Spain: Anarchism and the Struggle for the Emancipation of Women*, Bloomington, IN: Indiana University Press.

Enders, V.L. (1991) 'Nationalism and feminism: the Sección Femenina of the Falange', *History of European Ideas*, 15 (4–6): 673–680.

Fyrth, J. and Alexander, S. (eds) (1991) *Women's Voices from the Spanish Civil War*, London: Lawrence & Wishart.

Kelley, H. (1991) 'Unwed mothers and household reputation in a Spanish Galician community', *American Ethnologist*, 18: 565–580.

Lannon, F. (1991) 'Women and images of women in the Spanish Civil War' *Proceedings of the Royal Historical Society*, 213–228, London: The Royal Historical Society.

Longhurst, C.A. (1991) 'Women and social change in contemporary Spain', *Journal of the Association for Contemporary Iberian Studies*, 4 (1): 17–25.

Mangini, S. (1991) 'Memories of resistance: women activists from the Spanish Civil War', *Signs*, 17: 171–187.

Nash, M. (1991) 'Pro-natalism and motherhood in Franco's Spain' in G. Bock and P. Thane (eds) *Maternity and Gender Policies: Women and the Rise of the European Welfare States 1880s–1950s*, 160–177, London: Routledge.

Nash, M. (1991) 'Two decades of women's history in Spain: a reappraisal' in K. Offen, R. Roach Pierson and J. Rendall (eds) *Writing Women's History: International Perspectives*, Bloomington, IN: University of Indiana Press.

Uhl, S. (1991) 'Forbidden friends: cultural veils of female friendship in Andalusia', *American Ethnologist*, 18.

1992

Gibson, I. (1992) 'Women's rights', *Fire in the Blood: The New Spain*, London: Faber & Faber.

Instituto de la Mujer (1992) *Spanish Women in Figures*, Madrid: Ministry of Culture.

Kaplan, G. (1992) 'Revolution and radicalism in southern Europe: Spain', *Western European Feminism*, London: UCL Press/Allen & Unwin.

Seidman, M. (1992) 'Women's subversive individualism in Barcelona in the 1930s', *International Review of History*, 37: 161–176.

1993

Nash, M. (1993) 'Women in war: milicianas and armed combat in revolutionary Spain', *International History Review*, 15(2): 269.

1994

Brooksbank Jones, A. (1994) 'Feminisms in contemporary Spain', *Journal of the Association of Contemporary Iberian Studies*, 7 (2): September.

Camps, V. (1994) 'The changing role of women in Spanish society', *RSA Journal*, August/September, CXLII (5452), London.

Cousins, C. (1994) 'A comparison of the labour market position of women in Spain and the UK with reference to the flexible labour debate', *Work, Employment and Society*, 8 (1): 45–67.

Frotiée, B. (1994) 'A French perspective on family and employment in Spain' in M. Letablier and L. Hantrais (eds) *The Family–Employment Relationship*, Cross-National Research Papers, 4th Series, Loughborough, European Research Centre, Loughborough University.

Gallego Méndez, M.T. (1994) 'Women's political engagement in Spain' in B. Nelson and N. Chowdhury (eds) *Women and Politics Worldwide*, 660–673, New Haven, CT and London: Yale University Press.

Instituto de la Mujer (1994) *Spanish Women on the Threshold of the 21st Century*, Report to the 4th World Conference on Women, Beijing 1995, Madrid: Ministry of Social Affairs.

Kelley, H. (1994) 'The myth of matriarchy: symbols of womanhood in Galician regional identity', *Anthropological Quarterly*, 67.

Tobío, C. (1994) 'The family-employment relationship in Spain', *Cross-National Research Papers*, 4th Series, No. 2, 41–47, Loughborough: Loughborough University.

1995

Brooksbank-Jones, A. (1995) 'Women, work and the family: a critical perspective' in H. Graham and J. Labanyi (1995) (eds) *Spanish Cultural Studies: An Introduction*, 386–392, Oxford: Oxford University Press.

Gibson, I. (1995) 'Women's rights', *Fire in the Blood*, London: Faber and Faber/BBC Books.

Graham, H. (1995) 'Women and social change 1931–9' in H. Graham and J. Labanyi (eds) *Spanish Cultural Studies: An Introduction*, 99–116, Oxford: Oxford University Press.

Graham, H. (1995) 'Gender and the state: women in the 1940s' in H. Graham and J. Labanyi (eds) *Spanish Cultural Studies: An Introduction*, 82–116, Oxford: Oxford University Press.

Hooper, J. (1995) 'Sex', 'Women on the verge of a nervous breakdown', 'Relative values', Chs 10, 11 and 12, *The New Spaniards*, Harmondsworth: Penguin.

Instituto de la Mujer (1995) 'Spanish women on the eve of the 21st century', Spain's report to the IV World Conference on Women, Beijing 1995, Madrid: Ministerio de Asuntos Sociales.

Mangini, S. (1995) *Memories of Resistance: Women's Voices from the Spanish Civil War*, New Haven, CT: Yale University Press.

Montero, R. (1995) 'The silent revolution: the social and cultural advances of women in democratic Spain' in H. Graham and J. Labanyi (eds) *Spanish Cultural Studies: An Introduction*, 381–395, Oxford: Oxford University Press.

Nash, M. (1995) *Defying Male Civilization: Women in the Spanish Civil War*, Denver, CO: Arden Press.

Perriam, C. (1995) 'Gay and lesbian culture' in H. Graham and J. Labanyi (eds) *Spanish Cultural Studies: An Introduction*, 393–395, Oxford: Oxford University Press.

Valiente, C. (1995) 'Children first: central government child care policies in post-authoritarian Spain (1975–1994)' in J. Brannen and M. O'Brien (eds) *Childhood and Parenthood*, 249–266, London: Institute of Education.

Valiente, C. (1995) 'Rejecting the past: central government and family policy in post-authoritarian Spain (1975–94)', *Cross-National Research Papers*, 4th Series, 3: 80–96.

Valiente, C. (1995) 'The power of persuasion: the *Instituto de la Mujer* in Spain' in D.M. Stetson and A.G. Mazur (eds) *Comparative State Feminism*, 221–236, Thousand Oaks, CA: Sage.

Valiente, C. (1995) 'Family obligations in Spain' in J. Millar and A. Warman (eds) *Defining Family Obligations in Europe*, Bath: University of Bath Social Policy Papers, No. 23, 325–358.

1996

Molto, M.L. (1996) *Trends and Prospects for Women's Employment in the 1990s in Spain*, Spanish Report for the EC Network Women and Employment Equal Opportunities Unit, DGV, Commission of the European Union.

Threlfall, M. (1996) 'Feminist politics and social change in Spain' in M. Threlfall (ed.) *Mapping the Women's Movement*, London: Verso.

Valiente, C. (1996) 'The rejection of authoritarian policy legacies: family policy in Spain 1975–1995', *South European Society & Politics*, 1: 95–114.

Valiente, C. (1996) 'Partial achievements of central-state public policies against violence against women in post-authoritarian Spain, 1975–1995' in C. Corrin (ed.) *Women in a Violent World: Feminist Analyses and Resistance Across Europe*, 166–185, Edinburgh: Edinburgh University Press.

Valiente, C. (1996) 'Women in segmented labor markets and continental welfare states: the case of Spain', *Cross-National Research Papers*, 4th series, No. 4, 86–93.

Valiente, C. (1996) 'Men's family roles in post-authoritarian Spain (1975–95)' in U. Bjornberg and A.K. Kollind (eds) *Men's Family Relations: Report from an International Seminar*, Stockholm: Almqvist & Wiksell International.

1997

Brooksbank Jones, A. (1997) *Women in Contemporary Spain*, Manchester: Manchester University Press.

Cousins, C. (1997) 'Women and social policy in Spain: the development of a gendered welfare regime', *Journal of European Social Policy*, 5 (3): 175–197.

González López, M.J. (1997) *Do Modern Welfare States Foster Democratic Family Arrangements? Comparative Case Studies of Britain and Spain*, London School of Economics, Gender Institute, Working Paper Series, Issue 2.

Guerrero, T.J. and Naldini, M. (1997) 'Is the south so different? Italian and Spanish families in comparative perspective' in M. Rhodes (ed.) *Southern European Welfare States: Between Crisis and Reform*, London: Frank Cass.

Valiente, C. (1997) 'Gender, segmented labor markets, continental welfare states and equal employment policies, the case of Spain' in J. Holmer and J.Ch. Karlsson (eds) *Work – Quo Vadis?: Re-thinking the Question of Work*, 195–218, Aldershot: Ashgate.

Valiente, C. (1997) 'State feminism and gender equality policies: the case of Spain

(1983–95)' in F. Gardiner (ed.) *Sex Equality Policy in Western Europe*, 127–141, London: Routledge.

Valiente, C. (1997) 'The regulation of sexual harassment in the workplace in Spain: the role of state feminists in the elaboration of gender equality policies' in B. Hobson and A.M. Berggren (eds) *Crossing Borders: Gender and Citizenship in Transition*, 179–200, Stockholm: Swedish Council for Planning and Coordination.

1998

Baylina, M. and García-Ramón, M.D. (1998) 'Homeworking in rural Spain: a gender approach', *European Urban and Regional Studies*, 5 (1): 55–64.

Cousins, C. (1998) 'Social exclusion in Europe: paradigms of social disadvantage in Germany, Spain, Sweden and the UK', *Policy & Politics*, 26: 127–146.

Hart, A. (1998) *Buying and Selling Power: Prostitution in Spain*, Boulder, CO: Westview Press.

Moltó, M.L. and Domingo, T. (1998) *Women and the Labour Market in the Southern Countries*, València: Institut Universitari d'Estudis de la Dona, Universitat de València.

Ruivo, M., González, M. and Varejão, J.M. (1998) 'Why is part-time work so low in Portugal and Spain?' in J. O'Reilly and C. Fagan (eds) *Part-time Prospects: An International Comparison of Part-time Work in Europe, North America and the Pacific Rim*, London: Routledge.

Threlfall, M. (1998) 'State feminism or party feminism? Feminist politics and the Spanish Institute of Women', *European Journal of Women's Studies*, 5: 69–93.

Valiente, C. (1998) 'An overview of the state of research on women and politics in Spain', *European Journal of Political Research*, 33: 459–474.

Valiente, C. (1998) 'Sexual harassment in the workplace: equality policies in Post-Authoritarian Spain' in T. Carver and V. Mottier (eds) *Politics of Sexuality: Identity, Gender, Citizenship*, 169–179, London: Routledge.

1999

Alexander, G. (1999) 'Women and men at the ballot box' in V.L. Enders and P.B. Radcliff (eds) *Constructing Spanish Womanhood: Female Identity in Modern Spain*, Albany, NY: SUNY.

Cousins, C. (1999) *Society, Work and Welfare in Europe*, London: Macmillan.

Cousins, C. (1999) 'Changing regulatory frameworks and non-standard employment in Europe' in A. Felstead and N. Jewson (eds) *Global Trends in Flexible Labour*, London: Macmillan.

Cousins, C. (1999) 'Gender relations and changing forms of employment in Spain', *Journal of Southern Europe and the Balkans*, 1 (2): 199–215.

Enders, V.L. (1999) 'Problematic portraits: the ambiguous historical role of the Sección femenina of the Falange' in V.L. Enders and P.B. Radcliff (eds) *Constructing Spanish Womanhood: Female Identity in Modern Spain*, Albany, NY: SUNY.

Keene, J. (1999) 'Into the clear air of the plaza: Spanish women achieve the vote in 1931' in V.L. Enders and P.B. Radcliff (eds) *Constructing Spanish Womanhood: Female Identity in Modern Spain*, Albany, NY: SUNY.

Kelley, H. (1999) 'Enlacing women's stories: composing womanhood in a coastal Galician village' in V.L. Enders and P.B. Radcliff (eds) *Constructing Spanish Womanhood: Female Identity in Modern Spain*, Albany, NY: SUNY.

Morcillo Gómez, A. (1999) 'Shaping true Catholic womanhood: Francoist educational discourse on women' in V.L. Enders and P.B. Radcliff (eds) *Constructing Spanish Womanhood: Female Identity in Modern Spain*, Albany, NY: SUNY.

Puerolas, C. (1999) 'Masculinity versus femininity: the Sanfermines 1939–78' in V.L. Enders and P.B. Radcliff (eds) *Constructing Spanish Womanhood: Female Identity in Modern Spain*, Albany, NY: SUNY.

Sundman, K. (1999) *Between the Home and the Institutions: The Feminist Movement in Madrid, Spain*, Gothenburg: Acta Universitatis Gothoburgensis.

Trifiletti, R. (1999) 'Southern European welfare regimes and the worsening position of women', *Journal of European Social Policy*, 9: 49–64.

2000

Beadman, C. (2000) 'Illicit prostitution in 1940s Spain', *International Journal of Iberian Studies*, 13 (3): 157–166.

Cousins, C. (2000) 'Women and employment in southern Europe: the implications of recent policy and labour market directions', *South European Society and Politics*, 5 (1): 97–122.

García-Ramon, A.M. and Ortiz, A. (2000) 'The fixed-term contract, the Spanish route to flexibility? Women in the retail sector in the Barcelona region', *Economic and Industrial Democracy*, 21 (3): 311–333.

Hamilton, C. (2000) 'Re-membering the Basque nationalist family: daughers, fathers and the reproduction of the radical nationalist community', *Journal of Spanish Cultural Studies*, 1 (2): 153–171.

Morcillo Gómez, A. (2000) *True Catholic Womanhood: Gender Ideology and Franco's Spain*, DeKalb, IL: Northern Illinois University Press.

Valiente, C. (2000) 'Reconciliation policies in Spain' in L. Hantrais (ed.) *Gendered Policies in Europe: Reconciling Employment and Family Life*, 143–159, London: Macmillan.

2001

Hamilton, C. (2001) 'Activism and representations of motherhood in the autobiography of Dolores Ibárruri, *Pasionaria*', *Journal of Romance Studies*, 1 (1): 17–25.

Mangen, S. (2001) 'Welfare gender and the family', in *Spanish Society after Franco*, 148–161, Basingstoke and New York: Palgrave.

Threlfall, M. (2001) 'Women's political participation in Spain' in L. Twomey (ed.) *Women in Contemporary Culture: Roles and Identities in France and Spain*, 29–46, Bristol: Intellect Books.

Tobío, C. (2001) 'Working and mothering: women's strategies in Spain', *European Societies*, 3 (3): 339–372.

Twomey, L. (ed.) (2001) *Women in Contemporary Culture: Roles and Identities in France and Spain*, Bristol: Intellect Books.

Twomey, L. (2001) 'Licencia más amplia para matar: changes to Spain's abortion law and the traditionalist Catholic response' in L. Twomey (ed.) *Women in*

Contemporary Culture: Roles and Identities in France and Spain, 63–81, Bristol: Intellect Books.

Valiente, C. (2001) 'A closed subsystem and distant feminist demands block women-friendly outcomes in Spain' in A.G. Mazur (ed.) *State Feminism, Women's Movements, and Job Training: Making Democracies Work in the Global Economy*, 111–130, New York: Routledge.

Valiente, C. (2001) 'Do political parties matter: do Spanish parties make a difference in child care policies?' in T. David (ed.) *Promoting Evidence-Based Practice in Early Childhood Education: Research and Its Implications*, 97–114, Amsterdam: JAI Press.

Valiente, C. (2001) 'Gendering abortion debates: state feminism in Spain' in D. McBride Stetson (ed.) *Abortion Politics, Women's Movements, and the Democratic State: A Comparative Study of State Feminism*, 229–245, New York: Oxford University Press.

Valiente, C. (2001) 'Implementing women's rights in Spain' in J.H. Bayes and N. Tohidi (eds) *Globalization, Gender and Religion: The Politics of Women's Rights in Catholic and Muslim Contexts*, 107–125, New York: Palgrave.

2002

Preston, P. (2002) *Doves of War: Four Women of Spain*, London: HarperCollins.

Valiente, C. (2002) 'The value of an educational emphasis: child care and restructuring in Spain since 1975' in S. Michel and R. Mahon (eds) *Child Care Policy at the Crossroads: Gender and Welfare State Restructuring*, 57–70, New York and London: Routledge.

Valiente, V. (2002) 'An overview of research on gender in Spanish society', *Gender & Society*, 16 (5): 767–792.

Author index

Subject index